# Male Delivery
*Reproduction, Effeminacy,
and Pregnant Men
in Early Modern Spain*

# Male Delivery

*Reproduction, Effeminacy,
and Pregnant Men
in Early Modern Spain*

Sherry Velasco

Vanderbilt University Press
Nashville

© 2006 Vanderbilt University Press
All rights reserved
First edition 2006

10 09 08 07 06  1 2 3 4 5

Publication of this book has been supported by a generous subsidy from the Program for Cultural Cooperation between Spain's Ministry of Culture and United States Universities.

Library of Congress Cataloging-in-Publication Data

Velasco, Sherry M. (Sherry Marie), 1962–
Male delivery: reproduction, effeminacy, and pregnant men in early modern Spain / Sherry Velasco.—1st ed.
    p. cm.
ISBN 0-8265-1515-0 (cloth : alk. paper)
ISBN 0-8265-1516-9 (pbk. : alk. paper)
    1. Sex role—Spain—History—16th century. 2. Sex role—Spain—History—17th century. 3. Male pregnancy—Social aspects—Spain—History—16th century. 4. Male pregnancy—Social aspects—Spain—History—17th century. 5. Masculinity—Social aspects—Spain—History—16th century.
6. Masculinity—Social aspects—Spain—History—17th century.
7. Femininity—Social aspects—Spain—History—16th century.
8. Femininity—Social aspects—Spain—History—17th century.
9. Lanini Sagredo, Pedro Francisco de, 17th cent. Parto de Juan Rana. 10. Homosexuality, Male—Social aspects—Spain—History—16th century. 11. Homosexuality, Male—Social aspects—Spain—History—17th century.
I. Title.
HQ1075.5.S7V44 2006
306.874'3'09460903—dc22

2005023120

*For Brianna, Ben, and Andra*

# Contents

|   |   |   |
|---|---|---|
|   | List of Illustrations | ix |
|   | Acknowledgments | xi |
|   | Introduction:<br>Nothing Is Inconceivable | xiii |
| 1 | Comedy and Control:<br>Pregnant Men Throughout History | 1 |
| 2 | Performing Male Pregnancy<br>in *El parto de Juan Rana* | 28 |
| 3 | The Male Matrix: Appropriating<br>Reproduction in Early Modern Spain | 50 |
| 4 | The Fear of Effeminacy<br>in Early Modern Spain | 93 |
|   | Epilogue:<br>"Who's Laughing Now" | 123 |

**APPENDIXES**

|   |   |   |
|---|---|---|
| IA | "John Frog Gives Birth" | 129 |
| IB | *El parto de Juan Rana* | 135 |
| IIA | "Portrait of a Monster" | 145 |
| IIB | *Retrato de un monstruo* | 149 |
|   | Notes | 155 |
|   | Works Cited | 183 |
|   | Index | 201 |

# Illustrations

1. *Loco pícaro*   10
2. Arnold Schwarzenegger   16
3. Barbara Kruger's artwork   22
4. Leigh Bowery and assistant   25
5. "Aisha"   26
6. Cosme Pérez   36
7. Cantiga 17   51
8. Cantiga 184   53
9. Cantiga 89   55
10. God gives birth to the universe   59
11. Illustration of a problematic fetal position   67
12. Dorothy pregnant with several fetuses   83
13. Bearded lady Magdalena Ventura   102

# Acknowledgments

This book could not have been conceived without the happy coincidence of attending a classical theater conference in Almagro, Spain, when Peter Thompson presented a videotape of his students performing *El parto de Juan Rana*. I am eternally indebted to Peter for sharing this gem, his transcription of the only extant manuscript of the skit, as well as his encouragement and thoughtful advice during the past five years.

There are so many people who inspired and guided me throughout all stages of this project that it would be impossible to name them all. I would, however, like to express special gratitude to my friends and colleagues who read early drafts and gave valuable feedback: Harry Vélez-Quiñones, José Cartagena-Calderón, Lisa Vollendorf, Sidney Donnell, John Slater, Elena del Río Parra, Lourdes Torres, and Mary Daniels. I am also indebted to my colleagues at the University of Kentucky, especially Dianna Niebylski, Susan Larson, and Ana Rueda. Special thanks also go to Marta Vicente, Luis Corteguera, Jay Allen, and Joe Jones for their input on my translations of jokes, puns, and other challenging word play (without Marta's help, I would still be chasing false clues). I would also like to acknowledge the support of my dear friends Cindy Brantmeier and Nina Davis at Washington University in St. Louis during the initial stages of this project.

For financial support, I wish to thank the Program for Cultural Cooperation Between Spain's Ministry of Education, Culture and Sports and United States Universities as well as the University of Kentucky's generous support through the Summer Research Grant and the Major Research Grant. I am equally grateful to Joan Lipkin, Barbara Kruger, and Fergus Greer for sharing their artistic creations with me.

I am indebted to Betsy Phillips, Dariel Mayer, Peg Duthie, and everyone at Vanderbilt University Press who gave support and valuable editorial suggestions. Finally, my deepest thanks go to Jody Serkes and Dulce Velasco for their love and patience while I worked long hours on this project. They are as responsible as anyone for the gestation and delivery of this book.

Part of this book has been previously published. An early version of Chapter 2 appeared in as "Performing Male Pregnancy in Early Modern Spain: *El parto de Juan Rana.*" *Comedia Performance* 1, no. 1 (2004): 192–218.

# Introduction
## Nothing Is Inconceivable

In the mid-seventeenth century, Spain's most celebrated comedic actor, Cosme Pérez, alias Juan Rana (John Frog), played the part of a man nine months pregnant in a comic interlude by Francisco Pedro Lanini Sagredo.[1] By the end of the one-act play, the pregnant actor goes into labor and gives birth. The farcical comedy concludes with carnivalesque dancing and singing, whereby the newborn is recognized as his father's legitimate offspring by their shared dancing style. Most theatergoers in the early modern period would have accepted the over-the-top plot as typical of the upside-down world [el mundo al revés] characteristic of the *entremés* genre. Yet for twenty-first-century readers or spectators, Lanini Sagredo's *El parto de Juan Rana* (John Frog Gives Birth) (c. 1660) is revealing for its enactment of many of the anxieties related to women's reproductive health (such as conception, birth control, pregnancy, and childbirth) as well as issues of paternity, progeny, and power, not to mention what were considered abnormal births and other "monstrosities," including intersexed bodies, gender-blurring, and sodomy.[2]

This study explores the interdependent relationships among reproductive technologies, the politics of masculinity and male effeminacy, and the fluid nature of sex assignment and same-sex desire in early modern Spain. Using the one-act comedy *El parto de Juan Rana* as a point of departure, I argue that the pregnant man image is not merely a comical gimmick used to entertain but actually dramatizes serious and controversial issues that had significant consequences for Spain during the sixteenth and seventeenth centuries: the patriarchal invasion into the female sphere of reproductive medicine and the threat of a feminization of Spanish men, which was manifested in the body through unstable physiology, transgressive gender behavior, and criminalized sexual activity (i.e., sodomy). Consequently, the comical yet provocative spectacle of the pregnant man enacts the male fantasy of usurping women's reproductive power by eliminating the woman all together. At the same time, the interlude exposes society's fears of a change from male to female in gender roles, sex assignment, and sexual practices. In other words, effeminacy in men is linked to sodomitical culture and perhaps could lead to what would be considered an even more tragic horror: a physical male-to-female transmutation that could hypothetically (if not physiologically) allow for male pregnancy in the future. In this way, the metaphor of male pregnancy is paradoxically both fantasy and nightmare. By eliminating the need for women in human reproduction, the pregnant man gains complete control over procreation and paternity. Simultaneously, this image reveals the fear of the logical evolution of gender-bending and same-sex desire between men.

The belief that certain women could physically transmute into men was socially and scientifically sanctioned in the early modern period. Hence, there was no guarantee that the opposite could not also occur (despite misogynistic assurances that Nature tends only to improve itself by becoming progressively or instantaneously more masculine). While cases of men transforming anatomically into women were not common, this phenomenon, in fact, was discussed by various moralists, scientists, and other writers during the seventeenth century. For example, in his treatise on marvels and prodigies, Pedro Bovistau distinguishes between the natural spontaneous transmutations of women who become men and the unnatural provoked transformations of men who willingly turn into women. Furthermore, if men have the capacity to "degenerate" into women they could, in turn, become reproductive vessels.

Other narratives in Spain (such as a 1606 news pamphlet recounting a male pregnancy and monstrous delivery caused by a witch's potion) describe men who were impregnated without possessing female reproductive organs.[3] And yet other cases of mistaken male pregnancies and deliveries provide useful insights into the multiple cultural responses to this hypothetical situation. The pregnant man, I argue, emerges as one of the cultural figures that best symbolizes some of the more troublesome tensions among medical, legal, and social issues in early modern Spain.

In her book *Manly Masquerade*, Valeria Finucci argues that, in Renaissance Italy, the "fantasy of escape from the maternal matrix" is merely a stock feature of comedy, one that did not represent a serious concern for early modern society: "The idea of male pregnancy," says Finucci, "does not seem to have unduly preoccupied philosophers and doctors because it ran counter to cultural and biological stereotypes" (65). Yet a closer look at the anxieties behind the legal, scientific, and religious efforts to monitor cases of ambiguously sexed individuals, effeminate males, sodomites, and women's power in reproductive medicine in early modern Spain indicates that the issues that surface in male maternity actually provoked much concern and that the humor in which this figure was couched, in fact, was used as one of many strategies to control these nonconforming bodies.

The sixteenth and seventeenth centuries marked a crucial change in the practice of reproductive health, as it shifted from a female-controlled sphere to the gradual professionalization of reproductive medicine and medical discourse, which was dominated by male physicians, lawmakers, and moralists. New legislation attempted to eliminate the authority of female midwives and legitimize male authority in reproductive health, while secular laws and papal proclamations against birth control and abortifacients were upheld and formalized. The history of contraception and abortion demonstrates that the extensive knowledge about fertility control common in the ancient world was gradually lost or suppressed during the Middle Ages, becoming almost nonexistent in formal medical training by the early modern period. As a result, the Renaissance gynecological specialists had limited experience with women's reproductive options and therefore were ill-equipped (and likely resistant) to translate accurately ancient texts concerning abortifacients.[4] As Julie Sanders summarizes, the discourse of New Science would "lead by the end of the seventeenth century to the rise of the male midwife and to his colonization of the birthing room" (80). According to Ruth Gilbert, it is precisely the seventeenth-century scientific discoveries of women's central role in generation (and the new embryological debates) that necessitated strategies featuring a masculine matrix and male births in early modern England: "In spite of (or perhaps because of) these less confidently masculine subtexts, one of the implicit aims of the seventeenth-century scientific programme was to reinstate the supremacy of male creation" ("Masculine," 169).

Visual representations of pregnancy and childbirth at this time also underwent major transformations, as evident in the changing iconography depicting the virgin birth of Jesus. Medieval representations of Mary frequently had shown her pregnant or nursing her child, while Renaissance versions depicted her as an innocent maiden or sorrowing mother.[5] Accordingly, Francisco Pacheco, an authority on painting and portraiture during the seventeenth century, instructed artists to depict Mary without the child in her arms, as if she had not given birth (576). While popular medieval depictions of Mary pregnant or giving birth seemed to disappear during the early modern period, the cult of "Joseph as mother" transformed him from his pre-fifteenth-century persona as an impotent, old man into a virile and productive primary caregiver, thereby replacing traditional Marian iconography (Hale, 106). This male appropriation of maternity in pictorial representations demonstrates how the role of women in human reproduction is visually and symbolically minimized in favor of the father as primary progenitor.

Historical records (discussed in Chapter 4) leave no doubt as to the level of anxiety over the perceived feminization of Spanish men, which required legal, moral, and economic censures of the gender transgression. Not surprisingly, the numerous representations of male femininity were frequently associated with homosexual practices, namely sodomy. As a result, early modern Spain responded with stricter legislation of sexual activity deemed perverse or nonprocreative. Moreover, during a time when sex assignment could transmute before and/or after birth (or, in the case of intersexed individuals, was occasionally indeterminate), the need to control a possible male-to-female sex mutation that would match the feminine man "epidemic" was implied in various legal, medical, philosophical, moral, and literary texts. Like the "unspeakable" crime of sodomy, the tragedy of a male-to-female "degeneration" must have been looming as a subtext of the numerous narratives describing the fluid nature of sex assignment.

Since the enormously popular actor Juan Rana was known for his effeminate mannerisms and gender-bending performances (most likely used to enhance his comic persona in commercial theater), his arrest for sodomy in 1636 undoubtedly increased mainstream culture's anxieties regarding the consequences of men with excessively feminine traits. Therefore, the ridiculous and burlesque exhibition of a pregnant sodomite serves to police the potential spread of possible transgender-transsexual-homosexual outlaws. In the end, this hilarious yet complex interlude featuring the famous actor as pregnant man who gives birth on stage becomes a fascinating vehicle to explore the interrelated controversies involving women's reproductive health and nonconformity in gender roles, desire, and intersexed or non-fixed bodies.

This study begins by asking why the pregnant man image captivated such a wide range of cultures for so many centuries. In an attempt to answer this question, Chapter 1 ("Comedy and Control: Pregnant Men Throughout History") looks at various manifestations of male pregnancy in mythological, folkloric, religious, literary, scientific, political, philosophical, and psychoanalytical references, as well as examples from theater, film, television, illustrated sources, and cyberspace, in order to establish some of the major themes that emerge from these sources and thereby shedding some light on similar issues present in the seventeenth-century farce *El parto de Juan Rana*. What we find is that these pregnant man images, their strategies, and their cultural significance in a variety of contexts can be summarized in terms of power and humor: patriarchal control over procreation is suggested in the representations of man as sole progenitor and in the conflict over women's reproductive freedom. At the same time, male pregnancy frequently is featured in scenes designed for comic entertainment, whether to challenge traditional notions of gender, sex assignment, and sexuality or to defend the status quo.

Chapter 2 ("Performing Male Pregnancy in *El parto de Juan Rana*") focuses specifically on the issues implied in the pregnant man image as they appear in the comic interlude *El parto de Juan Rana*. My goal is to show how the dramatic farce acts out the cultural anxieties related to the understanding and control of female sexuality and reproduction and the gender-blurring of masculine traits as well as the attitudes toward and legislation of sodomy in early modern Spain. Counterposing an analysis of the interlude to a summary of the complex nature of the lead actor's professional and personal life, this section also raises questions regarding the political and didactic function of humor in this theatrical piece: Does the comic vision of a pregnant man giving birth merely dramatize the Aristotelian theory of laughter as a cathartic yet moralizing mechanism employed to maintain the established order, or does it open up the liberating potential of the Bakhtinian carnivalesque—a subversive early modern precursor to the campiness of a pregnant drag queen?

Chapter 3 ("The Male Matrix: Appropriating Reproduction in Early Modern Spain") addresses the implications of women's reproductive health suggested in *El parto de Juan Rana* by outlining the patriarchal fantasy of gaining control over pregnancy and childbirth in early modern Spain. The male appropriation of the womb is visible in artistic representations through the erasure of pregnancy and the emergence of Joseph as a much more central figure in the religious depictions of the Holy Family, as well as the popularity of visual images of newborn monsters. The previously exclusive female-only space of the delivery room is likewise invaded as the medical profession begins to assume the authority that was traditionally assigned to female midwives. Furthermore, as religious, scientific, legal, and philosophical theorists grappled with questions of generation and when (and how) human life begins, debates involving abortion, miscarriage, infanticide, and ovist versus animalculist preformationism had drastic repercussions for all women during that time. This chapter also shows how early modern discussions of maternity, pregnancy, and childbirth almost always addressed the topic of monsters or monstrous births. The freakish and startling descriptions and illustrations of monsters (including their conception and birth) justified the need for male intervention. In particular, concerns over resemblance became a key factor in the fear of false paternity. Following Aristotle's definition of a monster as that which fails to resemble its progenitor, the womb became a heavily contested battleground. Women's bodies (and minds through the maternal imagination) were seen as potentially dangerous spaces that must be controlled by men to ensure the legitimacy of the offspring's identity.

While Chapter 3 outlines the implementations and justifications for the male appropriation of reproduction that is implied in the pregnant man image, Chapter 4 ("The Fear of Effeminacy in Early Modern Spain") examines how mainstream society reacted to a perceived degeneration of traditional masculinity. Moralists, economists, and policy-makers were alarmed by the apparent increase in male effeminacy, especially given the association of gender-bending and sodomitical acts. It is not surprising that the early modern period saw a rise in the number of men accused and convicted of sodomy (and much stricter measures to punish them). As gender traits and sexual practices shifted toward what was considered more effeminate, sex assignment appeared to be equally unstable. Narratives and illustrations of intersexed bodies (such as hermaphrodites) and others with indeterminate or mutable sex identity were not only popular but facilitated the fear of an "unnatural" physiological transmutation from male to female. In this way, the unspeakable notion that men would some day be capable of procreating without women was undoubtedly in the cultural imaginary of early modern Spain.

At a time when there is heated debate about the rights of women versus the rights of an embryo or fetus, and just as much controversy over the ethics of reproductive cloning, stem-cell research, and other dramatic breakthroughs in the science of human reproduction in the twenty-first century, it is particularly relevant to examine how the politics of the womb during the early modern period also engaged in political and bioethical debates about reproductive issues such as precisely when life begins and whether or not birth control or abortion could be sanctioned by theologians, policymakers, or medical professionals. By the same token, the current trend in "metrosexual" maleness (which inevitably questions sexuality in its treatment of men who are interested in fashion and style) as well as political, moral, and legal battles over the rights of same-sex partners reveal an intriguing parallel to the controversy over sodomy and feminized men during the sixteenth and seventeenth centuries in Spain.[6]

# Male Delivery
*Reproduction, Effeminacy,
and Pregnant Men
in Early Modern Spain*

# 1
# Comedy and Control
## Pregnant Men Throughout History

Perhaps it is not by chance that, when we peel back the layers of the male matrix (from male pregnancy as metaphor for intellectual creativity to the control of women's reproductive health and the issues related to male effeminacy and homosexuality), we discover that these topics are played out in some variation in the early modern farce *El parto de Juan Rana*. At the start of the interlude, for example, a group of local government officials reviewing the scandalous crime of Juan Rana (mayor of the small town of Meco) begins a debate on the relationship between political power and men's (pro)-creativity or the ability to generate new concepts. They all agree that Rana is a transgression *contra natura*, but soon discover that he has also rejected traditional gender roles by allowing his wife to "wear the pants" in the family. Just as shocking, perhaps he has also participated in the even more serious crime of sexual relations with another man. After much slapstick debate, the five mayors decide that Juan Rana is guilty and that his punishment will be the shame and humiliation of parading publicly dressed in women's clothing in his present state of advanced pregnancy. Two-thirds into the one-act play, the (in)famous cross-dressed and pregnant celebrity appears on stage, bemoaning his plight in song while trying to exculpate himself for any wrongdoing (implicitly denying any innuendo of sodomy). He soon goes into labor, screeching in pain as two other men come to his aid by holding him up while he narrates the delivery. Suddenly his newborn son (who is played by a young actress) pops out from under his long skirt, as the witnesses comment on the strong resemblance, ironically calming any fears about the paternity of the male mother. The interlude ends with the lively song and dance by father and son, as the other officials quickly join in the festivities. Interestingly, Juan Rana has the final word, answering the "what if men gave birth" question by confirming the long-held fear that men can never really be sure of their children's identity as long as women are the ones who give birth.[1]

When considering the cultural significance of this intriguing interlude, we might begin by asking why the pregnant man image has been a source of continued fascination throughout the centuries. Mythology, folklore, religion, literature, science, politics, philosophy, anthropology, and psychology as well as theater, film, television, visual culture, and cyberspace all have scores of images and tales attesting to its appeal. Significantly, a review of the numerous versions of the pregnant man image throughout history indicates certain consistencies that transcend differences in context and ideology. Whether the case deals with a seventeenth-century man who gives birth to a monster in Granada or a twenty-first-century pregnant drag queen in Kentucky, what seems to emerge from the male capacity to generate children or to father ideas inevitably reflects core issues related to power and control (regardless of other strategies such as comic entertainment, repression or social justice and change). As a result, patriarchal control over procreation is played out in the conflict over women's sexual practices and their reproductive options as well as through a challenge to or defense of traditional notions of gender, sex assignment, and sexuality.

## Man as Sole Progenitor

The concept of male reproduction was not new in the seventeenth century and as a result *El parto* participated in a well-established tradition of male autogenesis. Scholars have long agreed that Athena's speech in Aeschylus condenses accurately the firmly held belief among Greek philosophers and scientists that "the male alone was the true parent, the true *genere*, since only the male was capable of the act of generation" (Zoja, 115). At the end of the *Oresteia* trilogy, motherless Athena voices what was obviously consensual agreement among the Greeks as to the paternity of offspring. The mother's womb is a mere vessel while the father's seed contains the embryo *in toto* (Athena proclaims: "For no mother had part in *my* birth" [Aeschylus, 161]). Nor were the Greeks alone in harboring this fantasy; in some Chinese images, Buddhas are shown with babies cuddling in their stomachs (Perreault, 305). Masculine generation is likewise featured in Lucian's *True History* (AD 2). As Ruth Gilbert reminds us, "men are born from the generative power of unmediated masculinity without the taint of passing through, or combining with, the female body. This idea, although expressed in the context of Lucian's satirical fantastic voyage, had a powerful hold on the imaginations of early-modern men" ("Masculine," 162).[2]

Male maternity is also found in the Bible (Psalm 109:3 and John 14:10, for example), in the writings of early Church fathers (such as Saint Augustine and Saint Thomas Aquinas), and was frequently invoked in medieval religious works when discussing God or male authority figures.[3] When referring to the birth of Eve from the side of Adam and the "birth" of Ecclesia from the pierced side of Christ, Barbara Newman notes that "in each case the symbolism of natural birth is inverted to display a female entity emerging from a male" (205). Likewise, one common characteristic of twelfth-century Cistercian writings was the recurrent metaphorical description of male figures conceiving, giving birth, and nursing (Bynum, 147). Caroline Walker Bynum describes the feminized yet nonsexual body of Christ in terms of male maternity in her study *Jesus as Mother*, while Karma Lochrie sees the homoerotic potential in representational art displaying feminizing features such as the wound of Christ. The practice continued for centuries, as is evident in the writings of the early modern Spanish mystic Juana de la Cruz (1481–1534). In her Trinity sermon (recorded in her principal work, *El libro del conorte* [The Book of Consolation]), Mother Juana uses *sui generis* images to describe how God the Father is pregnant with his Son while Christ is also presented as pregnant with the Father. As Ronald Surtz concludes, this narrative strategy can be read in terms of empowerment for women: "The pregnancy image is also a particularly striking case of role reversal and celebration of female fecundity through which Juana elevates the female experience of pregnancy and birthing into the domain of the divine" ("Privileging," 70).

In European folklore, legends of pregnant men have persisted in numerous versions and adaptations for centuries. Roberto Zapperi has collected dozens of medieval and early modern folktales related to male pregnancy in his anecdotal study *The Pregnant Man*. The folklore tradition of the "pregnant man of Monreale," for example, was inspired by religious iconographic images of the miraculous healing of a man suffering from dropsy, featured with swollen belly (37). Other folktales of men believed to be pregnant are frequently based on the confusion of a blood or urine sample obtained from a pregnant woman but attributed to a man. The pregnant man motif present in such texts as Boccaccio's *Decameron* and numerous variations of Aesopic fables is often employed for comic purposes while also revealing fantasies of male omnipotence (71).[4]

In Spain, tales of pregnant men began to appear in the Middle Ages and have continued to circulate for centuries through oral storytelling. In his review of some of the Spanish versions of male pregnancy, François Delpech demonstrates that this figure has been utilized for varying purposes that include serious and ennobling characterization as well as comical or grotesque representations. A few examples of male pregnancy through oral tradition that have continued to the twentieth century include a series of Spanish folktales from León involving pregnant priests ("The Priest Who Tries to Miscarry," "The Priest Who Thinks he is Pregnant," "The Pregnant Priest," "The Childbearing Priest," and "The Man Who Wanted to Give Birth" [Camarena, 144–50]) and a comical story recounted in Spanish-speaking areas of Colorado about a man who believes he has given birth to a calf.[5]

## Male Pregnancy as Metaphor for Mental Fecundity

Examples of childbirth as metaphor for the "labor" of literary invention abound throughout the early modern period.[6] It is not surprising, then, that *El parto de Juan Rana* begins its discussion of the male matrix by engaging early modern scientific theories of *ingenio* (wits), which interpret man's intelligence, creativity, and physiology in terms of his capacity to (pro)create.[7] Thomas Laquer reminds us that biological and intellectual conception are closely related in Aristotle (as well as his early modern followers). Therefore, "normal" conception involves the male having an idea in the uterus of the woman while abnormal conception (or the *mola*, which is a monstrous product of the womb attributed to self-insemination) is "a conceit for her having an ill-gotten and inadequate idea of her own" (Laquer, 59). In her study on male births and the scientific imagination in early modern England, Ruth Gilbert describes how men appropriated images of birth in their intellectual and technological aspirations while attempting to avoid the abject connection to women and the "messier" aspects of reproduction: "In such strategies the creative matrix is effectively transferred from the potentially appalling site of the female body (the womb) and becomes located instead in that part of the body which is seen to be the most masculine (the brain). The ideal male birth was thus clean, noiseless, bloodless and odourless" ("Masculine," 160). Raymond Stephanson likewise argues that there was a connection between the embryological debate and how male writers of the Enlightenment expressed their creative literary processes in terms of pregnancy and reproduction: "Just as preformationist theories gave way to more complex embryological views of fetal development and sequential growth from apparently unorganized material, tropes of the pregnant male brain turned increasingly to ideas of enigmatic but purposeful growth within the creative mind" (109–10). When discussing this practice in early modern France, Kirk Read similarly concludes that canonical male writers masculinize maternity in order to empower their writing: "What emerges is a set of conveniently crafted assumptions about gender, production, and reproduction that persistently favor male dominance and control—a preponderant iconography of men vested with women's maternal functions, supported and sustained in both poetic and anatomic constructs" (75). Katharine Eisaman Maus, on the other hand, argues that it is not so easy to decipher the cultural meanings behind the male pregnancy metaphors in English Renaissance poetry: "When a sixteenth- or seventeenth-century man lays claim to a womb, the precise character of his assertion is sometimes difficult to assess," which, according to Maus, ultimately encourages us to rethink "the ways we discuss literary creativity in a patriarchal society" (98, 106).

Perhaps one of the more famous cases of male pregnancy as a metaphor for intellectual fecundity in Spanish literature is found in the beginning of Cervantes' prologue to *Don Quixote*:

> Idle reader, you can believe without any oath of mine that I would wish this book, as the child of my brain, to be the most beautiful, the liveliest and the cleverest imaginable. But I have been unable to transgress the order of nature, by which like gives birth to like. And so, what could my sterile and ill-cultivated genius beget but the story of a lean, shrivelled, whimsical child, full of varied fancies that no one else has ever imagined. (25)[8]

While Cervantes initiates his novel by invoking the reproductive images recurrent in Juan Huarte de San Juan's 1575 scientific treatise on humors and intelligence (which describes men with superior intelligence and creativity in terms of fertility and childbirth), the male pregnancy theme resurfaces again in Chapter 47 during a conversation between the barber and Sancho Panza. When the barber accuses Sancho of being of the same humor or wit as Don Quixote (by engaging the previous image of reproduction and creativity), his comments also suggest Sancho's naïve lack of intellectual discretion: "For you've caught something of his humour and chivalry. It was an ill moment when you fell with child [*os empreñaste*] by his promises" (423).[9] Of course, Sancho is unable to recognize the other usage of *empreñarse* ("to be impregnated," as well as "to be guillible") intended by the barber:[10] " 'I'm not with child by anyone,' replied Sancho; 'and I'm not a man to let anyone get me with child, not the King himself' " (423).[11]

Although Sancho understands the barber's statement in terms of "procreative sodomy," other male pregnancy jokes in early modern Spain play on men's insecurities about paternity.[12] Juan Rufo, for example, in his 1596 collection of witty jests and aphorisms, *Las seiscientas apotegmas y otras obras en verso* [Six-hundred Maxims and Other Works in Verse], cites an anecdote about a man whose emotional cooing over a nursing baby prompted an onlooker to assume that he must either want children or was missing his own. When asked if he had children of his own, the admirer's response in the negative is surprising for its overstated protestations: "No Sir, certainly not. I have none nor do I have any intention of having them," to which the other gentleman quipped: "Well I didn't ask if you had given birth!" (Rufo, 210–11).[13]

Not long after Spanish audiences saw Juan Rana give birth on stage, John Dryden wrote his first play (*The Wild Gallant* [1663]), which also features a male pregnancy plot. Unlike the actual birthing scene in *El parto*, though, in Dryden's farce Lord Nonsuch is merely led to believe that he and three of his male servants are pregnant, and they consequently experience pregnancy symptoms through suggestion (Cody, 84). As Lisa Forman Cody explains: "By mocking a man gullible enough to believe he is carrying a child, the joke signifies his emasculated status and loss of patriarchal authority" (84).

Like both Lanini Sagredo's and Dryden's comical treatments of the male pregnancy plot, when the topic emerged in nonfictional sources during the same period, it frequently inspired jokes or derision. For example, in the 1651 English translation of James Primerose's medical treatise *Popular Errours, or the Errours of the People in Physick*, the description of husbands suffering from sympathetic pregnancy symptoms is diminished with the conclusion that these men are "most worthy to bee laughed at" (cited in Cody, 90). Likewise, Charles II was apparently amused when he found that one of his physicians, Dr. Edward Pelling, imagined himself to be pregnant. In fact, referring to Pelling's masculine wife, the King quipped that "if any woman could get her husband with child, it must be Mrs. Pelling" (cited in Cody, 91).[14]

During the same period on the English stage, Shakespeare also explored images of "male pregnancy" in reference to the fertility of the mind to produce ideas. In her discussion of *Measure for Measure*, Mary Thomas Crane notes the irony of the drama's content and the playwright's usage of the word "pregnancy" in the play: "Strikingly, in a play that has as its central image a pregnant female body, the word is never used to describe a woman but is instead used exclusively to denote the mental processes of men" (276). Janet Adelman also explores the fear and appropriation of maternal powers in Shakespeare's works, pointing out that in *The Tempest*, for example, through control of the maternal body, "Prospero seems able to reshape the world in the image of his own mind" (237). Following Adelman's conclusion, Peter S. Donaldson's analysis of Peter Greenaway's film version of *The Tempest* (*Prospero's Books*) argues that Prospero attempts to replace maternal birth ("both by literally creating many of the characters through his magic and by reinscribing others as his 'creatures' ") as well as control female sexuality (180). Similarly, according to Adelman, Juliet's pregnant body by the end of *Measure for Measure* is replaced by male power as the new site of revelation: "She is largely forgotten as the Duke increasingly commands center stage; her pregnant body—the visible sign of maternal origin and of female generative power—is replaced by his invisible and bodiless control" (89).[15] Of course, there is another level of the pregnant man theme in Renaissance English theater when the play features a female character "with child" (such as Helena in *All's Well That Ends Well*, Juliet in *Measure for Measure*, and Hermione in *A Winter's Tale*) since young male actors played the female parts. On the textual diegetic level, there is no transgression, while for the audience the visual and intellectual impact would necessarily involve a male pregnancy subtext.

In his discussion of the grotesque image of the body in Rabelais's work, Mikhail Bakhtin frequently uses images of conception, pregnancy, and childbirth. Citing an example of implied male pregnancy in Renaissance theatre through the "clownish" *commedia dell'arte* (first commented upon by G. Schneegans in his 1894 *History of Grotesque Satire*), Bakhtin describes how when a stutterer cannot pronounce a particular word, he begins to suffer physically as a result of his struggle to get it out (304). And when his impatient listener (Harlequin) knocks him in the stomach, the delayed word is finally "born." Bakhtin, then, interprets the birth of this word as a "degradation," since the word originates in the upper stratum of the body (in the mouth and the head) and is transferred to the lower stratum (abdomen):

> The stutterer enacts a scene of childbirth. He is pregnant, bearing the word that he is unable to deliver. Schneegans says that "it looks as if he were in the throes and spasms of childbirth." The gaping mouth, the protruding eyes, sweat, trembling, suffocation, the swollen face—all these are typical symptoms of the grotesque life of the body; here they have the meaning of the act of birth. Harlequin's gesture is also quite obvious: he helps to deliver the word, and the word is actually born. We specify that it is the word that is born, and we stress this fact: a highly spiritual act is degraded and uncrowned by the transfer the material bodily level of childbirth, realistically represented. But thanks to degradation the word is renewed; one might say reborn. (We are still within the cycle of delivery and childbirth). (308–9)

While labor and delivery are associated with the grotesque feminine, when the male producer of language appropriates childbirth as a metaphor for his intellectual productivity, these procreative images are elevated to a new spiritual plane.[16]

## Womb Envy

While many representations of pregnant men appear to eliminate the role of women in reproduction, a slightly different use of the metaphor has emerged in mainstream publishing in recent years. As "expectant fathers" are encouraged to become more involved in the childbirth and parenting process, many men have recorded their own experiences of "giving birth." *Birthing Fathers: The Transformation of Men in American Rites of Birth* (2005), *Pregnant Man: How Nature Makes Fathers Out of Men* (2000), *When Men are Pregnant: Needs and Concerns of Expectant Fathers* (1993), *Pregnant Fathers: Becoming the Father You Want to Be* (1997), and *Expecting: One Man's Uncensored Memoir of Pregnancy* (2000) are just of few of the titles published in the past decade. For example, Gordon Churchwell, the author of *Pregnant Man*, describes his decision to write about male pregnancy and its importance in the changing face of reproduction: "Men become 'pregnant' too, in a way that is much more concrete than just metaphor. Men undergo a bodily rite of transformation of their own that is cellular and permanent. The change is not as profound in physiology or purpose, not as large in scale or intensity as a woman's, but it is there. New thoughts, new priorities, new emotions, new love—all there and hardwired by nature" (284).

In fact, men have been performing their own version of pregnancy and delivery for centuries. During the early modern period in Europe, for example, the *couvade* was a symbolic ritual in which the husband of an expectant wife engages in mimetic childbirth, "pretending to have borne the baby himself. The man goes to bed and lives through the birth: he writhes and moans, his face is distorted with pain; when the labour is over, the baby is given to him to cuddle and soothe" (Gélis, 37). The *couvade* tradition, in fact, has a long history in Spain. Citing Posidonius's lost texts (135–151 BC), Strabo mentions the ancient practice in Iberia (AD 18–23), while others have noted male birthing activities throughout the nineteenth century in parts of the Basque Country (Reed, 34–36; Gélis, 37). Moreover, it is believed that the nineteenth-century fascination with the Basque men who took to the birthing bed with the newborn initiated usage of the term "couvades," most likely derived from the old French "couver" or "couvement," which according to Richard K. Reed is what "a hen does with her body when she broods a clutch of eggs! It draws a simple parallel between the attentive hen and the husband who takes on gestation and birthing" (34).

While these cultural rituals may be interpreted as inclusive and perhaps therapeutic for men who want to feel more involved in the childbirth process, some mental health workers have employed such diagnoses as "pseudocyesis" (false pregnancy) when working with those labeled psychotic, paranoid, and/or schizophrenic. The interpretation of male pregnancy as a psychological disorder is even portrayed in one of Francisco de Goya's nineteenth-century drawings titled *Loco pícaro* ("Crafty Lunatic") (c. 1824–1828): "This might also be called the 'disguised lunatic,' . . . With hat, ear-rings and fine shoes, he has disguised himself as a woman; then to make himself more interesting, he has imitated a well-advanced pregnancy by stuffing a thick cushion under his shirt" (Gassier, 567) (Figure 1).[17]

Consistent in some ways with the implied link between insanity, deviance, and male femininity evident in Goya's drawing of the *loco pícaro*, male pregnancy is understood by some as a clinically diagnosed psychological pathology and is frequently explained in terms of the patient's homosexuality. For example, in her study *The Pregnant Man and Other Cases from a Hypnotherapist's Couch*, Deirdre Barrett interpreted her patient George's false pregnancy symptoms (distended abdomen, enlarged breasts, morning sickness, etc.) as a metaphor for his grief over the death of his partner Alan (in a chapter titled "Mourning Sickness").

Undoubtedly the most famous precedent in psychoanalysis of a male body that perceives itself to be pregnant is found in Freud's 1911 case study of Daniel Paul Schreber (*Psychoanalytic Notes Upon an Autobiographical Account of a Case of Paranoia [Dementia Paranoides]*), which was based on Schreber's *Memoirs of a Neurotic* (1903). Freud attributes Schreber's paranoid psychosis to his inability to reconcile his homosexual desires, which resulted in his belief that he had transformed into a woman who was destined to procreate. Schreber writes:

> I became clearly aware that the order of things imperatively demanded my emasculation, whether I personally liked it or not, and that no *reasonable* course lay open to me but to reconcile myself to the thought of being transformed into a woman. The further consequence of my emasculation could, of course, only be my impregnation by divine rays to the end that a new race of men might be created. (Quoted in Freud, 96).

John O'Neill notes how Freud overlooked Schreber's "myth of parthenogenesis" through the misguided insistence on homosexualizing his "return

10   Male Delivery

Figure 1: Francisco de Goya's *Loco pícaro* ("Crafty Lunatic") (c. 1824–1828). (Reproduced by permission from the National Museum, Stockholm)

of the feminine" (84), while Cristina Mazzoni criticizes both Freud's and Lacan's interpretations of Schreber for having avoided the importance of his reproductive fixation and procreative fantasies: "Could maternity, womb envy, woman's ability to give life as object of desire and of scorn . . . could all this be what is at the bottom, so to speak, of Schreber's psychosis?" (118). Inevitably, debate over the origin of Schreber's desire to procreate ends in discussion of psychosis and homosexuality, while Juan Rana's pregnancy is explained through a combination of social, sexual, and biological perversions. Moreover, unlike Schreber's apparent womb envy, Rana presents himself as a reluctant participant in male autogenesis despite the interlude's implied patriarchal fantasy of appropriating control over reproduction.[18]

## Male Pregnancy as Metaphor for AIDS

A different approach to the male pregnancy metaphor associated with homosexuality (here employed as a strategy for confronting the pain, grief, and death associated with AIDS) is most poignantly invoked by Alberto Sandoval-Sánchez in his 1993 play *Side Effects*:

> Something is growing inside me.
> I feel it.
> My women friends laugh at me.
> I tell them I have nausea, feel dizzy, and weak.
> They say "you must be pregnant."
> It feels like it.
> Can a man give birth?
> I know that something is growing inside me.
> I feel it.
> It moves like a fetus from my stomach to my lungs.
> It swims in my blood trying to be born.
> What is inside me? What is it?
> Do women ever have a fear of giving birth to a monster?
> I incubate it.
> I feed it.
> I nurse it. [ . . . ]
> All I can think of is horror movies.
> I sit on the edge on the bed.

> On the wall all I see is all kind of aliens hatching
> in my body. [ . . . ]
> I scream: The Alien is inside me.
> What's inside me? What is it? (6–7)

When discussing his very personal and poetic exposition of the devastating side effects of AIDS, Sandoval-Sánchez connects the male matrix (perceived as a diseased monster) to political issues that involve other aspects of his identity, such as being a gay Latino scholar: "And given that I do scholarship with my body, my writing is the umbilical cord to abjection, to my migrancy, to my mariconería, and to my Latinidad. In such terms, abjection is the only way to recover my corporeality from a system of knowledge that always procures to transcend and sublimate the materiality of the body, its biological processes, the experience of suffering, and the reality of mortality" (Sandoval-Sánchez, 8). Consequently, in this intriguing variation on the painful curse of pregnancy and childbirth, Sandoval-Sánchez defends his homosexuality, ethnicity, and even his mortality by reconnecting these rejected spaces to an intellectual production that traditionally is elevated above the inferiority of lower-body function of generation.

## Pregnant Man as Comic Entertainment

Departing from the serious representations of abject male pregnancy, other depictions of the masculine matrix follow the strategy featured in *El parto de Juan Rana* by highlighting the curse of painful childbirth for comic effect. In fact, it is this desire to escape the burden of pregnancy, labor, and delivery that motivated Sherry Millner to include the *female* fantasy of male pregnancy in her 1983 film *Womb with a View*. In this comic project the woman resents her reproductive biological "destiny" and prefers that a man carry and delivery the baby instead:

> This is the first time since I began menstruating that I've felt trapped by the biological order. I really wish that Ernie could be pregnant instead of me . . . I mean, he's so much more suited to do that—he likes to cook, he's so much more comfortable with his body. He likes physical changes. It seems totally unfair to me that I have to carry this child. Though I want this child—but it seems like it should be, or could be, in his body. (Millner, 209)

However, when the male character in Millner's film does become pregnant, he enjoys the attention and publicity of being one of the first pregnant males in the U.S., fantasizing about whether Dustin Hoffman would play him in the film based on his life (217).

More than twenty years after Millner's pregnant man utopia, an episode of the popular television sitcom *Scrubs* (aired on January 24, 2006) featured a brief fantasy scenario in which Carla dreams of winning the lottery to pay for a procedure allowing her husband Turk to carry their future baby in *his* stomach instead of hers. In the dramatization of her imagined lottery win, Turk appears in late stages of pregnancy as Carla relishes her escape from pregnancy and childbirth.

The female fantasy of male pregnancy is likewise comically portrayed in Karen Rostoker-Gruber and Gail Panzer-Salmanowitz's illustrated book of jokes titled *If Men Had Babies* . . . but in an exaggerated and ideologically conservative manner. While written by women, the book's narrations all confirm and defend traditional gender roles and the misogynistic heterosexuality of the hypothetical pregnant man, since most of the depictions (and the cartoons by Jim Gallagher) objectify women as sexual objects for the expectant father. For example, one typical narration states: "If men had babies . . . all OB nurses would be required to wear fishnet stockings, stiletto heels, and white miniskirts" while the drawing shows a stereotypical playboy model who flirtingly asks the pregnant man, "Is there anything else I can do to ease your pain?" (38). One might conclude that these images of "What if men had babies" (unlike the suggestion of sodomy in *El parto de Juan Rana*) actually reflect an implied heterosexual male fantasy that seems more interested in confirming the non-homosexual nature of the potentially dangerous implication of male pregnancy than with proposing any political or personal agenda based on women's reproductive choices or questioning traditional gender roles.

The feature-film industry seemed to take advantage of the *Roe v. Wade* controversy in the 1970s by producing a series of questionable movies about "the world's first pregnant man." During the same year as the landmark decision of 1973 (with its convincing case for the legalization of abortion), Jacques Demy wrote and directed the French film *A Slightly Pregnant Man*, starring Catherine Deneuve and Marcello Mastroianni. In this "what if" fantasy, a heterosexual man named Marco discovers that he has become pregnant, which is explained in terms of a gradual transformation in human physiology as a result of certain factors and changes in the modern world (such as the effects of eating hormone-fed animals). Some of the consequences and concerns that surface in the film include jokes about a homosexual relationship that resulted in his pregnancy, discussion of legalized abortion now that men also give birth, politicians who propose immediate funding for childcare centers, and worries about overpopulation and gender role reversal. One of the more developed episodes involves a new business venture pitched by a prenatal clothing designer and manufacturer targeted at future pregnant men. With Marco as the spokesperson, the marketing campaign parades numerous male maternity outfits for a diverse group of pregnant men in various social, professional, and recreational situations. Nonetheless, despite the apparent outbreak of other cases of male pregnancy around the world, Marco's condition turns out to be an error made by the gynecologist's lab; Marco was merely experiencing symptoms psychologically induced by the suggestion of pregnancy. In the end, the biological transgression is "corrected" as his wife announces that *she*, in fact, is pregnant.

Undoubtedly inspired by Demy's *A Slightly Pregnant Man*, the 1977 flop *Rabbit Test* (written by Joan Rivers and Jay Redack, directed by Joan Rivers, and starring Billy Crystal) is an even more confused comedy about a young man who inexplicably becomes pregnant. The film tries to explore the hypothetical "what would happen if men could give birth" but only succeeds in reaffirming negative stereotypes based on race, ethnicity, gender, and religion. Written during a pivotal time in the legislation of women's reproductive rights, *Rabbit Test* seems to parody all sides of the debate without making any thought-provoking statement that could engage the issues more thoroughly. For instance, in the film's story, after a period of publicity and hype surrounding the novelty of the world's first pregnant man, politicians begin to consider the consequences on the world's overpopulation if both men and women could give birth. The film then portrays the general public as bloodthirsty abortion activists when the protagonist refuses to abort the fetus (which by that time was only a few weeks from delivery). The movie ends with a parody of the birth of Jesus, as the protagonist and his wife (having been rejected by society) hide in a barn-like structure during the Christmas holidays. The protagonist Lionel miraculously gives birth as a voice-over of God announces that the baby is a girl. Apparently the unsuccessful and highly problematic film was trying to capitalize on the current debate over reproductive rights and the questioning of traditional gender roles in society during the women's movement of the seventies.

The possibility of male pregnancy also appears in an episode of the television program *The Cosby Show* (first aired on November 9, 1989) as part of a dream sequence, creating an absurd yet humorous scenario peppered with social commentary. Cliff dreams that he, his son Theo, and his sons-in-law

Elvin and Martin are all pregnant as the result of the eruption of a volcano in Peru that sent spores into the drinking water. Following stereotypes traditionally associated with female pregnancy, the pregnant men become very emotional and complain about their discomfort, while the women act insensitive to their plight. Theo deals with stares and cruel comments because he is an "unwed father." Lamenting that the mother wants nothing to do with the baby, he realizes the importance of men using birth control. The four men eventually go into labor, but they are denied actual childbirth experiences, since Martin gives birth to a toy sailboat, Theo has a mini sports car, and Cliff gives birth to a six-inch hoagie. In the final scene, Cliff appears to have gained some insight as the result of his pregnancy dream. Upon awaking, he tells his wife Clair how much he appreciates her and how much he admires all women.

When critiquing the 1994 Hollywood comedy *Junior* (directed by Ivan Reitman and featuring Arnold Schwarzenegger as a pregnant scientist), Ernest Larsen argues that this male fantasy of male pregnancy, like the horror film genre, exhibits a fear of female sexuality and of women's reproductive capacity. Referring first to Mary Shelley's *Frankenstein* (and the association of monsters and a male scientist who "gives birth"), Larsen emphasizes the importance of casting in *Junior*, given the identification of Schwarzenegger as a "cyborg technomonster," but here now nine months pregnant and disguised as a woman to facilitate the controversial pregnancy (Figure 2). Kelly Oliver likewise highlights the actor's previous roles when discussing *Junior* ("Conan the Barbarian becomes the sensitive man and our model of motherhood") while arguing broader political implications: "This science-fiction story suggests a future where women have no more to do with reproduction than donating eggs—of course in this story the egg was stolen. This is a story of men stealing all control over reproduction from women" (188). Given Schwarzenegger's recent career change to politics (as governor of California), the ironic similarities to the seventeenth-century farce *El parto de Juan Rana* become even more apparent since the early modern protagonist is both pregnant and a local politician.

While some believe that *Junior* attempted to capitalize on recent advances in fertility research at the end of the twentieth century, others see feature-length films on the theme of male pregnancy as another response to the gradual acceptance in the iconography of the pregnant body during the 1990s and the consequent sensationalizing of the topic through depictions of pregnant men (Larsen, 242). Sandra Matthews and Laura Wexler, for example, argue that Annie Leibovitz's photograph of a nude and pregnant Demi Moore on the cover of the August 1991 issue of *Vanity Fair* inspired

16    Male Delivery

Figure 2: A pregnant Arnold Schwarzenegger in the 1994 film *Junior*. (Reproduced by permission from Universal Studios)

a series of "clones" imitating the controversial photo. Among the most sensational imitations were the humorous images of "pregnant men," such as Moore's then-husband Bruce Willis, who (taking advantage of the publicity opportunity) appeared pregnant in a computer-generated image on the cover of *Spy* magazine one month after Moore's *Vanity Fair* cover (Matthews and Wexler, 205). Other pregnant man photographs designed for their shock value include those in the advertisements for the film *Naked Gun 33 1/3: The*

*Final Insult* and in the July 7, 1992, issue of the tabloid *Weekly World News*, which featured an article titled "Man Gives Birth to a Healthy Baby Boy!"[19]

Following the tabloid's example, but enhanced with online "medical" details of "The First Male Pregnancy," website www.malepregnancy.com outlines the pregnancy of Mr. Lee Mingwei (a Taiwanese-born man purported to have volunteered to have an embryo implanted in his abdominal cavity), complete with photos and links to a spoofed *Time* magazine cover, CNN headlines, and internet reader response. This "interactive" site even invites the visitor to "join physicians and scientists around the world in monitoring Mr. Lee's pregnancy online." The website was "conceived" and designed by the artists Virgil Wong and Lee Mingwei, who David Emery describes as members of a "multidisciplinary arts group developing work about the human body as seen through medicine, society and technology." On his "Urban Legends and Folklore" website, Emery concludes that this cyberspoof of male pregnancy fails to escape "the fact that historically the idea of a man bearing a child has been considered laughable . . . It's just the same old joke retold in a brand-new medium."[20]

An episode of the television medical drama *Grey's Anatomy* (which aired on November 6, 2005) also exploits the tabloid-carnivalesque characteristics of male pregnancy through a pseudo-scientific treatment of the topic. When the husband of a pregnant woman is admitted to the hospital's psychiatric ward (because he is convinced that he, too, is pregnant), the interns and other hospital staff quickly become curious voyeurs of the medical "freak show." However, when he tests positive on a pregnancy test, he then becomes a "surgical" patient, and they soon discover that his growing abdomen is the result of a teratoma, a type of tumor containing cells that can result in tissue growth; some teratomas have been known to grow hair and teeth and others even secrete the "pregnancy hormone" (see "Teratoma," at wikipedia.org). Despite the plausible medical explanation for the man's pregnancy symptoms, the episode plays more like a circus sideshow, as crowds of onlookers take photos of the "pregnant man" while interns sell tickets to the surgical removal of the "creature."

## Technology and Procreation

When discussing the recurring fantasy of a child born from man alone, Rosi Braidotti judges the pseudo-science of alchemy to be the *reductio ad absurdum* of the male desire for self-reproduction, as the homunculus (a tiny man-made male) pops out of the alchemist's laboratory, fully formed and endowed with language (*Nomadic*, 87).[21] Accordingly, when Paracelsus, the master theoretician of alchemy, is certain that a man should and could be born outside a woman's body, Braidotti concludes: "The assumption is that the alchemist can not only imitate the work of women but they can do it better because the artificial process of science and technique perfect the imperfection of the natural course of events and thus avoids mistakes. Once reproduction becomes the pure result of mental efforts, the appropriation of the feminine is complete" (87–88). Interesting, especially in light of "John Frog's" autogenesis, is William Newman's analysis of alchemy and the homunculus, in which he describes how the fifteenth-century treatise attributed to Thomas Aquinas (*De essentiis essentiam* [*On the Essence of Essences*]) plays down the need for females in the business of reproduction by referring to the "spontaneous generation of frogs–they sometimes burst from wet soil with such speed that the vulgar believe them to rain from the sky. No female is required here" (Newman, *Promethean*, 189).

In the nineteenth and twentieth centuries, technology and medicine also provided ample inspiration for real and fantastical attempts by men to create life without the need for women. For some, Mary Shelley's portrayal of this process in *Frankenstein* serves as a cautionary tale, a feminist critique of science through the horror story of "what happens when a man tries to have a baby without a woman" (Mellor, 40). However, for other readers and spectators, *Frankenstein* merely propagates the representation of the homosexual as monster. In his study of homosexuality and the horror film, Harry Benshoff argues that, in both the novel and cinematic versions,

> *Frankenstein* itself has become something of a counter-hegemonic classic; feminists and queers alike have plumbed its depths to underscore a scathing critique of male hubris in which the attempt to create life without the aid of procreative sexual union results in disaster for all . . . this core idea—that of a mad male homosexual scientist giving birth to a monster—can be found to a greater or lesser degree in almost every filmic adaptation. (18)

Following Shelley's model of what many considered a new literary genre (gothic sci-fi), science fiction has explored numerous versions of the manmade creature. In her discussion of monsters and male maternity, Rosi Braidotti notes that "extra-uterine births are central to science fiction texts" (*Metamorphoses*, 192). From the misogynistically horrific portrayal in *The Stepford Wives* (1974) to cloning and other new reproductive technologies, the usurpation of traditional modes of human reproduction frequently erupts in controversy. Andrea Dworkin, for example, in the late 1970s wrote ominously of the certain future of male maternity in a society in which "female life is determined by its reproductive value":

> And what is going to happen to women, these women and all women, when the tools of reproductive control of women are no longer technologically (medically) crude? When the technology catches up with the political and legal leap into the Orwellian future? What is going to happen to women when life can be made in the laboratory and men can control reproduction not just socially but also biologically with real efficiency? ... What is going to happen to women who have only one argument for the importance of their existence—that their reproductive capacities are worth a little something (shelter, food, solace, minimal respect)—when men can make babies? (172–73)

Still others look enthusiastically to the unstable and evolving nature of humanity as a way of explaining the "posthuman age."[22] In her "Cyborg Manifesto," Donna Haraway defines the present in terms of the cyborg: "By the late twentieth century, our time, we are all chimeras, theorized and fabricated hybrids of machine and organism; in short we are cyborgs" (150).

Not surprisingly, reproductive technology has finally caught up with the fantastical metaphors of male pregnancy that have been circulated and marketed for centuries. Robert Winston describes in his study *The IVF Revolution* how an embryo can now be implanted in the abdomen of a man, much like women's ectopic pregnancies. While the procedure is simple (yet dangerous), the pregnant man must take female hormones and he runs the risk of developing breasts and hemorrhaging in the implanted placenta. Although Winston presents the possibility of male pregnancy as another advantage of the medical advances in reproductive medicine, he laments some of the "inappropriate" responses in the media, quoting one writer who claimed that the procedure undermines "conventional moral values" (207).

Given the scientific plausibility of male pregnancy, it is not unexpected that a 2006 publication combining science and humor chose the pregnant man question for its title: *Can a Guy Get Pregnant? Scientific Answers to Everyday (& Not-So-Everyday) Questions* (Sones and Sones). Upon further perusal, the curious reader learns that the answer to the title's question is "amazingly enough, yes, in the sense of carrying to term an already fertilized egg implanted in the body" (Sones and Sones 27). Quoting the science writer David Bodanis, the text remains unflinching toward the apparent oxymoron: "There is no good reason why a properly implanted and hormone-supplied zygote could not enjoy the same normal nine-month growth inside a man" (quoted in Sones and Sones, 27). Other questions in Sones and Sones's text include: "Can men breastfeed babies?" and "Are there 'false pregnancies' in men?" (41, 46).

## Pregnant Man as Political Vehicle

While the manipulation of science and technology is what gives the male pregnancy website the illusion of authenticity, recent advances in medical research have also intensified the political cultural war between pro-life advocates and those who defend women's reproductive rights. As Laura R. Woliver argues, the political geographies of pregnancy have shifted and increasingly we find reproductive power in the hands of medical professionals, lobbyists, and policymakers. Not surprisingly, since *Roe v. Wade*, feminists have utilized the pregnant man metaphor in a variety of images. Helen Forelle, for example, published a collection of letters in 1982 titled *If Men Got Pregnant Abortion Would Be a Sacrament*. These letters were written by women after they had an abortion in an attempt to voice the "pro-choice" argument "to counteract misleading and exaggerated claims by so-called 'pro-life' activists" (viii).

Theorizing along similar lines, in her 1994 study *Pregnant Men: Practice, Theory, and the Law*, Ruth Colker decided to ask whether equality theory could be used to redress women's subordination in the reproductive health arena. Colker examined the courts' treatment of "pregnant men" or men who are similarly situated to women in the context of reproductive health (male sperm donors, for example) and found that these "pregnant male persons are treated much better than pregnant female persons. Such a result occurs because the courts devalue or ignore women's experiences of pregnancy" (137). Colker encourages her readers to learn how to talk about "pregnant men" in order to reveal this deliberate attempt to harm women's (but not men's) reproductive freedom. When discussing rights such as abortion, Colker concludes that "we need to find practical ways to demonstrate that the pregnant man would never be denied access to a service so fundamental to their reproductive freedom" (207).

Visual images that employ the pregnant man figure are also used to stimulate the viewer to consider complex issues surrounding motherhood, legal abortion, birth control, and women's rights. The work of Barbara Kruger at the end of the twentieth century, for example, serves to interrupt and challenge cultural assumptions about gender, sexuality, and power. Particularly appropriate for the topic of male pregnancy are the images Kruger designed for a bus shelter project in 1991. In an interview with Therese Lichtenstein, Barbara Kruger describes the billboards for this project:

> I try to visualize a site, a world where men are just as responsible for reproductive responsibility as women. So I've used three images of men—a construction worker, a high school student, and a young professional and his child—and try to invert the procedures of having these people get anecdotal about their lives and tell you that they just found out that they are pregnant. I am trying to deal with a serious topic in an anecdotal and comedic way, to engage viewers and make them laugh but also to rearrange their conceptions of what is possible. (203)

Kruger published a similar version of the bus shelter posters in the op-ed page of the *New York Times* on June 4, 1991. The caption under an image of a young George W. Bush reads: "I've worked hard. Business is booming and I've decided to enter politics. The campaign is going really well and I just found out I'm pregnant. What should I do?" Emblazed across the middle of the photo in huge letters is the word "HELP!" and above the photo, the artist engages the reader with the question "Any Suggestions?" (Figure 3). In her study on abortion and social responsibility, Laurie Shrage proposes an updating of Kruger's George W. Bush pregnancy image with the caption, "The war on terrorism is going great, my approval ratings are soaring, and I need to get Saddam but I just found out I'm pregnant." as well as a version featuring John Ashcroft: "I'm moving the conservative Christian Agenda forward, I've got hundreds of detainees to get rid of while liberals are screaming about civil rights, but I just found out I'm pregnant" (158).

Male pregnancy with a similar political message but through a very different vehicle is explored in Joan Lipkin and Tom Clear's 1990 pro-choice musical comedy *He's Having Her Baby*. This satirical approach to the abortion debate employs the pregnant man premise through gender role reversal and musical comedy to demonstrate the importance of reproductive freedom and choice for women during the controversial post-Roe v. Wade debate over fetal rights and women's reproductive autonomy.[23]

While *He's Having Her Baby* is a creative "what if . . ." approach to the abortion debate, the casting and performance choices are surprisingly reminiscent of the seventeenth-century musical comedy *El parto de Juan Rana*. Like Juan Rana in *El parto*, the lead actor Paul Tomak portrays a feminine gender-bending but apparently heterosexual male (Joey), who is impregnated by his butch (captain of the field hockey team) and sexist girlfriend Liz. Also similar to the seventeenth-century comedy, the campy performance

Figure 3: Barbara Kruger's artwork for *The New York Times* op-ed page (June 4, 1991). (Reproduced by permission from Barbara Kruger)

of the effeminate and pregnant Joey creates a queer subtext that inevitably connects the issues of women's reproductive freedom and homosexuality, which is deepened even further for those audience members who are aware of the lead actor's own gay identity.

Women's reproductive health, especially when adversely impacted by conservative legislation, is also treated in a fascinating three-minute political film created by the Spanish director and actress Icíar Bollaín.[24] Part of a collective project involving thirty-two filmmakers before the 2004 presidential elections in Spain, Bollaín directed the short video *Por tu propio bien* (For Your Own Good). This intriguing short features a pregnant man who gives birth in a hospital while the attending doctor and nurses (rather matter-of-factly and without much emotion) direct the suffering and scared father-to-be through the birth of his son.[25] After the humorous yet "uneventful" birthing scene, the final frame reads: "Childbirth is Ours. Give it Back to Us!" [El parto es nuestro. ¡Que nos lo devuelvan!] As each short film was created to show a critical view of a particular issue in Spain before the elections, Bollaín's video intended to criticize how in recent years José María Aznar's conservative government had handled maternity issues and the workplace. Nonetheless, the plea to take the control over reproductive health out of the hands of men and give it back to women could also invoke other issues such as abortion rights as well as support for maternity leave and daycare centers. In this way, Bollaín's twenty-first-century Spanish version of male pregnancy can be seen as a feminist response to the misogynistic message at the close of the seventeenth-century *El parto de Juan Rana*.

## The Pregnant Man as Gay Camp

The first episode of the 2003–2004 season of the popular television program *Will & Grace* begins with gay friends Jack and Will in bed together, waking up to the disturbing thought that they had inadvertently had sexual relations during a night of excessive drinking.[26] After the initial shock, Jack announces that he would need to purchase an EPT (early pregnancy test) and that he would not go through the pregnancy ordeal alone. In fact, in an earlier episode, Jack actually takes a home pregnancy test (initially intending to support Karen, who feared she might be pregnant), but when the results of Jack's test are negative, he humorously has to deal with his sadness and disappointment.[27] It's not unexpected, then, when we learn in another episode how a young Jack had placed a football under his shirt and told everyone that he was pregnant with George Michael's baby.[28] Although the joke about male pregnancy resulting from sex between men also appears in the heterosexual feature films *A Slightly Pregnant Man*, *Rabbit Test*, and *Junior*, in the television comedy *Will & Grace* the humor now originates from gay characters. During another episode that links male pregnancy with gay identity, Grace's need to know any other shocking secrets about Will (as unsettling as his confession of being gay) inspires Will to lighten the moment with "I'm pregnant!"[29]

In fact, some of the male matrix jokes in this popular series play on campy inversions related to the physiological effects of pregnancy. For example, when Will and Grace discuss the possibility of having children in the future, Grace claims that he will need her, to which Will quips, "Right. I'm not going to the gym ten hours a week just to wind up with stretch marks" (similar to a comment made by one of Will's friends in a subsequent episode when clarifying why he adopted his son: "I didn't want to lose my figure").[30]

Not to be out-done by the popular network sitcom, Showtime's "groundbreaking" program *Queer As Folk* also took advantage of a male pregnancy joke in the last episode of its final season (aired on August 7, 2005). When Brian and Justin suddenly (and uncharacteristically) decide to get married, their friend Emmett quips sarcastically that Justin must be pregnant.

Much less mainstream and sanitized than the male pregnancy jokes in *Will & Grace* and *Queer as Folk* are the outrageous performances of the Australian-born fashion designer, gay nightclub icon, and performance artist Leigh Bowery (1961–1994) in various clubs as well as in the 1993 gay New York drag festival "Wigstock," which was captured in the feature film *Wigstock: The Movie* (1995) and included in the 2003 documentary directed by Charles Atlas titled *The Legend of Leigh Bowery*.[31] The delivery scene, in which Bowery "gives birth" to a full grown woman, is as over-the-top as it is campy and grotesque, as well as visually, musically, and theatrically hilarious. Moreover, like the cross-dressed actor in *El parto de Juan Rana*, this drag queen gives birth to his female assistant, who is hidden under the performer's skirt:

> He came out wearing a dark green, floral printed, velvet knee-length skirt with matching jacket, looking larger than life. Rather than wear make-up he had on a nylon face-mask that zipped up the back with three holes in front, two for the eyes and one for the mouth . . . Nicola his long suffering assistant was strapped to his body under his outfit in a cloth harness. She was covered with red body paint and KY Jelly and wrapped with a string of sausages. She was curled in an embryo position with her feet up by Leigh's shoulders and her head in his smelly sweaty crotch. At the end of his number he shocked the crowd by pulling up his skirt and giving birth to Nicola who popped out of his Velcro womb while his arms and legs flailed in the air all the time belting out an amazing on-key rendition of Beatles' song "All You Need Is Love." (Tilley, 203–4)[32]

Fergus Greer's photograph in Figure 4 demonstrates the under-garment position of Bowery (and his assistant, who must hang upside-down under his costume) prior to giving birth on stage.

Figure 4: Drag queen icon Leigh Bowery and assistant reveal their positions before the birthing scene. (Reproduced by permission from Fergus Greer)

Perhaps the performance of male pregnancy that best epitomizes the campy display of a man dressed in women's clothing and nine months pregnant is the 2004 drag queen performance of "Aisha" lip-synching and dancing to Whitney Houston's rendition of Chaka Khan's song "I'm Every Woman." During the musical number, performed at the gay club "Connections" in Louisville, Kentucky (whose customers are generally familiar with drag but nonetheless are pleasantly shocked by the unexpected sights), Aisha appears on stage clothed in an elegant floor-length wrap with ruffles, thus covering "her" body so she can then shock the audience by dropping the coat to reveal the silhouette of a woman nine months pregnant. The gimmicky yet ironic performance concludes with the agony of the pregnant singer going into labor, in beat to the moaning and groaning of the song's sounds of sexual pleasure, but from the mouth of a pregnant drag queen the utterances

Figure 5: "Aisha" goes into labor while performing "I'm Every Woman." (Photo by Jody Serkes)

announce her pre-delivery pain and panic. In a brilliant portrayal of the ultimate challenge to traditional notions of gender, sex assignment, and desire, this performance makes the viewer consider the significance of a pregnant drag queen who represents "every woman" (Figure 5).

Like the pregnant drag numbers, the seventeenth-century performance of the comic interlude *El parto de Juan Rana* also concludes with the dramatic appearance of a pregnant man dressed in women's clothing and who is about to go into labor. While all three acts end with music, singing, and dancing, the gimmick of a pregnant "drag queen" who gives birth is only part of the early modern presentation. What comes before as well as after the climactic birthing scene engages the audience to consider how issues related to the control of gender roles and the legislation of sexual and reproductive practices impacted everyone's lives. And while the political, scientific, and moral debates have developed and shifted over the centuries, these topics consistently have surfaced in various contexts in different cultures, thus demonstrating that there is something about the pregnant man that continues to be an effective image for multifaceted engagement of controversial sexual and reproductive issues.

# 2
# Performing Male Pregnancy in *El parto de Juan Rana*

After reviewing such divergent representations of male pregnancy (from classical mythology to twenty-first-century drag shows), we might be surprised to find a similar variation of themes that emerge in the seventeenth-century dramatic text *El parto de Juan Rana*. While the predominant function of the interlude is to entertain through carnivalesque humor, the one-act play also reveals a multiplicity of interrelated and contentious issues that were being played out in early modern legal, religious, scientific, and literary venues (which will be discussed in Chapters 3 and 4).

## Intellectual Fecundity and Procreation in *El parto*

Like the prologue to *Don Quixote* (in which Cervantes employs a paternity and childbirth metaphor to describe his talent for engendering literary works), Lanini Sagredo's *entremés* begins by highlighting the relationship between biological procreation and patriarchal intellectual fecundity.[1] As the play opens and the local officials are discussing Juan Rana's crime of having transgressed gender, anatomical, and sexuality proscriptions by becoming pregnant, their dialogue reflects the scientific theories of "ingenios" (wits) detailed by Juan Huarte de San Juan in his highly influential 1575 *Examen de ingenios para las ciencias* (Examination of Wits for the Sciences). According to Huarte, man's ability to conceive new ideas and give birth to them is the result of the male body's humoral makeup, which predetermines each individual's mental and creative aptitudes. Like the mayor Berrueco in *El parto*, Huarte uses the language of procreation to explain what makes men *ingeniosos* (intellectually fertile): "He gets pregnant, gives birth, and has children and grandchildren ... they are called geniuses for being fertile in producing and engendering concepts related to science and knowledge"

(188–89).² Moreover, it is not by chance that women are absent from the sexual/textual reproductive metaphor: "The erasure of the woman in the biological metaphor is a clear symptom of her erasure from the social sphere" (Montauban, 43). The bottom line, then, is the connection among bodily composition, intelligence, and gender. Since brain power is tantamount to social power, in *El parto* the dilemma created by an individual who (as a man) should not have the biological capacity to bear children but who (as a political leader) should possess the intellect to give birth to new concepts and solutions, is carried to farcical proportions:

> **Berrueco:** Would it not be a greater crime for a mayor, having been fertile, now to be sterile?
> **Court Clerk:** What strange nonsense. Do you want him to be fertile?
> **Berrueco:** What good is a mayor's staff if it doesn't bear fruit?
> **Clerk:** Now you're comparing a staff to his member?
> **Berrueco:** Clerk, you don't understand. A staff conceives thousands of things and later can deliver them prodigious.

> [**Berrueco:** Alcalde siendo, aun más delito era
> siendo fecundo, que hay estéril fuera?
> **Escribano:** ¡Necedad es bien rara!
> ¿Fecundo queréis sea?
> **Berrueco:** Pues la vara
> a un alcalde absoluto
> ¿de que provecho le es, si no da fruto?
> **Escribano:** ¿La vara comparáis agora al sexo?
> **Berrueco:** Vos, escribano, no entendéis bien de eso;
> una vara concibe dos mil cosas
> luego puede parirlas prodigiosas.]

Of course, in the interlude, the *vara* (staff) of patriarchal power and authority also serves as a phallic symbol of the protagonist's sexual behavior that led to the present scandal.³ Peter Thompson notes, however, that the pregnant man must combine both phallo- and gynocentric images: "Juan Rana's *vara* symbolizes phallocentric powers, but the fact remains that Juan Rana's pregnancy is proof of his female fertility. What is implied here is that Juan Rana's character in *El parto* is a fruitful example of both genders in one, namely, that his double-sexed condition makes him a hermaphrodite" ("Crossing," 324).⁴

## Gender Inversion and Sexuality in *El parto*

So how do the other characters in *El parto* explain this "most hideous and lewd crime" [más liviana fea culpa]? One attempt to justify the inexplicable condition incriminates Juan Rana's nontraditional marriage to his *marimacho* (manly) wife Aldonza:[5]

> **Court Clerk:** First of all, being married to Aldonza, John Frog has never given any indication of being a man, he is but a plaything, so Aldonza was the one who ordered him (the aforementioned) around; she scolded him and sometimes beat him. By fighting with him she got him to do all the housework: the sweeping, scrubbing, cooking—and he even did her errands for her.
>
> **Berrueco:** Proof of the pregnancy ascribed to John Frog is plain. For if he allowed his wife to wear the pants on occasion, then it's not so incredible that he get pregnant since he did what she should have done.
>
> [**Escribano:** Primeramente,
> el que siendo casado
> Juan Rana con Aldonza nunca ha dado
> indicios de ser hombre, pues Aldonza
> (al susodicho) siendo una peonza
> era quien le mandaba,
> le reñía y a veces le pegaba,
> logrando en sus contiendas
> que él hiciera de casa las haciendas,
> que barriese, fregase y que pusiese
> la olla, y aun a sus mandados fuese.
>
> **Berrueco:** La probanza esta llana
> del delito que importa a Juan Rana
> del preñado supuesto
> que si el permitió que los calzones
> su mujer se pusiese en ocasiones,
> ser el preñado él no es demasía,
> pues hizo lo que ella hacer debía.]

The court clerk's reference to Juan Rana as a *peonza* (literally, "spinning-top") reengages the comical treatment of the political debate over power, control, and masculinity. As Antonio Martínez Ripoll notes in his discussion of authority, leadership, and force, the image of both the *vara* and *peonza* are joined in Covarrubias's *Emblemas morales* through the emblem depicted with the saying "Non nisi percussus" (Only by force).⁶ The pictorial image reveals a top that spins only by the whip of the stick shown above while the commentary explains: "How tiresome to always have to carry a staff or whip in hand so that the servant or vassal does what is expected and what his master commands" (Covarrubias, *Emblemas*, 176v).⁷ Of course, in *El parto*, this sociopolitical lesson is inverted when Aldonza is depicted as the staff-bearing authority figure who controls her "servant" Juan Rana (symbolized by a spinning top) through *her* own rod. So the logical conclusion, taken to the extreme, reasons that if she possessed the staff (while he was doing all of the other womanly duties), then why wouldn't *he* be the one to get pregnant and give birth?

We might also wonder, then, if Rana's dishonor also serves as a warning to others who transgress traditional gender roles in ways that suggest unorthodox sexual practices. In other words, gender nonconformity can also lead to or at least indicate possible sodomitical activity, which in turn can result in anatomical sex transmutation. Not surprisingly, *El parto* reveals numerous references to and jokes about same-sex desire. At the beginning of the *entremés* Berrueco announces that Juan Rana is a "better woman than he is a man" [para hembra es mejor que para hombre] while it is also confirmed that in no way is he a real man ("he has never given any indication of being a man" [nunca ha dado indicios de ser hombre] and "John Frog is not a man in any regard" [por no ser Juan Rana hombre en nada]). Later, when Juan Rana speaks in his own defense, he refers to himself in the feminine: "It is important also that I confess to you that I [as a woman] am not guilty of anything" [Valga también confesaros / que no soy culpad*a* en nada]. While the audience waits during much of the interlude for the climactic entrance of the pregnant Juan Rana (who Thompson describes as "an over-the-top, pregnant drag queen" ["Crossing," 326]), the other visiting mayors participate in burlesque homoerotic gags. One mayor, for example, sits on the lap of another, which inspires jokes about him being a packsaddle on a donkey, as another makes a suggestive pun distinguishing which *alcalde* is the top and which is the bottom.⁸

An interesting twist on the top/bottom dilemma contributing to male pregnancy (as well as a popular precursor to *El parto*) is found in the third story of the ninth day in Boccaccio's *Decameron*.⁹ In this tale a gullible husband is convinced by a couple of tricksters (looking to make some fast and easy cash) that he is pregnant. The panic-stricken husband immediately blames his pregnancy on his wife for assuming the dominant role during sex: " 'Ah, Tessa, this is your doing! You always insist on lying on top. I told you all along what would happen' " (694). He implies, then, that his phallic pregnancy is really not so phallic after all, since his usual sexual position on the bottom is frequently associated with a passive female role during sex.

Since the only sanctioned sexual position had the woman on the bottom, the man who agrees to assume this position was considered effeminate (Pérez Escohotado, 80). This inverted sexual position with "the woman on top" traditionally had been viewed with "horror by theologians and by medical practitioners, who thought that reversing the proper downward flow of semen could not only damage the fetus because the womb is 'turned over,' but may also cause harm to the man" (Camille, 76). The woman on top motif is also evident in early modern interpretations of Ovid's story of "Salmacis and Hermaphroditus," pictorially and verbally representing the destructive force of women's aggressive lust, men's passivity, and the "fragile nature of masculinity." As Salmacis assumes the active role of sexual predator, Hermaphroditus degenerates into the passive role of "a blushing feminized virgin" (Gilbert, *Early,* 58–61).

Displaying the misogyny implied in the Ovidian tale, the husband in Boccaccio's story not only condemns the transgression of gender roles in bed, but he also blames his pregnancy on his wife's rampant female sexuality:

> Ah, what a terrible fate! What am I to do? How am I to produce this infant? Where will it come out? This woman's going to be the death of me now, with her insatiable lust, I can see that. May God make her as miserable as I desire to be happy. I swear that if I were fit and strong, which is far from being the case, I should get up from this bed and break every bone in her body. It serves me right, though; I should never have allowed her to lie on top: but if I ever get out of this alive, she certainly won't do it again, even if she's dying of frustration. (694)

In the end, the "pregnant" husband pays for a remedy that will induce what he believes is a "painless miscarriage," since his biggest fear is related to pain:

> "Get on with it then, doctor, for the love of God," said Calandrino. "I have two hundred pounds here with which I was going to buy a farm, but you can take the whole lot if necessary, provided I don't have to bear this child. I simply don't know how I could manage it, when I think of the great hullabaloo women make when they are having babies, even though they have plenty of room for the purpose. If I had all that pain to

contend with, I honestly think I should die before I ever produced any child." (694–95)

Far from representing an implied version of "womb envy" inherent in the male pregnancy image, Boccaccio's story (like many other depictions of childbirth) emphasizes the painful curse of having to give birth through its farcical representation of a "pregnant" man who (unlike Juan Rana) opts to abort the fetus.

## Female Sexuality, Frogs, and Homosexuality

Reminiscent of the pregnant husband's fear of his wife's active sexual desire in Boccaccio, film critic Ernest Larsen notes the symbolic rejection of female sexual agency through the male pregnancy plot in the 1994 Hollywood comedy *Junior*, but here his comments serve to preface a gay subtext in the relationship between the pregnant scientist (played by Arnold Schwarzenegger) and his business partner (played by Danny DeVito). During the impregnation scene, after DeVito suggestively injects Schwarzenegger using a long syringe, the men admire the mobility of the future maternal father's "tadpoles" under the microscope. Interestingly, around the time when *El parto* was first performed, the recent invention of the microscope created a new association between sperm and tadpoles. Accordingly, consistent with the descriptions and illustrations in later seventeenth-century scientific treatises on reproduction, there are numerous references to frog and tadpole-related imagery in *El parto* (Pinto-Correia). When the first visiting mayor comes from the town Pozuelo (small well or pond), Berrueco observes, "What a famous fish-hook" (¡Qué famoso anzuelo / de pescar!). When the second mayor arrives, Berrueco jokes that he might have emerged from the lagoons of his town as a tadpole instead of a mayor. The imagery here, playing on the tadpole in the lagoon (while implying a connection to both the ambivalent frog-nature of the protagonist and perhaps anticipating a possible sperm reference provided by reproductive technologies), humorously evokes another meaning of *renacuajo* (tadpole), defined in Covarrubias's *Tesoro* as "a disfigured and annoying boy" [Un muchacho mal tallado y enfadoso] (904). The suggestive imagery in this scene continues as the third mayor arrives from "Guesos" (Bones), whose inhabitants Berrueco describes as *capones* or eunuchs. Of course, with the invention of the microscope and the dramatic changes in reproductive medicine that resulted from the embryological findings during the last half of the seventeenth century, performances of the interlude during and after that time would inevitably have created (for some spectators) another opportunity for same-sex humor, referencing the "animalcules" (frequently described as tadpoles) engendered in semen through the frog and tadpole jokes in *El parto*.

The audience of *El parto* may not have known this, but frogs (*ranas*) were not only etymologically linked to the term "buffoon" ("from the Latin word for toad . . . for spitting venom of malice and shamelessness to entertain fools" [Covarrubias, *Tesoro*, 243]) and the related *buffo* (male singer of comic roles in opera), but the aquatic creatures likewise have been used to represent the uterus and female sexuality for centuries.[10] The Church, in particular, has manipulated the image of frogs and toads as symbols of fornication and immorality, frequently associating them with female sex organs and demonic involvement (Lovkrona, 117). In fact, frogs and toads commonly appear in narratives relating the grotesque birthing or engendering of monster-like creatures. Paré explains, for example, that "many animal forms are likewise created in women's wombs (which are often found with fetuses and well-formed young), such as frogs, toads, snakes, lizards, and harpies" (56). Other frog images associated with androgyny, sodomy, fertility, and sin are depicted in the iconography of Bosch and Bruegel as well as their literary and visual sources. In "The Frog's Wedding" (in Bosch's *The Temptation of St. Anthony*), the outstanding feature of the white-bellied frog is his bisexuality and reproductive powers: "In its female capacity the androgynous frog is fertilized from above; at the same time in its masculine capacity it impregnates the witch, thus bringing her into a filial relationship with the primal mother" (Fraenger, 412). Referring to the idolatrous worship of the frog that inspired certain images in Bosch's artwork, Wilhelm Fraenger describes a thirteenth-century bull attacking the rite of initiation of a medieval batrachite (frog-worshipping) sect: "He was forced to venerate this frog with a shameful kiss. The bull ends with an allegation that cult members of both sexes mingled in licentious orgies, the most shameful feature of which was the sin against nature" (469). The association between frogs and "swamplike promiscuity"[11] continued into the early modern period in Spain, as the term *rana* or frog was also linked to female sexual transgression: "Let's remember that 'frog' was a generic word for loose women, prostitutes, and madams" (Luna, 153).[12]

According to ancient and medieval versions of the legend of Nero, the Roman emperor was associated with any number of perversions. Prime among them were sodomy and male effeminacy. Among other crimes and vices, Nero was known for participating in at least two homosexual marriages. It was also believed that his transgressive sexual behavior caused his stomach to swell so much, creating such pain that his doctors believed him to be pregnant. However, he reportedly died when they opened his belly in the vain attempt to remove a fetus (Zapperi, 112–13).

Not surprisingly, the emperor's image was also linked to that of the frog. Other medieval German and Latin versions of Nero's life recount how his intense wish to give birth to a child helped convince his doctors to prescribe him a magic potion which would enable him to become pregnant. The medical treatment proved effective but when it came time to give birth he only succeeded in delivering a frog from his mouth (Frazer, 215).[13] Undoubtedly an interesting precedent for Juan Rana's performance in *El parto*, the story of Nero's pregnancy most likely was inspired by the role that the emperor played on stage in *Canace in Childbirth* (told in Euripides' lost tragedy *Aiolos* and in Ovid's *Heroides*). As R. M. Frazer notes, "Imagine the ruler of the Roman Empire playing on the public stage a woman in childbirth!" (215). Referring to the significance of the frog in Nero's pregnancy tale, Frazer argues that it can be interpreted in terms of an ill-willed critique of his "rather froggy-sounding" singing voice (217).

The two actors Nero and Juan Rana appear to have shared certain physical features that could be compared to a frog-like physique. Suetonius, for example, describes Nero as "regular rather than attractive, his eyes blue and somewhat weak, his neck overthick, his belly prominent, and his legs very slender" (quoted in Frazer, 217). Similarly, Hannah Bergman suggests that the stage name "Juan Rana" was inspired by the physical attributes featured in the actor's portrait "with such a round and swollen body and a big, fat head, even a slight suggestion of being hunch-backed; he actually looks like a frog" (67) (Figure 6).[14] On the other hand, critics such as Peter Thompson and Harry Vélez-Quiñones argue that Rana's name resonated more with its connection to frogs' amphibian nature, thus referring to the man/woman duality frequently featured in the celebrity's professional roles.[15]

## Male Femininity and Sodomy as Spectacle

Like the readers and spectators of the pregnant Nero drama, the seventeenth-century Spanish audience would have been fully aware of the suspicions of homosexuality associated with Cosme Pérez, the actor behind the stage name Juan Rana. Scholars such as Peter Thompson, José Cartagena-Calderón, and Frédéric Serralta argue that the 1636 sodomy charges against the actor as well as his frequent gender-bending roles on stage prove that the public undoubtedly must have assigned a gay subtext to Juan Rana's performances. Cartagena-Calderón, for example, cites a line from Agustín Moreto's 1662 play *El lindo don Diego* (The Dandy Don Diego) to show how Juan Rana's

Figure 6: Anonymous seventeenth-century portrait of Cosme Pérez (Juan Rana). (Reproduced by permission from Real Academia Española)

celebrity icon had become a symbol for homosexuality: "The 'sodomitic' sexuality of Don Diego becomes even more obvious when in the middle of an argument he reproaches his rival, Don Juan by saying 'you mistake me for a frog,' an allusion that in the context of this performance the audience of that time would not have had any difficulty associating with the theatrical figure of Juan Rana [John Frog]" (166).[16] In fact, Francisco Sáez Raposo argues that the sodomy charges against Juan Rana had a decisive impact on the actor's career (given that the theme of sexual ambiguity became one of the most exploited topics in the dramatic works written for the famous performer after 1636), but without creating the accusatory suspicions that one might expect after a legal incident involving sexual relations between men (33). While Peter Thompson agrees that this incriminating event served as a thematic point-of-departure for the actor's writers, the scholar also stresses that it was Juan Rana's homosexuality, in fact, that provided the key to his stage performance/presence (*Triumphant*, 25).

We might also assume that the audience would have been exposed to the public spectacle of men convicted of sodomy on parade, dressed in women's clothing and with their hair curled as they marched to their deaths.[17] Therefore, the spectators surely must have made a connection between those men and the visual image of an actor (one who had been arrested for the same crime) now on stage dressed as a woman as punishment for being a man who becomes pregnant. Interestingly, both male pregnancy and the sentence of having to parade publicly in women's clothing can be read as possible legal and (hypothetical) physiological consequences of homosexual behavior.

And while there were few dramatic roles requiring male actors to dress as women (especially compared to the frequency of women dressed as men on stage),[18] the seriousness of the social taboo is reflected in a recommendation by the Council of Castile in 1600 to the king regarding the prohibition of public theater:

> They say that women should not perform on stage because in such a public venue their shameless actions incite sin; and instead of women, young men could appear on stage dressed as women but without wearing makeup or displaying indecent actions. However, it is the Council's belief that it is much less offensive for women to act on stage in public than to have male actors dressed as women (playing the female roles), even if they don't wear makeup. (Quoted in Cotarelo y Mori, *Bibliografía*, 164)[19]

And yet, despite the comic element that motivated female impersonation in theater ("men dressed as women ... guaranteed big laughs from the audience" [Restrepo, 201]), the fashion inversion was, nonetheless, associated with serious castigation for same-sex transgressions.

The perversion associated with male cross-dressing is presented as an interesting dilemma in Tomás de Trujillo's 1563 *Libro llamado reprobación de trajes* (Book of the Critique of Clothing), as the author attempts to hypothesize why any man blessed with male privilege would want to give that up for the lower status assigned to women:

> There are some men who are so unchaste and poorly disciplined that they are given to another unusual practice: dressing and disguising themselves as women. Not knowing the favor that God granted them by making them men (something so noteworthy and advantageous in human nature) ... How many women in the world would give everything they own to be a man like you and to have the freedom that you have? (92–93)[20]

In a desperate plea directed explicitly to the would-be cross-dresser, Trujillo urges him to abandon such habits, as they are interpreted as an indication of criminal sexual practices (i.e., sodomy): "Give up this clothing to save your life, Brother. You should be ashamed of these dresses since they are proof of little honor and of great lewdness. Furthermore, they are like a banner that announces perversions and sins" (94).[21] Accordingly, when Juan Rana is forced to wear women's clothing in public, the audience undoubtedly would have interpreted the female garb as a sign that his pregnancy was the result of his same-sex desire and the practice of sodomy.

Regardless of the symbolic castigation in *El parto* for the unpunished sexual transgression in the private life of the lead actor, Juan Rana's overwhelming popularity with the royal family as well as with the general public surely influenced the decision to release the actor from jail instead of enforcing the death penalty normally expected for the crime of sodomy.[22] In fact, despite the potential scandal, Rana was later granted a pension for life from the Queen "in consideration for how much he makes her laugh" [en consideración de lo que la hace reír] (quoted in Bergman, "Juan," 68). This royal favor is likewise believed responsible, in part, for an existing portrait of the actor, given that portraiture of thespians in early modern Spain was extremely rare. (Bergman, "Juan," 70) (Figure 6). Rather than assume that the portrait reveals a faithful resemblance to Cosme Pérez, Evangelina Rodríguez Cuadros links the artistic proscription for painting the figure of the "stupid, silly, or simple-minded man" [bobo, necio o simple] described by Vicente Carducho in his *Diálogos de la pintura* (Dialogues on Painting) (1633) with the "almost caricaturesque" nature of the anonymous artist's portrait of the famous actor, with "his sagging neck, the huge outline of his entire body, which is accentuated by the curve of his stomach, his short limbs, his droopy expression, his suggestive big lips" (Rodríguez Cuadros, 273).[23]

In accordance with Aristotelian theory for dramatic comedy, asserting that laughter is provoked by ugliness and stupidity (described as "ridiculous" in terms of a physical deformation or deviation from social decorum), a man dressed as a woman on stage was considered both humorous and "ugly" and therefore worthy of social and moral correction in early modern Spain.[24] Along similar lines, the representation of gays in films in the past often utilized character actors who, like Cosme Pérez, look funny "in that they look comic and in that they look in a real sense deformed" (Saunders, 8). This "comic ugliness of the sissy," described by Michael William Saunders in his study on gay monsters in film, is also referenced by Ernest Larsen in his analysis of the casting of Danny DeVito opposite Arnold Schwarzenegger as a pregnant scientist in the comedy *Junior*. Saunders argues that DeVito's homeliness defuses the transgressive potential of the implied homoerotic undercurrent in the plot: "An actor in the role who was in the least conventionally attractive would have propelled the film into dangerous territory" (243). We might wonder, then, if the "comic ugliness of the sissy" associated with the early modern actor Cosme Pérez helped to avoid similarly dangerous territory. Moreover, the mere physical appearance of Juan Rana evoked laughter: "Just walking on stage, without speaking, caused laughter and applause" [Sólo con salir a las tablas, y sin hablar, provocaba a risa y al aplauso] (quoted in Cotarelo y Mori, *Colección*, clxi).

Like the emblems of gluttony (represented by a man with a protruding abdomen), the "beer belly" visible in the portrait of Juan Rana and referred to in the play was not a far cry from his role as pregnant man. Therefore, we might assume that the actor did not need to pad his stomach for his pre-delivery appearance. While his affection for food and liquor previously was the reason for his extended abdomen, his new aversion to eating cannot stop his growing stomach from announcing the imminent delivery:

**Clerk:** John Frog's stomach has grown so much that he's as big as a barrel.
**Third Mayor:** Full of wine he used to be.
**Clerk:** And he no longer feels like eating, which is a sure sign of pregnancy.
**Fourth Mayor:** And for him, being a glutton, it's even more notable.

[**Escribano:** Juan Rana le ha crecido
el vientre de manera
que una cuba parece.
**Alcalde Tercero:** Antes lo era
de vino.

| Escribano: | Y le han faltado |
| --- | --- |
| | las ganas de comer, que en un preñado |
| | son las señas fatales. |
| Alcalde Cuarto: | Y en él, que es un glotón, son más señales.] |

Just as Huarte de San Juan described the effeminate male as being flabby and having a soft-spoken voice (622), Rodríguez Cuadros notes that references to the actor's high-pitched voice [voz atiplada] have been used to speculate on his possible homosexuality but also point to his ability to comically "manipulate certain physical disadvantages for a clever construction of a theatrical persona" (273).[25] Accordingly, in his 1639 text, Jiménez Patón discusses the linguistic consequences of male effeminacy, as he laments the affected accent adopted by these men:

> The men described here as sissies and "dandies" usually add to these womanly effeminacies another practice no less worthy (I'm not sure out of laughter or out of mockery) which is to speak effeminately in a false voice and accent altering their speech by switching the "s" to "z" and "z" to "s" as well as the "j" to "h" and other blameworthy affectations . . . You are (he says) soft-spoken, you have effeminate speech; even a girl has a deeper voice . . . whoever would hear him talk would swear beyond any doubt that he is a woman. (*Discurso*, 32–32v)[26]

While Jiménez Patón complains of a transgression of traditional gender behavior, his subtext associates male femininity through grooming and speech patterns with homosexual identities. The author criticizes effeminate men for spending too much time with hairdressers, accusing them of being like Ganymede and Narcissus:

> No where can you find more vain men than in the barber shop. These Ganymedes and Narcissuses have the patience to spend two hours in the hands of the barber, with such exquisite diligence they wish to be groomed and they spend more time fixing their beards and mustaches, styling their toupees, combing their locks, and fluffing up the hair on their necks than the most beautiful lady . . . and when any little hair is out of place or a bit disheveled they swear that they [the barbers] made they look like ugly devils. (26v)[27]

As James Saslow demonstrates in his study on Ganymede in the Renaissance, "the very word *ganymede* was used from medieval times well into the seventeenth century to mean an object of homosexual desire" (2).[28] Likewise, the terms "lindo" and "narciso" were not only used to describe effeminate men but were linked to sodomitical practices.[29] As a result, the high-pitched voice Juan Rana used in his successful performances undoubtedly participated in the construction of an early modern theatrical version of a gay icon.

In fact, Juan Rana's feminine voice and gender-bending on stage are mentioned in Agustín Moreto's *Loa de Juan Rana* (Juan Rana's dramatic prologue):

Rana imitates Escamilla's voice, so *he* should play the ladies' roles and she the comic male roles.

[A la Escamilla imita
Rana en los tonos,
pues haga él las terceras,
y ella graciosos.] (440)[30]

When Juan Rana finally gives birth, however, it is the actress Manuela de Escamilla, as a young girl, who plays the part of his newborn son Juan Ranilla [John Frog Jr.] (Cotarelo y Mori, *Colecció,n* cclxxii). Therefore, following Moreto's verses quoted above, in *El parto* Juan Rana appears on stage dressed in women's clothing and nine months pregnant while the young female actress is cast and dressed as a boy. According to the early modern theater documents compiled in the *Genealogía*, Manuela de Escamilla was born in 1648 and began acting on stage at the age of seven, playing *terceras damas* [minor women's roles] in *sainetes* [burlesque one-act comedies] and later returned to Madrid to play the recurring role of Juan Ranilla (Shergold and Varey, 421, 561). Following Cotarelo y Mori's assertion that Manuela de Escamilla was still a child when acting in *El parto*, we might assume that the interlude was performed long after news of the actor's sodomy charges were common knowledge for theatergoers.[31]

As a result, the male pregnancy plot surely must have resonated with the audience in terms of the consequences of Cosme Pérez's sexual behavior, perhaps more with other men than with Juan Rana's domineering wife Aldonza and their gender role reversal. In fact, his own humorous pleadings while in labor play on references to same-sex partners in the past. As Juan Rana screams with pain and begs for relief, his water breaks and he bemoans the absence of a midwife to assist with the birth: "Gentlemen, have mercy, my water just broke! How can I give birth without a midwife, having known so many" [Señores, piedad, ¡que rota / tengo ya la fuente! ¡Qué haya / de parir yo sin comadre / habiendo tenido tantas!] The term *comadre*, most commonly meaning "midwife," was also used to describe a blunt and perhaps difficult woman, one who always tells it like it is: "the angry woman who, even without getting mad, cannot hold her tongue" (Covarrubias, *Tesoro*, 340).[32] Therefore the joke might refer to his experience with women like his bossy and controlling wife Aldonza. Another big laugh here, nonetheless, might likely come from the implied play on words between *comadre* and *comadrero*, who according to Covarrubias is "the man who spends time with women and only enjoys chatting with them for pleasure; typical of old men, unmanly and feminine men" (340).[33] This clear reference to the description of the effeminate male most likely registered with the audience in terms of *el pecado nefando* (sodomy).

## The Physiology of Male Delivery

Despite his doubts about the personal compatibility of a "manly" wife with a feminine husband, Huarte suggests a coupling that greatly resembles the Juan Rana-Aldonza marriage for masculine women seeking successful fertility results. In the chapter "What woman should marry what man so she can conceive" [Qué mujer con qué hombre se ha de casar para que pueda concebir], Huarte recommends: "The woman with low levels of coldness and moisture, whose characteristics we noted were admonishing, ill-tempered, deep voice, muscular, olive-skinned, hairy, and ugly. This woman will easily get pregnant from a man who is foolish, good-natured, soft-spoken, chubby, and with soft, white skin and little body hair" (624),[34] despite the fact that the author also claims that such men are "unfit to procreate. These men are not very fond of women nor are women of them" (622).[35]

Of course, in *El parto*, it is not just the gender role confusion in marriage that leads to Juan Rana's pregnancy. The female announcer suggests that a biological failure in the mail (male) delivery is the root of his "faults":

> Mother Nature wrote John Frog, but he missed the letters. He has shown his mistakes and with nine missed menstrual periods everything he says now are pregnant words.[36]

[La naturaleza humana
escribió a Juan Rana antes
ya le faltaron las cartas.
Sus faltas ha descubierto

y en nueve faltas,
cuantas palabras pronuncia
son ya palabras preñadas.]

The suggestive use of "pregnant words" is described by Covarrubias as "words that literally communicate much more than they mean" [las que contienen virtualmente mucho más de lo que espressan] (*Tesoro*, 880). Therefore, the audience is invited to read between the lines and discover what is "missing." Likewise, the author humorously plays with variations of "faltar" (to miss): missing letters, mistakes, and nine missed periods. While the idea of a "menstruating man" may seem like an oxymoron, some early modern Iberian physicians and theorists (such as Andrés de Laguna, Juan de Quiñones, and Isaac Cardoso) wrote about (or against) male menstruation as a sign of the consequences of being idle, effeminate, and/or a judaizer: "If Jewish males menstruate they are, in effect, no longer men but women, and the crime of deicide has been punished by castration" (Yerushalmi, 128).[37]

Given all this historical baggage, I argue that *El parto de Juan Rana* exposes the transgression of both the gender and sexual boundaries that led to the protagonist's condition of being "with child" as well as the cultural preoccupation with patriarchal control over reproductive practices. Once Juan Rana gives birth ("John Frog Jr., wearing a tunic, comes out from under John Frog's skirts" [Sale por debajo de las faldas Juan Ranilla con sayo]), the new debate centers on issues of paternity—whether he is really the child's father—despite the fact that the birth was witnessed by six mayors, a court clerk, and the female announcer. Medieval civil law, in fact, recognized the indisputable identity of one's mother when determining certain inheritance rulings: "Mothers are always certain of the children born of them, and for this reason every child, together with the legitimate children born of her shall inherit the property of its mother, whether it is legitimate or not" (Alfonso X, *Partidas*, 1273). Accordingly, these paternity fears led many early modern writers to emphasis the need to monitor women's sexual activity "in order for us to be certain of our offspring" (Castiglione, 330). Juan Rana, following suit, tried to exculpate himself by implying that his child was not conceived by any external participant or any impropriety on his part. Like the Virgin Mary's Immaculate Conception, Juan Rana was not impregnated by man:

> It's important also to confess that I am not guilty of anything. This living bump didn't come from any fall. Finally, it's worth mentioning

that if mares can conceive by the wind, then John Frogs can do the same.

[Valga también confesaros
que no soy culpada en nada
pues este chichón viviente
ningún tropezón le causa.
Y por fin, valga advertiros
que si en las yeguas se halla
concebir del viento, pueden
lo mismo hacer los Juan Ranas.]³⁸

In this way, Juan Rana becomes the "monstrous mother" described by Marie Hélène Huet: "a blasphemous parody of the cult of the Virgin Mary. In erasing all traces of the progeny's legitimate father, the monstrous mother replicated, and derides, the Immaculate Conception" (30).³⁹ Of course, Juan Rana also serves as a farcical reminder of Eve, given his dramatic resistance to the curse of pain in childbirth.

Considering the early modern male pregnancy jokes in *El parto de Juan Rana* that bring into play images as diverse as the silhouette of a glutton's beer belly, an immaculate conception, and the inversion of gender roles and the politics of women's reproductive health, it is interesting to find that the finalists in *The New Yorker* cartoon caption contest (February 13 and 20, 2006) also engage similar themes for humorous purposes. The cartoon drawing (by J. B. Handelsman) portrays a man in what looks to be late stages of pregnancy while talking to a coworker. The three jokes that form the group of finalists are:

"She told me she had protection."
"The ultrasound says it's a keg of Bud Light."
"No one expects an immaculate conception until it happens to him."
(178)

And despite the thematic similarities, the seventeenth-century versions of these jokes in *El parto* are much more explicit about the homoerotic implications of the pregnant man image.

The burlesque image of a man writhing in pain while in labor also appeared in a text on monsters published in Lima at the end of the seventeenth century. Joseph de Rivilla Bonet y Pueyo's 1695 *Desvíos de la naturaleza o tratado de el origen de los monstruos* (Nature's Deviations or Treatise on the Origin of Monsters) recounts an anomalous event that took place in 1330 in the Netherlands. A husband who frequently enjoyed making fun of his wife's pain and discomfort during each pregnancy and delivery also joked about wishing to experience labor himself in order to mock childbirth even more. As a result, God decided to punish him by making him pregnant and after nine months of "the same anxiety and nausea that pregnant women feel . . . he experienced labor pains, whose intensity forced him to give birth through his thigh to a true and perfect child" (Rivilla Bonet y Pueyo, 78).[40]

## Paternity Anxiety and the Role of Resemblance

Consistent with the early modern passion for monster-gazing and the absence of a physical likeness of monsters to their progenitors, in a pre-DNA paternity testing era, resemblance became a determining factor when linking fathers to their offspring. Accordingly, one of the witnesses quickly confirms the physical resemblance after Juan Ranilla pops out from under his father/mother's skirt: "The boy is the spitting image of his father, in body and face" [Su retrato es el muchacho / en talle y en rostro]. While the child recognizes Juan Rana as his parent ("Mommy, won't you hug your little John Frog?" [Mamá, ¿no abraza a su Juan Ranilla?]), one witness notes the indisputability of his paternity according to the "newborn": "He doesn't deny his father at all" [No niega / en nada a su padre]. Although the proud childbearing father greets his offspring with joy, he soon begins to look for proof that this boy is truly his: "I still need to know if he is my son, since it's possible that another man made him in my absence" [Aun falta / el saber si es mi hijo, pues / puede ser que otro lo haya / hecho en mi ausencia]. When asked how he can prove his paternity, he responds that the test will be a father-son comparison while dancing the *zarambeque* (a lively and joyful African dance commonly performed in the interludes) (Cotarelo y Mori, *Colección*, cclxxi-iii).[41] As they dance together and are soon joined and imitated by the other mayors, Juan Rana celebrates the similarity: "How he takes after me, my little John Jr., in the zarambeque dance!" [¡Que se me parece, / ay, mi Juan Ranilla, / en el zarambeque!]

Based on Aristotle's definition of a monster as that which does not resemble its progenitors ("they generate offspring which, owing to its imperfect state, is unlike its parents:—for monstrosities come under the class of offspring which is unlike its parents" [425]), theories of false resemblance were frequently attributed to the relationships between procreation, art, and the mother's imagination. Referring to illustrations such as Paré's drawing of a frog-faced boy (born to a mother who had been holding a frog in her hand during conception),[42] Marie Hélèn Huet discusses the role of visual images during both conception and again after birth through the artistic rendition of the monstrous newborn: "These drawings had a twofold importance: they provide concrete evidence for tales of extraordinary births, and they possessed a tangibility that was more striking than words. Most of all, they duplicated in frightening detail the workings of the maternal imagination" (16).

Huarte de San Juan, on the other hand, rejects the Aristotelian belief that a visual image could impact the mother's imagination and thereby the physical appearance of her offspring: "It is also told that a woman gave birth to a son who was darker than he should have been because she had stared at a black face on a tapestry. I consider this a great joke and if it is true that she did give birth to a black child I would say that the man who fathered it was the same color as the figure in the tapestry" (653).[43] Nonetheless, like his contemporaries, Huarte is also preoccupied with issues of resemblance and anxieties about infidelity and paternity, even offering suggestions to fathers who want their children to take after them and not the mother:

> If the father's seed predominates then the child will have his appearance and manners but when the mother's seed is stronger then the same reasoning applies. For when the father wants his child to be formed from his own seed he must refrain from sexual relations for a few days so that his fluids cook and age. Then it will be certain that he will provide the procreative material while the women's seed will serve merely as nourishment. (669)[44]

Juan Rana's pregnancy, while freakish in nature, includes many common experiences that normalize his predicament, such as food aversion, nine missed menstrual periods [nueve faltas], extreme pain (not to mention his water breaking), and promises of never getting pregnant again. While these experiences are likewise highlighted in early modern medical publications dealing with pregnancy and childbirth, the narrative strategy that most aligns *El parto de Juan Rana* with other births is found in the descriptions of monstrous deliveries and the emphasis on witness and spectator shock when the newborn child emerges. Although the audience watches as the actor gives birth, the father (whose arms are supported by two of the mayors) must narrate his own painful delivery: "Hold me, it's coming, the head is crowning but after this hell I will never get pregnant again, ever" [Tengan, que del parto está / la cabeza coronada, / mas ya parir con mil diablos / no me haré otra vez preñada, / no mas en mi vida]. Once little John Jr. comes out from under his father's skirt, all those present shout "Heavens! He just gave birth!" [¡Cielos, / que ha parido!] Juan the father naturally responds to their surprise by asking, "Why do you look so shocked?" [¿Qué se pasman?] This initial fear of what kind of creature might have emerged from his womb is alleviated by the reassurances of the non-monstrous resemblance between father and son (the boy is the spitting image of his father, in both body and face).

The end of this incredible reproductive fantasy answers the hypothetical question, "What if men could give birth?" as a singing woman announces that only by giving birth themselves can men be sure of their children:

> **Singing woman:** If men gave birth it would be a great thing—since they would be certain of all of their offspring.

> [**Cantando mujer:** Si los hombres parieran
> fuera gran cosa
> pues tuvieran por ciertas
> todas sus obras.]

Of course, Juan Rana ends the *entremés* by blaming women for taking advantage of men and being deceptive about the identity of their children's father:

> **John Frog:** There is no doubt that we've seen lots of women who give their kids to other fathers for feeding.

> [Juan Rana: No hay duda pues que muchas
> mujeres vimos,
> que a mamar a otros padres
> los dan los hijos.]

While the protagonist indicts women for being deceptive about their offspring's paternity, early modern ecclesiastics and moralists frequently recommended a "don't ask, don't tell" policy to married women who had given birth to a child not fathered by their husband. Fray Martín Azpilcueta wrote in his 1556 manual for confessors that such a woman can be absolved of sin without telling the truth to her husband if she fears that he will kill her or if the family's reputation will be damaged (179). In his 1682 confessional guide, Pedro Galindo advises adulterous mothers to confess the truth about the child only if he is to inherit a princedom and she feels that the false inheritance might be harmful to the nation (457). In this way, the Church also contributed to the general mistrust of women and paternity. The same moralists who believe that adulterous mothers may suppress the truth about false paternity (under certain circumstances) also maintain that nobody can ever be fully certain of the paternity claims of these women. Consequently, inheritance issues and other financial concerns become very complex for the husband, the lover/biological father, and even the child who cannot ascertain the truth. Galindo frequently reminds his readers that the husband "thinks the child is his" while the actual father may have his own doubts about paternity:

> So in order for the adulterous third party to comply with his obligation to compensate expenses to the husband, he must be completely certain that the child is his. If there is equal doubt between two possible partners then they both should share the costs. If the doubt is between the husband and the third party then the latter should pay half of the expenses. (457)[45]

Azpilcueta likewise gives the lover the right to question the woman's claims (as she may be sleeping with other men), thereby avoiding any financial obligation for the child (180). Even the child may question his mother's confession of infidelity when his own inheritance is affected: "The child of an adulterous affair is not obligated to believe his mother if she reveals the infidelity, unless he is convinced by the explanation or the circumstances; for example if she swears on her death bed or if reliable witnesses can confirm that the reputed father was absent during the time of conception" (Galindo, 457).[46]

The mistrust of pregnancy and paternity is not just the result of adulterous affairs. Married women were also known to fake pregnancies by stealing another woman's baby, pretending to give birth, and eventually passing it off as her own (Azpilcueta, 178). Not surprisingly, this fear is played out in other seventeenth-century interludes. In his study on humor in early modern theater, Javier Huerta Calvo describes how women manipulated men with false claims of pregnancy for a variety of purposes. For example, Quevedo's Bárbara (in the interlude of the same title) confesses: "When these men left, I led them to believe that I was pregnant. I have great talent for faking nausea, pretending to faint, and for suffering morning sickness while craving one thing or another" (20).[47] In fact, Bárbara acquires a small fortune by convincing various men that she had given birth to their child, thus enabling her to accumulate the money for the dowry she needed to get married (26). Reminiscent of the paternity lies and doubts common among the *pícaras* in the picaresque genre, Juan Rana's accusations at the close of *El parto* are played out by women in other *entremeses*, as they pretend to be pregnant or tell more than one man that her child is his in order to collect gifts from multiple fathers (Huerta Calvo, 71).

Ultimately *El parto de Juan Rana* is both a carnivalesque representation of man's desire to appropriate reproduction by eliminating the woman and an insightful precursor to other new reproductive technologies that force us to reconsider how we view women's bodies in procreation. In this way, Lanini Sagredo's interlude methodically reveals a complex and interconnected list of cultural anxieties related to the control of procreation, gender transgression, homosexuality, monsters and abnormal births, and perhaps the not so inverisimilar fear that an anatomical transmutation can occur in the reverse, "unnaturally" from male to female.

# 3
# The Male Matrix
## Appropriating Reproduction in Early Modern Spain

The patriarchal fantasy that emerges from the image of male autogenesis in *El parto de Juan Rana* involves a reproductive configuration that eliminates woman as the primary protagonist in childbirth. Not surprisingly, this androcentric reproductive scenario takes on a life of its own in early modern iconography and literature, as well as in gynecology, obstetrics, teratology, and in legal and philosophical debates. Yet, as this chapter makes clear, this patriarchal utopian view of procreation is itself a response to a variety of fears involving reproductive technologies, female sexuality, paternity, and progeny.

### Visualizing Pregnancy in Medieval Spain

To fully understand the impact of the changes during the early modern period in the context of the representation of women's reproductive issues, we must first look to the cultural heritage from the Middle Ages. As the cult of the Virgin Mary and Marian iconography took center stage in medieval spirituality, pictorial depictions of Mary frequently had shown her pregnant or nursing her child.[1] Likewise, in medieval miracle plays that involved childbirth, Mary was often the labor coach and midwife. In fact, these dramatic birthing performances were fascinating demonstrations of the openness with which childbirth was represented in medieval European culture, their visual impact on the spectator inevitably resulting in curious portrayals of male pregnancy. Since the role of the pregnant woman was played by a male actor, the actual birthing scene most likely resembled the farcical moment of the burlesque delivery in *El parto de Juan Rana* in the seventeenth century: "The actor would heave and groan, while the Virgin Mary in attendance encouraged him roundly. At the appropriate moment, she would bend down and draw from between the actor's legs a doll wrapped in swaddling clothes"

(Warner, 277). Despite the potential for humor, in the medieval miracle plays the labor and birthing scenes were intended as serious portrayals of Mary's omnipotence.

Unlike many early modern artists, medieval illustrators did not shy away from depicting all aspects of procreation: conception, pregnancy, labor, and childbirth.[2] For example, in Cantiga 17 (one of Alfonso X's thirteenth-century illustrated songs, relating daily life problems solved by the miracles of Mary), the artist's drawings follow the author's text through their open portrayal of incestuous sexual relations, childbirth, and infanticide. When a noble woman's husband dies, she cannot cope with her grief and "unwisely took comfort with a son she had by him, who got her pregnant" (26) (left panel of Figure 7).[3] Later, when she discovered that she was pregnant, she was "much distressed" but did nothing until after the birth of another son, at which time she "locked herself in her house where no one could see her and killed him" (26).[4] The right panel of Figure 7 is divided into two parts, with the left side depicting the woman seated on a birthing stool while she delivers the baby, and on the right side (in sequential narrative form) the mother quickly disposes of the newborn in the latrine, symbolically representing the shameful fruit of the illicit relationship.[5]

Cantiga 184 deals with both infertility and child mortality but the real drama might involve a fetal-rights issue that is currently debated in the courts today. The married woman in Cantiga 184 is said to have lost multiple new-

Figure 7: Incestuous relations lead to pregnancy and infanticide in Alfonso X's Cantiga 17. (Reproduced by permission from the Patrimonio Nacional, Madrid)

borns, all of whom died soon after birth. When the woman becomes pregnant once again, she asks Mary to protect her child. Months later, when her husband becomes embroiled in a violent fight with a group of men and is wounded, the courageous wife (now in late stages of her pregnancy) attempts to save her husband by intervening in the fight. As a result, she is fatally stabbed. Miraculously, "the child came out through the wound, in need of a plaster for the cut that he had on his cheek made by the knife which had killed his mother" (220) (Figure 8). The message to the readers seems to focus on the miraculous survival of the fetus ("a little boy who still lay in the womb of his mother") as the answer to the woman's prayers, even though both parents die in the process. With this goal in mind, the text ignores how the mother herself endangered the life of her unborn child when intervening in the bloody fight.

Not surprisingly, the medieval civil legal code (Alfonso X's *Las Siete Partidas*[6]) legislated fetal homicide, but only after six weeks from conception for a male fetus and three months for a female: "We decree that a man shall suffer the same penalty who knowingly strikes his wife while she is pregnant, so that she loses her child by reason of the blow. If a stranger should do this, he shall suffer the penalty of homicide if the child was living when it lost its life through his fault, and if it was not living at the time, he shall be banished to some island for the term of five years" (page 1347, Partida VII, Title VIII, Law VIII).[7]

While the crimes of homicide perpetrated against the father and the mother are undeniable, we might consider current questions debated by bioethicists, activists, and legislators today when reading or viewing this medieval text in terms of the fetus. In particular, what rights does a fetus have? Can a fetus be a crime victim? How should the law treat someone who knowingly attacks a pregnant woman? Writing about medical ethics, Bonnie Steinbock defends a pro-choice position but also acknowledges certain fetal rights involving violent crimes:

> So it is consistent to say that a woman has a constitutional right to terminate a pregnancy up until viability [about 24 weeks] and even afterwards if her life or health is in danger. But if somebody attacks a pregnant woman and beats her viciously and causes her to have a miscarriage, that could very easily be seen as a crime ... A number of states have done something I think is very sensible; they talk about whether the attacker should have known. So, if a reasonable person should have known that he [or she] was attacking a pregnant woman and was putting her pregnancy at risk, then he should be responsible. But the attacker didn't know she

was pregnant—or it's so early that no one could know—then it's probably not relevant. (Quoted in Rosenberg, 47)

If we consider Steinbock's position in relation to the visual representation of Cantiga 184 in Figure 8, we could conclude that the attackers must have known that the woman was pregnant (given that the illustrations depict her in late stages of pregnancy). At the same time, however, it is not clear whether the armed men actually intended to injure the woman, since she purposefully intervened to protect her husband. If this were the case, the mother (had she survived) might have been found criminally negligent for the endangerment of her unborn child. Of course, in the end, neither the attackers (nor the pregnant woman) in Cantiga 184 would be responsible for fetal homicide since Mary intervenes to save the baby.

Less dramatic but no less fascinating is the graphic depiction of child-

Figure 8: Pregnant woman is stabbed and dies in Alfonso X's Cantiga 184. (Reproduced by permission from the Patrimonio Nacional, Madrid)

birth in Cantiga 89 titled "This is how a Jewess was near death in childbirth and called on Holy Mary and was delivered at that moment" (Figure 9). The first panel shows a pregnant mother attending to her older child while experiencing labor pains, as her midwife enters the room to assist. The third panel clearly depicts the woman giving birth while seated on a birthing stool with her knees apart as the baby emerges from below.[8]

Pregnancy was thus not a censored or hidden event in religious visual culture in the Middle Ages. Depictions of both Mary and ordinary women in medieval works reveal that the representations of midwifery, unwanted or difficult pregnancies, infertility, infanticide, child placement, and so forth were not only recurrent but narrated verbally and visually with great candor and surprising sympathy, even when the actions would normally be punishable by civil law through Alfonso X's legal code *Las Siete Partidas*.[9]

## Pregnancy Erased from Early Modern Iconography

By stark contrast, during the early modern period, visual representations of pregnancy and childbirth were infrequent, while the images that did circulate underwent major transformations, especially in the religious context of Mary, Joseph, and Jesus. Whereas medieval iconography frequently depicted Mary pregnant, nursing, or serving as midwife to other women who were giving birth, in the sixteenth and seventeenth centuries she more often appeared as innocent maiden or sorrowing mother. Not surprisingly, the seventeenth-century authority on painting and portraiture, Francisco Pacheco, instructs artists to depict Mary according to her virginal maternity: "not only without the Child in her arms but even without having given birth" (575).[10] In her study of maternity images in baroque painting, Alba Ibero analyzes the gradual disappearance of pregnant and birthing women (both Mary and ordinary women) in early modern paintings, arguing that sixteenth- and seventeenth-century iconography focused on the post-birth scenes, which served to redefine and revalue a new image of ideal maternity that emphasized obedience and submission (103–5).[11]

Perhaps the best example of the trend to visually and ideologically separate pregnancy from women is found in the early modern iconographic cult of Mary as symbol of the Immaculate Conception. As the dogma of the Immaculate Conception became an obsession in sixteenth- and seventeenth-century Spain, a new iconography of Mary emerged (Stoichita, 97). The shift in representation now featured (or implied) God as the divine creator who

Figure 9: Alfonso X's Cantiga 89: "This is how a Jewess was near death in childbirth and called on Holy Mary and was delivered at that moment." (Reproduced by permission from the Patrimonio Nacional, Madrid)

engenders Mary as well as the entire universe. While artistic representations of the Immaculate Conception were diverse (depending on changes in the theological debate), one variation of these images depicted a bearded male figure positioned in the top portion of the painting looking down and directing his finger, representing his divine power and capacity to create (98).[12] In her study of the Immaculate Conception in Spanish art, Suzanne L. Stratton describes how Spain quickly adopted the iconography of the Virgin *tota pulchra* (all beautiful) during the sixteenth century, frequently depicting the image of God as father above Mary "emphasizing the creation of the Virgin in the mind of God, before all things" (43). Accordingly, Pacheco reminds his readers that when representing the Immaculate Conception, artists "usually place God the Father or the Holy Spirit at the top of the painting" (577).[13]

According to Ibero, the Immaculate Mother figure also communicated another message: if Mary does not need male intervention to conceive her child, her image ultimately (and ironically) functions to subordinate and repress women: "In fact, the role of the Immaculate Mary is reduced to nothing more than the receptacle of the son of God, and in this way becomes a vehicle to deny women's role in the process of biological reproduction and consequently becomes an image of feminine passivity" (112).

Popular medieval depictions of a pregnant Mary or of the Virgin giving birth seemed to disappear during the early modern period. In their place one sees the rise of the Counter-Reformation cult of Joseph as a "universal parental figure" transformed from his pre-fifteenth-century persona as an impotent older man into a virile and productive primary caregiver. The change in iconography is as notable as it is relevant. In earlier medieval biblical plays, Joseph's depiction in the childbirth scene would often inspire humor, as "the aged Joseph who in comic *couvade* groans about the 'travayl' that men must suffer" (Gibson, 19). Rosemary Drage Hale has noted that in early nativity plays, Joseph was portrayed as a comic, inept, cuckold, and feeble old man, but by the sixteenth century he was made into a man in his prime, an economically strong and physically fit tradesman (106).[14] Pacheco also discusses Joseph's age when he instructs artists that Joseph should be depicted as a man of thirty or thereabouts, since a much older man wouldn't have had the strength or energy for travels or the hard labor of supporting his family (592). All this changes dramatically in the early modern period, with its new emphasis on the father's role in the family and the emerging empire: "The figure of the father," states Ibero, "acquires a major presence in the domestic sphere and in the socialization of genealogy in an attempt to limit an activity in which women had always been the protagonists, redefining at the same time patriarchal authority" (107). Even more telling is the fact that traditional symbols associated with the virginal purity of Mary in medieval times (such as lilies) are now applied to Joseph. As Marina Warner explains, in early modern paintings "his virginity stemmed from a holy purpose, not the debility of old age" (189).[15] Similarly, images of the solitary Joseph and child reinforced the ideological notion that men could play center stage in reproduction and child care. As a result, the male appropriation of maternity in pictorial representations demonstrates how the role of women in human reproduction is visually and symbolically diminished in favor of the father as primary progenitor.

## The Professionalization of Reproductive Medicine

Reflecting on and participating in these cultural shifts, medical authorities also began to monitor and eventually minimize the role of female health care providers in gynecology and obstetrics. While the practice of these medical fields had been the exclusive domain of women during the Middle Ages, the early modern period witnesses the invasion in this area by male scholars, theologians, and medical practitioners. Even the frequent illustrations of midwives ("acting so competently and energetically") practicing Caesarean operations prior to the fifteenth century disappeared and were replaced by male surgeons: "The slow incursion of men into obstetrics via the Caesarean operation thus found its own pictorial history" (Blumenfeld-Kosinski, 90). In effect, the sixteenth and seventeenth centuries proved to be pivotal in the context of reproductive health since it marks the beginning of the shift from a female-controlled sphere to the professional formalization of procreative medicine, which was dominated by male physicians, lawmakers, and moralists. In her study of early modern midwifery, Julie Sanders describes the importance of this transition in terms of gender and the distinction between formal theory and the actual practice of women's reproductive health care:

> The professionalisation of medicine and medical discourse effectively excluded women from a world they had previously gained access to due to that world's continuing involvement with traditional and local (and by implication amateur) practices which were handed on within communities rather than disseminated through the world of textbooks. (78)

Even though during much of the early modern period midwifery was still practiced by women (given that "tradition and prevailing morality forbid examination of women patients by men" [Ortiz, "Hegemony," 299]), the sixteenth and seventeenth centuries saw the gradual encroachment of this field by men who were not yet widely practicing reproductive medicine in the birthing rooms but who began to establish their authority through the written word, in medical, religious, and legal texts. Accordingly, Sanders argues that "one of the ways in which the male scientific community began to harness midwifery and the space of the birthing room for its own purposes was through language" (77). It is not surprising, then, that three manuals on childbirth written by male physicians were published in Spain during the sixteenth and seventeenth centuries: Damián Carbón's 1541 *Libro del arte de las comadres o madrinas* (Book of the Art of Midwives), Francisco Núñez's 1580 *El libro del parto humano* (Book of Human Delivery), and Juan Alonso de los Ruyzes's 1606 *Diez previlegios de preñadas* (Ten Privileges for Pregnant Women).

Like most other midwife manuals published in Europe during this time, Carbón's study is largely a Spanish adaptation of Eucharius Rösslin's *Rose Garden for Pregnant Women and Midwives* [*Rosengarten*], which was written in 1513. Widely reprinted and translated, *Rosengarten* remained the authority on midwifery in Europe throughout the sixteenth and seventeenth centuries (Arons, 3).

Wendy Arons explains why this influential model is problematic: it was "written by a man who had never attended a delivery and who was dependent on ancient sources for his information, the book did not necessarily reflect the actual practice of midwifery at the time" (1). The author attempts to justify his text by arousing in his readers the fear of possible malpractice at the hands of incompetent midwives and the hope that some of the pain and risks of childbirth could be alleviated with male intervention. In the introductory poem, "Admonition to Pregnant Women and Midwives," Rösslin's alarmist tone shows little respect for the experience of female midwives:

> Midwives I mean especially
> Who should be trained for their duty
> So that they earn their salary
> Just when they do things properly
> Now there is so much negligence ...
> And since no midwife that I've asked
> Could tell me anything of her task
> I'm left to my medical education
> Which takes such things in consideration
> I've put it down quite pleasantly. (34–35)

Carbón's 1541 manual on midwifery was the first such text published in Spain and the second in Europe after Rösslin's study, largely repeating its predecessor's tone and material.[16] Carbón explains that since midwives are not formally trained, they need the guidance of male physicians to avoid mistakes. Consequently, the focus of his book features the remedies for common problems associated with pregnancy and childbirth (2- 2v). Again the author reminds the reader of the biblical origin of pain in childbirth and how God bestowed on men the intellectual capacity for scientific learning, thus justifying their intervention in obstetrical medicine (5v-6). Having established women's weakness and men's superiority, Carbón laments that female midwives are still required for the actual delivery process because of social decorum: "Due to chastity issues it was necessary to leave these concerns in the hands of women" (7).[17] Along similar lines, all three pregnancy manuals published in early modern Spain affirm that female babies are more difficult to deliver than male infants and that one job of the midwife is to give words of comfort and encouragement so the woman in labor will give birth to a boy.[18]

Through pictorial representation, Carbón's manual dramatizes the direction that reproductive practices that would take throughout the early modern period. The first woodcut (featured on the title page) depicts two women standing with arms joined in a casual embrace, implying the traditional all-female network in the business of childbirth. However, the women in this scene are not located in the private space of the birthing room but outside in public. This pictorial message of female solidarity is quickly reversed, nonetheless, when the reader turns the page to Chapter 1. The new image depicts God as the true creator of life, occupying the top half of the woodcut and below him (in a symbolic birthing position) lies the newborn child (Figure 10). Like the attempt throughout the narrative to minimize the midwife's

Figure 10: God as Father gives birth to the universe from *Libro del arte de las comadres*. (Reproduced by permission from the Biblioteca Nacional, Madrid)

authority in reproductive medicine, here women are erased from the only illustration that involves a newborn.

Although there were exceptions to this growing trend (as Caroline Bicks has demonstrated in her study on midwifery in Shakespeare's England), the practice of excluding women from reproductive textual authority continued in the next two manuals published on childbirth in early modern Spain.[19] As Teresa Ortiz observes in her article "From Hegemony to Subordination: Midwives in Early Modern Spain," Núñez's and Alonso de los Ruyzes's texts were more learned and contained numerous passages in Latin, with the obvious intention of being little help to those who were not formally educated, including midwives (97).[20] When considering possible reasons why male physicians began to publish works on midwifery, Ortiz doubts whether midwives even read such books, adding that perhaps these physicians

> actually wrote for themselves, aspiring to possess a new knowledge rather than to devote themselves to it. Given that cultural and social circumstances did not make their works readily accessible to midwives, putting them forward as advice books for this group was rather rhetorical, and may have been an attempt to overcome the obstacle of morality and customs which placed childbirth within the female domain. It is here that one of the origins of the transformation of childbirth into an aspect of medical science may be found. (98)

Like other scholars of early modern midwifery, Julie Sanders is right to note the importance of this change in the cultural imaginary regarding the private space of the delivery room and the distrust of women:

> Fear of women's ability to exploit this female space of the birthing room was culturally rife. The ability to tamper with the 'evidence' of childbirth which this private space provided them with added to the social myths of subversion that built up around midwives. They were credited with the ability to practice magic and witchcraft, or, more pragmatically, with the provision of birth control and abortifacients to women in the community who were in need. (77)

While the birthing room was typically a female-only space, in the case of royal or noble births the presence of a male physician signified honor and social importance. It should not come as a surprise, then, that during the mid-seventeenth century when Spain was anxiously awaiting the conception, birth, and survival of a male heir to the throne, all the details of Queen

Mariana's reproductive health were documented in public news items written by Jerónimo de Barrionuevo. The following are a few excerpts from the news items in *Avisos* recording the reproductive state of the Queen:

"There is a chance that the Queen is pregnant with a girl—why bother? We have enough women already" (Sept. 23, 1654).[21]

"Since Sunday, the King has been sleeping with the Queen. May God give them blessed sons for the peace of Spain" (Jan. 15, 1656).[22]

"The Queen got her period, which clouds the pregnancy. It must not be God's will that she have sons." (Sept. 6, 1656).[23]

"Today the Queen entered into her ninth month and the entire pregnancy was free of anxiety, grief, and queasiness like in the other pregnancies, from which the doctor and midwives want to infer (out of flattery) that she is carrying a son. Soon we will all make it through this pregnancy." (Nov. 7, 1657).[24]

"The Queen hasn't had her period for eighteen days. It seems that if this continues, she will give birth every year." (Feb. 13, 1658).[25]

When they finally get a male heir to the throne, on the day of the baptism the baby was presented nude. When asked why, they responded that "it was done on purpose so that all can see that he is truly a boy" (Dec. 17, 1657).[26] As these commentaries show, it is not just the birthing chamber that is invaded by the controlling male gaze. The reader is coerced into becoming a voyeur to the Queen's body and sexual life (through menstruation, reproductive intercourse, pregnancy, and miscarriage) precisely at the time when theatergoers first saw an interlude about a man who takes control over procreation by giving birth himself.

In other cases involving the status of inheritance and property rights as contingent upon the sex of the newborn heir, male officials were invited to witness the birth and to testify that the pregnant mother or her midwives had not deceived others by bringing in someone else's newborn male. The recorded public account of the labor and delivery of Isabel de la Cavallería in 1490, for example, demonstrates both the patriarchal fear of female collusion as well as the social and economic advantages to having a son. The written testimony of Domingo de Cuerla (a notary in Zaragoza) not only documents the physical details of the delivery (so that the new mother could avoid accusations of reproductive fraud) but also show how he intervenes physically to confirm his observations:

> To the request of Isabel I, the aforesaid Domingo de la Cuerla, notary, and in front of all the witnesses named below, touched with my hands their [the two midwives] bodies and between their legs, with their skirts and clothes up to their shirts so that I could see and examine if the midwives were bringing any baby fraudulently, or if Isabel had any under her skirt ... And having done this, a bed which was in the room was uncovered and I, the aforesaid notary and the witnesses, saw that there was nothing in it except the necessary and appropriate linen for its dressing.[27]

The notary continues to provide a detailed description of the birthing stool and other instruments used to assist the birth as well as specifics about the actual delivery: "I, the notary and the witnesses seeing it, saw that the umbilical cord was hanging from the placenta within the body of the aforesaid Isabel de la Cavallería and was affixed to the navel of the aforesaid newborn baby, ... and saw that the newborn baby was a man, since he had all the male organs that men have, that is, his member and its companions, alias popularly called willy and balls."[28] Far from a private affair, this very public, invasive, and voyeuristic narrative demonstrates the fear of women's potential social and economic control in reproductive issues and paternity.

The anxiety over how women could interfere in the legalities of procreation continued as long as the birthing room continued to have secrets. On January 9, 1658, for example, Barrionuevo wrote in a news item that a group of more than sixty women who had previously been incarcerated were released. However, the only female inmate mentioned specifically is the midwife named "la Cuenca." She had been convicted and sentenced to life in prison for having participated in a falsified birth that affected the inheritance of the first born son (Barrionuevo, vol. 2, 148). As Mary Elizabeth Perry concludes when discussing the early modern suspicion of midwives and their power: "The sin of the midwives, then, was not their ignorance in matters of giving birth, but their knowledge, which seemed so close to magic and could facilitate illicit sex" (*Gender*, 28).

Thus, while the male medical community was reaping the benefits of the new printing presses by appropriating the craft of midwifery, new legislation attempted to eliminate the authority of female midwives and to legitimate male authority in reproductive health. The highest medical authority, known as the *Protomédicos* were decreed to examine and license all medical practitioners (including midwives) between 1477 and 1523. After 1523, however, these medical officials were allowed only to license physicians, surgeons, apothecaries, and barbers but ordered not to bother licensing midwives, spicers, or druggists, "thus creating a dividing line between some groups of practitioners and others" and ultimately resulted in marginalizing midwives from dignified obstetrical authority (Ortiz, "Hegemony," 98).

Not unexpectedly, while midwives were still allowed to assist deliveries (provided that they were under the supervision of local physicians), by the mid-eighteenth century the tribunal of the royal *Protomedicato* intervened in obstetrics to redefine the art of midwifery as a male surgical science through new examinations and qualifications that favored surgical experience in obstetrical practices (Ortiz, "Protomedicato" 118).[29] Accordingly, Juan de Navas followed suit in his 1795 *Elementos del arte de partear* (Elements of the Art of Midwifery) by redefining midwifery as a surgical field: "The art of midwifery is the part of surgery taught by known doctors to help Nature facilitate the delivery of the child" (1).[30] In her study of the subjugation of midwives in the Low Countries between the fifteenth and seventeenth centuries, Myriam Greilsammer reminds us that the "exclusion of women from universities as from other guilds must have contributed further to the decline of the midwives' knowledge, power, and status. Among the other causes of this decline is an increasing recourse to physicians and surgeons as a mark of social status" (320). As Ortiz summarizes, the mission to educate midwives actually "became an instrument more of subordination or submission than of liberation since surgeons used the campaign for their own professional agenda and gain while it resulted in separating midwives from their expertise, from their language, from their culture, and without a doubt from their social power" ("Educación," 156).[31]

## Theories of Human Reproduction and When Life Actually Begins

Although the first published works on midwifery emerged during the sixteenth century, male philosophers and physicians had been writing about reproduction since ancient times.[32] Prior to the mid-seventeenth century, theories of generation relied on Greek philosophy and medicine. For Aristotle (*Generation of Animals*), the creation of life was male-centered since the man provided the seed while the mother was a mere receptacle, thereby implying that the father was more the "true parent" than the mother.[33] Aristotle argues, moreover, that it is the male who provides the "soul" in every living creature: "the male always completes the business of generation—it implants sentient Soul, either acting by itself directly or by means of semen" (207). Unlike Aristotle, Hippocrates and Galen believed that women also had a significant role in generation, as they likewise contributed semen or seed, which was necessary but weaker than that of males.[34] As Valeria Finucci notes, even while postulating the two-seed theory, "medical thought was adamant in denying woman too much importance in procreation" (*Manly*, 13).

Along with theories of conception arose discussion about when life begins, which became (and continues to be) the center of numerous medical, legal, and moral debates. In his *Natural History*, Pliny ascribes gender value to women's pregnancy and childbirth, as well as the formation and movement of the fetus, which was different for males than females: "If the child is male, the pregnant mother has a better colour and an easier delivery, and movement begins in the womb on the fortieth day. If the child is a girl all the symptoms are the opposite: the weight is hard to carry, there is a slight swelling of the legs and groin, and the first movement is on the ninetieth day" (81). Also referred to as the "quickening" or "animation," the moment when the fetus was "well developed" and "animated" became a moral issue related to the soul and the definition of human life. The early modern surgeon Diego Antonio de Robledo affirms that the first stage in fetal development is "spermatic," beginning seven days after conception and developed by thirty days for males and forty days for females. As Robledo explains, "the fleshy parts that are formed from menstrual blood are fully developed in the third month for males and the fourth month for females. Once the fetus is developed, it is 'animated' and starts to move" (quoted in Granjel, 145).[35]

Citing Galen and the early medieval Arabic doctor Avicenna (following the theories of Aristotle), in his 1589 *Diálogos familiares de la agricultura cristiana* (Familiar Dialogues of Christian Agriculture), Juan de Pineda outlines the connection between embryology, the termination of pregnancy, and Christianity:

> Avicenna, like Galen, refers to the fetus after quickening as a child because it is formed at thirty-five days and it moves at seventy days after conception. . . .If the child is formed at forty-five days after conception, it will move at ninety days and will be born two hundred and seventy-some days, which is usually nine months . . . Galen said that prior to thirty days after conception (before the fetus is well formed) it is not possible to terminate what would be considered a complete male (nor a complete female

before forty days) since before this time the fetus is not complete nor well developed. . . . he says that the male moves three months after conception and the female after four months . . . Aristotle and Saint Thomas say that a male does not have a rational soul until forty days after conception and a female until the fourth month (usually believed at eighty days). (73)[36]

The debate over when life actually begins continued throughout the early modern period. Fray Antonio de Fuentelapeña, for example, in his 1676 publication summarizes the various sides of the polemic, mentioning those who believe that an embryo has a rational soul within three days after conception, those who believe that a child has life only after birth, and others who believe that only a fetus capable of moving and feeling ("when the fetus in the uterus moves and cries" [222]) can be considered an individual soul apart from the mother, which he concludes occurs after forty days for males and eighty for females (218–26). Fuentelapeña's consideration of when life begins, not surprisingly, leads to a discussion of the legal-moral issues related to abortion: "The fetus has a rational soul in the mother's womb, so those who abort an *animated* fetus are guilty of homicide" (226; italics mine).[37]

In the history of embryology, nonetheless, the mid-seventeenth century (around the time when *El parto* first appeared on stage) was crucial since it produced decisive discoveries about the ovaries, sperm, and the procreative process that countered the widely held notions inherited from classical sources.[38] Even as the reproductive technologies of the mid-seventeenth-century New Science discovered that life was developed within the female egg (thus implying that men were almost "incidental participants"), the textual and iconographic response again was a reinscription of masculinity into generation (Gilbert, "Masculine," 168–69). Referring to the key role of William Harvey's *Exercitationes de generatione animalium* (1651) in establishing that all life comes from the female's egg, Ruth Gilbert argues that it was "framed textually and pictorially by representations of male births that reclaimed creation as masculine. The frontispiece image, which depicts Zeus opening the cosmic egg, summarizes the tension between scientific heroism and the reproductive female body . . . If female nature was to be effectively subdued by masculine science then creation had to be authoritatively coded as male" ("Masculine," 169, 171).[39] Along similar lines, in her study of early modern sex, science, and politics, Lisa Forman Cody explains the numerous seventeenth-century allusions to pregnant men as a cultural response to a "contemporary curiosity about what made a man physiologically a father and what exactly his biological powers might be" (94).

## The Iconographic Disembodied Fetus as Mechanism of Control

While depictions of pregnant women seemed to diminish in the sixteenth century, it is worth mentioning that the common practice of illustrating fetuses during the early modern period duplicates another visual strategy frequent during the late twentieth and early twenty-first centuries: the separation of the fetus from the body of the pregnant woman.[40] Although these images imitated the illustrations of the autonomous fetus depicted in Soranus's second-century *Gynecology* (which were reproduced later in Muscio's thirteenth-century manuscript), this visual disembodiment during the early modern period acquired new meaning. Factors such as the disappearance of pregnancy and childbirth illustrations that had been common during the medieval period, as well as the encroachment of male physicians in midwifery facilitated the medical, legal, and ecclesiastic authorities to view the fetus as a separate individual. This autonomous being was distanced from issues related to women's control over their own bodies, which then justified the need for patriarchal intervention to "protect" the fetus. For example, borrowing the drawings from Rösslin's *Rosengarten* (1513), Francisco Núñez's *Libro del parto humano* (1580) includes fifteen different images of problematic fetal positions prior to delivery (Figure 11).[41] Similar to current ultrasound images (which are viewed on a monitor while looking away from the actual pregnant woman's belly), these early modern drawings are illustrated to look like tiny adults who are completely disconnected from the female body. Karen Newman describes the ideology implied in these fetal images as consistent with gendered notions of female inferiority and passivity:

> The entire series of disembodied wombs from the Soranian tradition through the many editions of Rösslin and into the handbooks of the late seventeenth century suppress completely fetal dependence on the female body by graphically rendering that body as a passive receptacle, the scriptural woman as "vessel"—a visual rendering in keeping with the medical belief in "preformation," in which the fetus was conceived of as preformed, a fully fashioned though tiny adult that simply grew in size. (33)

Like the early modern erasure of representations of "normal" female pregnancy and childbirth, it is not by chance that Núñez's text does not include the only drawing in Rösslin's text that depicts an actual birthing scene, even though it copies more than a dozen of the fetal illustrations from his

Figure 11: Illustration of a problematic fetal position from *Libro del parto humano*. (Reproduced by permission from the Biblioteca Nacional, Madrid)

predecessor's midwife manual. For example, one illustration featured in the *Rosengarten* shows the pregnant woman in labor right before the delivery, as she sits on the birthing stool accompanied by her midwife and another attendant. Núñez's text, however, offers only a small drawing of the birthing stool alone. While the woodcut featured on the text's cover shows the commonly reproduced post-birthing scene of the mother resting in bed and the female attendants bathing the newborn, the reader/viewer is denied access to the pregnant woman or the actual birth. Unlike the medieval images of pregnant women giving birth, early modern iconography disembodies the fetus from its mother (or, as we will see, monsterizes the pregnant woman).[42]

## The Abortion Debate in Early Modern Spain

The connection between embryology and religion proved crucial for the legislation of women's reproductive health during the early modern period. Legal and ecclesiastical doctrine regarding birth control, abortion, infanticide, child placement, miscarriage, and infertility frequently depended upon the medical definitions of fetal formation, as they informed moral debates that implied fetal rights and women's reproductive control. Medieval secular laws and papal proclamations against birth control and abortifacients were revised and formalized during the early modern period. Gregorio López's sixteenth-century revision of medieval civil law from Alfonso X's *Las Siete Partidas* (Partida VII, Title VIII, Law VIII) relies on Aristotelian concepts of when the fetus has developed enough to be considered "ensouled." The statute declared that the punishment for any abortive measures before the fetus is animated or considered "alive" is exile for five years (Alfonso X, *Partidas*, 1346–47). If the fetus had developed beyond three months (and therefore believed to have life), then the punishment was death (Lopez, 30–31).

A series of papal decrees reflect shifting and perhaps conflicting views on abortion. Prior to a 1588 decree, only aborting a male fetus after 40 days or a female fetus after 80 days was punishable with excommunication. However, Pope Sixtus V's 1588 bull (*Effraenatum*) attempted to enact a more conservative and harsher position on abortion by criminalizing any intervention in women's reproduction that resulted in termination of the pregnancy, regardless of how far along the fetus was.[43] The 1588 bull was short-lived, nonetheless, since his successor Gregory XIV annulled it in 1591. In 1679 Pope Innocence XI condemned 65 proposals, two of which pertained to the abortion debate (and the Spanish Inquisition soon followed suit). One of these (Proposal 34) rejected the claim that it was acceptable to induce abortion before fetal animation in order to save the life or the reputation of the pregnant woman. Another (Proposal 35) denounced the belief that the fetus did not have a rational soul while in the womb but starts to have a soul only after birth and therefore abortion could not be considered homicide.[44] These censures, as Javier Pérez Escohotado reminds us, historically are a delayed reaction to ideas that had been circulating and that had persisted in the mentality of Christians throughout the sixteenth and seventeenth centuries (97).

While early modern theologians and legislators grappled with the moral and biological issues involving reproduction and women's bodies, civil law and many penitentials maintained that the abortion of an "inanimate" fetus did not constitute homicide, especially if the pregnant woman's life or health is at risk. Pedro Galindo, in his 1682 *Directorio de penitentes* (Directory of Penitents), argues that even if the fetus is "animate" (which he defines at 40 days for a male and 80 for females) the pregnant woman can abort if the pregnancy endangers her life, since the abortion would be "pardonable homicide" due to the need for self defense, much like "running from a bull or a beast" to save one's life (164). However, any woman or anyone else who assists or counsels her in aborting the fetus when her life is not at risk is guilty of the mortal sin of homicide (Galindo, 164).

Anxiety about what rampant abortions would do to the social fabric seemed no less prevalent in the seventeenth century than it is for some today. Francisco de Osuna believed that a married couple who used abstinence to avoid pregnancy were practicing a form of abortion "as if they killed their child"; Fray Martín de Azpilicueta affirmed that a woman sins against the fifth commandment if she attempts to abort her fetus by taking any potions, by working too much or by doing any other method that terminates pregnancy; and Vicente Mejía compares couples who abstain from sexual relations (due to anxiety about having too many children and not enough inheritance) to a land owner who doesn't sow seed in his soil (Vigil,138).

The notion that unwanted pregnancies could be avoided through various methods of birth control or terminated with abortive measures obviously frightened moralists of the time. Popular news items reporting cases of unwanted pregnancies aborted by priests, doctors, or even female celebrities were circulated and occasionally surfaced in print. On February 13, 1658, Barrionuevo writes about a priest who deceived a young girl into believing that the pope would give him permission to marry her. When she became pregnant for the first time, the priest gave her an abortifacient. After she became pregnant a second time, he sent her to a witch, who gave her a potion that allowed the unwed "illicit" couple to continue the affair without her father noticing the assault to the family's honor. The remedy even created an auditory illusion of silence that rendered the cries of the newborn child undetectable by the family. According to the story, the couple eventually poisoned her father. In the end, the priest was arrested while the young woman entered a convent (Barrionuevo, 2:162).

News reports of royal reproductive scandals likewise were of great interest to the early modern public, again implying an awareness of transgressive options for unwanted pregnancies as well as an implied justification for the need to control these errant women. Barrionuevo reported on September 13, 1656, that Queen Christina of Sweden was impregnated by a cardinal in Rome. According to the account, she "secretly" aborted the pregnancy before arriving in Paris. Christina's reputation was already tainted by that time, but the author chooses to blame her gender rather than her personality for her immorality: "After all, she is a woman—anything is possible" (Barrionuevo, 1:314).[45] Consistent with other narratives about Queen Christina, this news item demonstrates how her enormous popularity in Spain during the seventeenth century was based on a non-traditional tabloidesque lifestyle that proved entertaining for the scandal-thirsty public of that time.

According to Merry E. Wiesner's case study of midwives in sixteenth- and seventeenth-century Nuremberg, these women participated on both sides of criminal investigations involving abortion, infanticide, child abandonment, and illegitimacy (since "illegitimate children would be those most likely to be aborted, killed, or abandoned") ("Early," 107). Wiesner's findings show that midwives were not always suspected of criminal collusion, given that they were also required to become detectives to help solve the reproductive crime by investigating, interviewing and examining suspects, searching for bodies and other evidence: "Thus we find midwives active in a broad spectrum of medical, legal, and religious activities. Their opinions and judgments were taken seriously and their essential power over life clearly recognized. No other group of women received more frequent consideration by the city council or was more closely watched as to conduct, numbers, and skill" ("Early," 110).

Wiesner's conclusions emphasize the potential power that midwives could wield in towns and cities during this period. It is precisely this potential for control over women's reproductive practices that made midwives seem so dangerous. Not unexpectedly, then, the obstetrical manuals published in Spain during the eighteenth century reveal the widespread fear that midwives might actually aid in promoting immorality, or at least in hiding it. In Antonio Medina's 1750 *Cartilla nueva*, for example, the question-and-answer format reveals this persistent fear:

> **Question:** And what should be done if the woman who becomes pregnant due to an illicit affair requests that the midwife facilitate an abortion through any means possible, giving as excuses the scandal, dishonor, and other serious concerns?
>
> **Answer:** All midwives should surely believe (no matter how many justifications they are capable of imagining) that it is not licit for them to give any advice or interference that may suggest abortion. For this reason alone they would be excommunicated through the gravest censures by the Highest Priests and by Secular Judges, punished with the death penalty without recourse to the excuse that the abortion was enacted during the time before the fetus was animated. Other than the fact that no one is capable of knowing

this for certain, even if it were true, from the moment of conception the embryo has the aptitude or potential to possess a rational soul. (34–36)[46]

Medina's answer in the passage just cited demonstrates the power that midwives could wield as reproductive counselors—as the author attempts to remind women of the moral and legal repercussions of assisted abortion, regardless of the particular circumstances of the young woman as well as any differences in the stage of the embryo or fetus.[47]

Looking at the changes in medical practices concerning conception and abortion, John M. Riddle argues that the shift began in the twelfth century, when medical training moved from clinical apprenticeship to theoretical university study. The gynecological practices that had been in the hands of midwives who were not destined for formal university studies were gradually lost, especially given the Renaissance distrust of orally transmitted medical wisdom: "By the fifteenth and sixteenth centuries, few physicians knew about birth control agents, simply because it was not part of their training in becoming doctors, nor was there a ready means to learn about them during regular practice" (Riddle, 157). As a result, the Renaissance gynecological specialists had limited direct experience with a wide range of women's reproductive options and therefore lacked the particular training (and the incentive) necessary to accurately translate ancient texts concerning abortive measures. Moreover, in addition to the changes in medical training, the continuing debate in theology and secular law undoubtedly was an influencing factor in the obstacles to reproductive options during the early modern period.[48]

For Riddle, one of the lamentable consequences of this shift is that the extensive knowledge about fertility control widely held in the ancient world was gradually lost over the course of the Middle Ages, becoming nearly extinct by the early modern period. Riddle explains that Hippocratic authors had passed along information about how to have a safe abortion. For example, in his *Natural History*, Pliny mentions various contraceptives and abortifacients to induce sterility, and Galen described a number of prescriptions to terminate pregnancy (Riddle, 82–86). Nonetheless, according to Riddle, Renaissance authors seemed to know very little about birth control compared to classical and medieval sources (144–46).

In early modern Spain, the suppression of abortive medicine was evident in the Inquisition's censorship of medical texts. Interestingly, the excised passages related to abortifacients and antifertility agents actually created a paradoxical controversy, since the elimination of this information from medical texts could result in placing a pregnant woman at risk when she unknowingly used a plant or herb with abortive powers for other ailments. For example, when Andrés Laguna's Castilian translation of *Materia Medica* by Dioscorides (*Pedacio Dioscórides Anazarbeo, acerca de la materia medicinal*, first published in 1555) was reprinted in a censured edition in 1632 (without such passages as those explaining the abortive properties of cardamom [in Book 1, Chapter 5] and parts of the laurel plant [Chapter 86]), critics reluctantly opposed the "correction" due to the unintentional miscarriages that could result (Pardo Tomás, 216–18). Despite opposition, the excised passages regarding abortifacients were not reincorporated in subsequent editions since, as José Pardo Tomás concludes: "The general public's knowledge of practices such as abortion was more feared than any possible consequences of not knowing the risks of applying the medical remedy" (218).[49]

## The Miscarriage Debate as Means to Control Women's Bodies

The term *aborto* in Spanish means both "abortion" and "miscarriage," depending on whether the loss of pregnancy is intentional or unintentional. As I have shown here, pregnant women who attempted to miscarry intentionally were criminalized for their behavior. Juan de Pineda, for example, cites Hippocrates' text describing an "evil woman of ill-repute who being newly pregnant began to jump up and down so much that she expelled the mass in the form of an egg white with a thin membrane with many small dots of blood and red threads in the center that looked like the belly button" (78).[50]

During the early modern period, the debate over ways to avoid miscarriage became a hotly debated topic in many medical and moral treatises. One factor involved the need to ensure descendants for the future, as infant mortality was extremely high during the sixteenth century, with a rate of 40–45% of children dying before their seventh birthday in some rural areas (Vigil, 137).[51] Most discussions surrounding pregnancy and miscarriage, then, addressed married women who miscarried because of unintentional "negligence" on their part or because of their unfortunate physiology. Francisco Núñez's publication on childbirth and difficult deliveries, for example, describes possible causes of miscarriage and ways to avoid it (43v). According to Núñez, reasons for miscarriage include the following: the womb opening is too big, too slippery, or is ulcerated; the pregnant woman has a bad cough; or, she has taken a purge before the fourth month. After the seventh month, avoiding these things can help prevent miscarriage: excessive vomiting, not eating enough, eating too much, too many chills, a bath that is too hot, too much vigorous movement (such as work, dancing, or an accidental fall), too much sex, or a sudden flash of anger, fear, or happiness (43v-47v). Núñez also explains that one can know if the fetus has died in the womb if the woman's breasts wrinkle, the baby stops moving, or if when the woman moves back and forth the baby "follows like a rock" (51).

Like Núñez's obstetrical treatise, numerous moralists wrote at length about the causes for miscarriage. In his 1529 *Relox de príncipes* (Dial of Princes), an expanded version of his enormous bestseller *Libro áureo de Marco Aurelio*, Antonio de Guevara includes four chapters about the dangers of miscarriage and ways to prevent it. While he notes the irony of a celibate clergy member giving pregnant women advice about something he has never experienced, Guevara claims authority through his formal education, since practice without theory is insufficient: "I could be excused from speaking about this topic since I am a member of the clergy and I have never been married . . . but frequently a learned man can provide a better analysis of something that he has read than would a simpleton even though he has experienced it" (392).[52] Guevara begins by urging pregnant women not to be too active. He advises them to avoid running, dancing, or jumping, reminding them that women who "bounce around" acquire a bad reputation anyway (393). Other recommendations for pregnant women proposed by Guevara include not eating too much at one sitting, avoiding sudden and shocking news, and not attending overly crowded events for fear of being crushed. While the author assigns blame for the miscarriage to the woman ("this all happens because of women's actions, they become the author of their own homicides . . . It is their own fault that they miscarry" (401)[53]), he also includes a specific section on the role that men can play to ensure the successful pregnancy of their wives: "The husband should keep his wife from doing a lot of work and the wife should be careful not to indulge in too much leisure since it is a rule for pregnant women that too much work makes them miscarry and too much leisure is also dangerous . . . because idleness is not only reason to be denied eternal life but it also causes women to miscarry" (402–3).[54] Likewise, the husband should not upset his pregnant wife by making her angry, and when she is advanced in the pregnancy, he should stop having sexual relations with her, whether out of necessity or virtue (404).

Not surprisingly, given Guevara's and other moralists' recommendations that husbands do not deny their pregnant wives anything they request (when the craving is not unhealthy) (409), the Countess D'Aulnoy observed while traveling in Spain during the seventeenth century that Spaniards tended to indulge the cravings and whims of pregnant women for fear of miscarriage (219). In fact, while emphasizing the impact of the Spanish respect for the wishes of pregnant women, D'Aulnoy recounts an anecdote that employs a "pregnant man" scenario:

> I was told that there was a young man at Court who was desperately in love with a very fine woman, whose husband continually kept [her] under his eyes, so that finding no other way to speak to her he disguised himself like a woman big with child, and so went to her house. He addressed himself to the jealous husband, and told him he had the *antajo* [sic] (which is the word for longing [craving]) to discourse with his wife in private. The husband, deceived by this appearance, made no question that this was a young big-bellied woman, and immediately consented that his wife should make this person happy with a long and pleasant audience. (220)

Another important cause of miscarriage that was expounded by Guevara involved pregnant women who wore extravagant clothing to indulge the desire to look attractive. Guevara's advice was repeated and expanded in numerous treatises, as it touched on issues related to nation, gender, morality, and economics. Reviewing these anecdotes in Guevara's *Relox*, Emilie Bergmann reminds us that "each reproductive disaster is narrated in graphic physical detail, involving such female excesses as gluttony or vanity . . . The receptivity and the threat of violence with which the maternal body is invested are here exaggerated to render it truly 'monstrous.' " (43–44).

In his 1636 treatise on the dangers of fashion, *Rogación al Rey D. Felipe IV . . . en detestación de los grandes abusos en los trajes* (Petition to King Philip IV . . . Critique of the Widespread Abuses in Clothing), Alonso de Carranza goes so far as to state that some items of clothing are "a threat to the propagation of Spaniards," referring especially to platform shoes [chapines], big hoop skirts [guardainfantes], and form-fitting stockings (20). Tall shoes were dangerous for walking since women could easily fall (Guevara also notes, "I saw a pregnant woman miscarry merely because her platform shoe tripped her" [400]). Likewise, the *guardainfantes* were heavy and could cause sterility "because the fullness brings much air and coldness to the uterus where the human body is formed . . . it is a complete impediment for reproduction" (20–20v). [55] Tight stockings were harmful because they created too much heat, which produces humoral dryness and consequent infertility. Carranza's list also warns pregnant women that it is very easy to miscarry from a cough, a shock, and the smoke from a candle poorly extinguished; but the greatest risk, nonetheless, came to those who wore large and heavy clothing. The fear of women's fashion as a cause of infertility continued throughout the sixteenth and seventeenth centuries, as is evident in Fray Antonio de Ezcaray's 1691 *Voces de dolor nacidas de la multitud de pecados . . . trajes profanos* (Voices of Pain Born of a Multitude of Sin . . . Profane Clothing), which also associates popular tight-fitting attire with infertility: "These ornaments and outfits attract many sins and impediments to health since they cause infertility and sickness given that these women walk around with the gut of a whale and constant torture from its tightness" (39).[56]

This fear of miscarriage also surfaces in Pedro de Luján's 1550 *Coloquios matrimoniales* (Colloquies on Matrimony), as he repeats the same seven reasons why women suffer miscarriages that are outlined in Guevara's text. The difference is that in Luján's book the discussion originates from the perspective of two women, one of whom already had experienced multiple miscarriages. Interestingly, the pregnant Eulalia is worried about having a third miscarriage and asks advice from Dorotea, who has not experienced pregnancy. Dorotea agrees to speak on the subject since they are alone and can express themselves freely. As the author hides behind the personal stories of two women characters, his text fails to offer a different perspective on women's reproductive health. Dorotea merely repeats the same argument developed in Guevara's *Relox de príncipes*:

> You had much to blame in this. Certainly because of two lewd things, such as squeezing the body and getting angry about nothing, you killed the child you conceived and put your own life at risk . . . There are two ways that a miscarriage occurs: one it the fault of the woman and the other the fault of the man. Since we are only women here I will tell you the woman's part . . . Surely people could ask me how I dare speak bad about something that I have not experienced but I say that doctors have not had every illness either but because of their education and what they have observed and cured they can heal, so I too can speak about what I have seen, heard and even read. (178)[57]

Luján's book also contains advice for expectant fathers. When Eulalia's husband Marcelo arrives and joins in the discussion, Dorotea offers guidance for his behavior to ensure a healthy pregnancy. First, he should not make her work too much but not spoil her either since too much leisure causes a difficult delivery (187). Likewise, husbands should not leave home when their wives are pregnant "because one of the rules for a good husband is that he should use his eyes to watch out for her, his hands to serve her, his fortune to care for her, and his heart to please her" (187).[58] Dorotea concludes by warning Marcelo that more women miscarry from getting angry at their husbands than from their diet.[59] Yet, whether these manuals indict women for reproductive problems or merely provide passing comments regarding the husband's role in ensuring a healthy pregnancy, the recurrent discussions involving women and miscarriage during the early modern period contributed to the increasing invasion by men into women's reproductive health issues.[60]

## Infanticide as Solution to Unwed Motherhood

A 1667 survey of the poor in Seville reveals that poverty was frequently inextricable from the struggles of single mothers. Perry notes that unwedded mothers were a reality to be reckoned with: "Pregnancy and dependent children appeared to be the most common attributes of people identified as the 'deserving poor' . . . seldom was the name of the husband included with that of the pregnant woman" (*Gender*, 173). Since the consequences of unwed motherhood in early modern Europe could be socially and economically disastrous, it is not surprising to read that unmarried women were able to hide their pregnancies and give birth in "outhouses, cow stalls, hay mounds, and dung heaps hoping to avoid public notice," attempted to relocate the infants for placement or kill them (Wiesner, *Women*, 51). The ability to give birth without public notice, however, required certain conditions. For example, various moralists accused women's fashion as an accomplice in the crime of hidden pregnancies. When Carranza wrote of women's clothing as dangerous for morality, especially the *guardainfante* or large hoop skirt, he emphasized how it allowed hidden pregnancies, given its wide and puffy design, "so disproportionate from the waist that it gives unmarried women much room to go around nine or ten months pregnant without being noticed" (22). Carranza even explains that the term "guardainfante" originated from a French woman who needed to hide her pregnancy, so she used a wide skirt to "*guard enfant*" ("to keep the baby") (22).

In his 1638 treatise *Reforma de trages* (Reform of Clothing), Bartolomé Jiménez Patón also blames the *guardainfante* for facilitating illicit pregnancies and provoking the miscarriage of legitimate ones (6). In fact, Jiménez Patón (citing Fray Hernando de Talavera) claims that the large hoop skirt was invented precisely to hide the pregnancies that resulted from adulterous relations (*Reforma*, 44v). Considering the *entremés*' generic reputation for portraying explicit sexual content, it is not surprising that Jiménez Patón uses the controversial one-act interludes as proof of the origin of the *guardainfante* as the object that allows women to hide illicit pregnancies (*Reforma*, 44v). Talavera takes this argument even further by stating that when men see a woman wearing a *guardainfante* they become much more aggressive in their quest to seduce her: "It is a scandalous outfit that easily incites lust because, since men know that it can cover pregnancies, they more freely attempt to convince this type of woman to engage in sexual relations" (quted in Jiménez Patón, *Reforma*, 46).[61]

In the case that the reluctant mother is able to successfully hide both the pregnancy and the delivery, she must then contend with the consequences of unmarried motherhood or separation from the newborn. As James Casey describes, the early modern period showed increased efforts to care for foundlings. Charitable confraternities were established in numerous cities "to remedy the frequent distress of finding in its streets and squares and at the gates of its temples innumerable newborn children, who were often killed by the cold or by scavenging dogs" (Casey, 215). Although it is difficult to establish accurate illegitimacy ratios, Casey estimates that 2–3% of the newly born in rural areas and 10% or more in cities would have had to grow up with unrecognized parents (215). According to Maureen Flynn's study of foundling confraternities in early modern Spain, hospices to care for foundlings and poor children abandoned at chapel doors "involved hiring wetnurses to raise the minors until they reached the age of seven, when they were placed in schools and trades" (58). Local theatrical productions in Valladolid, for example, raised enough money to support annually an average of 100 children with wetnurses, dowries, and religious and educational services (Flynn, 59).[62]

In the context of infanticide, most European countries equated it with homicide and penalized it by death. According to Merry Weisner, more women were executed for infanticide in early modern Europe than for any other crime except witchcraft, and in some areas women accused of infanticide were more often executed than those accused of witchcraft (*Women*, 52). In fact, the line between intentional and unintentional infant deaths was not always clear. Sixteenth- and seventeenth-century confessors' manuals indicate practices that were dangerous for newborns, as they inadvertently mention ways of getting rid of unwanted births. The most frequently cited examples are cases of suffocation or crushing, especially involving babies who slept in the same bed with their mother (Pérez Escohotado, 100).

In María de Zayas's 1637 story "El prevenido engañado" (Forewarned but not Forearmed), the consequences of societal restrictions placed on women's reproductive options and unwed motherhood are painfully evident.

When Serafina gets pregnant out of wedlock, she feels her only option is to conceal the pregnancy, deliver the child in secret, and abandon the newborn in a vacant shack after giving birth: "Serafina ducked into the dark space . . . there she struggled to stifle her moans and she cried out to God and all His saints to help her . . . Serafina gave birth to a baby. As soon as she saw herself free of her burden, she gathered up her skirts and returned home, abandoning the little creature to its fate (*Enchantments*, 118).[63] Zayas's reader might be inclined to judge harshly Serafina's initial lack of motherly love. Her subsequent attempts to find out what happened to the baby (who had been rescued) and her ensuing guilt and trauma later make her an object of sympathy. In any event, Zayas's tale makes readers reflect on the personal tragedy that arises from the lack of reproductive options for women: "She was haunted by the nightmare of the abandoned baby, for, if it had died or the dogs had eaten it, her conscience would have to bear that crime" (119–20).[64]

As in Zayas's story, in which the birthing scene is observed through the eyes of a male, the representation of childbirth in cultural texts frequently has little to do with the personal perspective of the mother in labor. In fact, the opportunities for observing childbirth are generally limited to the sensationalist moments of problematic deliveries or other anomalies that create a spectacle for the curious gaze of the observer. Not surprisingly, many scholars have noted that the figure of the mother is typically absent or minimized in early modern literary works of Spain. Ruth El Saffar, for example, argues that

> by the end of the sixteenth century, the figure of the mother virtually disappears from the Spanish stage and from the literary texts. The daughters appear, like Athena, to have emerged directly from the heads of their fathers. The mothers, for their part, seem to have been entirely swallowed up in the patriarchal social structures that prescribed for them roles of silence and obedience. (68)

Conversely, Christiane Faliu-Lacourt challenges this belief by discussing cases in early modern Spanish theater that reveal mothers who talk openly about or make references to the movement of their fetus, their growing pregnant stomachs, the screams and cries during labor and the delivery, and the emotion of holding their child for the first time (46). Faliu-Lacourt argues that the dramatic function of these positive images of pregnancy and childbirth was to move the male spectators to feel paternal pride and the women as well so that their maternal role would be valued (43). While these moments may celebrate nonproblematic aspects of women's reproduction, they are somewhat infrequent in classical Spanish theater and more importantly, the actual childbirth scene (indicative of the sociopolitical climate yet unlike the outrageous male birthing scene in *El parto de Juan Rana*) takes place off stage.[65]

## The Monsterization of Motherhood

When considering the possibilities for narrating pregnancy, labor, and delivery in most early modern medical, scientific, and certain popular texts, we discover that they frequently resort to discussions of monsters to talk about the specifics of childbirth. All three obstetrical texts published in Spain during the sixteenth and seventeenth centuries, for example, not only focus more on the potential problems during pregnancy and childbirth (than they do the normal deliveries) but they also relate maternity to the monstrous.[66] In *Libro del arte de las comadres o madrinas* (Book of the Art of Midwives), Damián Carbón repeats anecdotes about women giving birth to monstrous fleshy masses formed in various shapes, some alive, others not. Beginning with Aristotle's definition of a monster as a "deformity of some aspect outside the natural custom and therefore to be different from the norm" (11v, 12), he then cites classical authors such as Galen, Averoes, Avicenna, and Aristotle. The author explains the existence of these *mola* as the result of the "lack of informative efficacy in the spermatic humour and also because of corruption of the matter ... And therefore Aristotle said ... that such a monstrosity is created when the man's seed does not converge and when the woman's vessel is not attended by the male, which results in the generation of a similar monster" (12v).[67] Carbón also includes graphic descriptions of women who gave birth to pieces of flesh in the shape and nature of fish (one of the women delivered twenty-five fish-shaped forms because the hour of conception aligned with the sign of the fish) and of how, after a woman from Mallorca delivered a boy missing one arm, a creature resembling a live hedgehog with teeth emerged from her womb: "it was a marvel to see such a frightening figure" (13).

Francisco Núñez continues the tradition of narrating monstrous births in his 1580 medical treatise on childbirth. He mixes ancient anecdotes with contemporary stories of hybrid creatures born to women in Spain:

> A body with two heads has been born and not long ago in another town a monster with horns, teeth, and a tail was born. Another woman in Seville, who is from my hometown, after a long and difficult labor gave birth to a

monster who looked like a lizard and then suddenly escaped. According to Pliny, a woman named Alcipe gave birth to an elephant while a slave woman delivered a serpent, and that in Monviedro a boy was born and then turned into the wind. (8v-9)[68]

While Juan Alonso's 1606 treatise *Diez previlegios de preñadas* also begins with a discussion of what constitutes a monster, he argues that (despite Aristotle's statement "we should look upon the female state as being as it were a deformity") women should not be considered monstrous merely because they are dissimilar from the perfection of being male. His defense of women is based on resemblance logic: since some people do not resemble either parent, or a bit of one or the other or both, we all would be considered monsters given that we can't completely resemble both the male and the female (9).

Just as the manuals on motherhood and childbirth are quick to address the issue of monsters, early modern teratologies inevitably discuss the central role of mothers in the generation of monsters. Ambroise Paré's introductory description of what constitutes a monster in his popular text *On Monsters and Marvels* (first published in 1579) orients the reader to anticipate the emergence of the marvelous creature, thus inviting the reader/viewer to participate as voyeuristic witness to the shocking births:

> Monsters are things that appear outside the course of Nature (and are usually signs of some forthcoming misfortune), such as a child who is born with one arm, another who will have two heads, and additional members over and above the ordinary. Marvels are things which happen that are completely against Nature as when a woman will give birth to a serpent, or to a dog, or some other thing that is totally against Nature, as we shall show hereafter through several examples of said monsters and marvels, which examples I have gathered along with the illustrations from several authors. (3)

The author then outlines thirteen causes for the existence of monsters: nine involve the pregnant woman or specifics of generation, two are attributed to God's will, and two are explained by evil forces. The nine causes related to reproduction include: too great or too little a quantity of seed, the imagination during conception, the narrowness or smallness of the womb, the improper position of the mother (as when being pregnant, she has sat too long with her legs crossed, or pressed against her womb), through a fall, or blows struck against the womb of the mother, being with child, through hereditary or accidental illnesses, through rotten or corrupt seed, and through mixture or mingling of seed (3–4). According to Paré's descriptions of monsters, the body of the pregnant women is extremely vulnerable to becoming the target or scapegoat for various reproductive complications or physical discrepancies between newborn and its parents. For example, Paré includes stories and illustrations of petrified children trapped in the mother's womb for decades and other tales of the influence of diet and activities that can result in the birth of monsters: "Some have attributed monsters to being procreated from the corruption of foul and filthy foods that women eat, or want to eat, or that they abhor looking upon just after they have conceived or that someone may have tossed something between their teats, such as a cherry, plum, frog, mouse, or other thing that can render infants monstrous" (46).

## Visualizing Mothers and Monsters

While artistic depictions of pregnant women were less common during the early modern period than in the Middle Ages, the pictorial representations of newborn monsters were frequently published and circulated. Paré's work, as we see in its introduction, emphasizes the role of the mother and the moment of delivery in terms of a pictorial spectacle, which necessitates the inclusion of illustrations of the newborn for the reader who was not present at the birth. Accordingly, the etymology of the term monster (from the ancient Greek root of the word *teras*, which implies both aberration and adoration, as well as from the Latin *monstrum*, "to show") indicates the ambivalent and visual nature of the monstrous exhibition. It may not be surprising, then, that Paré's text includes seventy-nine illustrations of monstrous creatures. Interestingly, only one visual image is that of a pregnant body, despite the dozens of narrations of monstrous births. In the chapter titled "On Women Who Carry Several Children During One Pregnancy," Paré includes a drawing of a pregnant woman from Italy named Dorothy who "gave birth to twenty children in two confinements, namely nine children at one time and eleven at another, who carrying such a great load, was so heavy that she held up her stomach, which hung down as far as her knees, with a great hoop which hung over her neck and shoulder, as you see in this picture" (24–25) (Figure 12). Like the other illustrations of the "freakish" figures, as if on display in a carnival side show or in a tabloid magazine, Dorothy's exaggeratedly pregnant belly is considered monstrous in its excess. Along similar lines, Barrionuevo writes on October 13, 1655, of a local woman who also has an abundant pregnancy:

> On Mayor street, in front of my mother's house, . . . there is a woman pregnant with such excess that it is a monstrosity and it looks like she carries a large earthen jar instead of a belly. I was amazed to see her. She, her husband, and all the other neighbors told me that last year she had given birth to four babies, all male, one after the other and how she now felt just as many if not more, as she pointed out the outlines of all their heads on her stomach. After four months they all died. At present she is pregnant again in her eighth month . . . I have talked to her and have seen her in person and can testify that it is a bizarre case (1:265).[69]

Barrionuevo mentions the local details of the street name near his mother's home and the fact that he had witnessed the spectacle in person in order to enhance both its credibility and the fear of this oddity being so close to home—that such a sensational occurrence could happen to anyone among us.

In seventeenth-century Spain, the accounts of monsters were illustrated more frequently than any other class of news pamphlet, and "an essential feature of these relations is that they outdo each other in *admiratio* and, almost by definition, seek to present their subjects as unexampled" (Ettinghausen, "Illustrated," 127). In a 1688 *relación* (news pamphlet), for example, the description of the recent birth of an intersexed child with both primary sex characteristics manipulates the reaction of disbelief of those present at the birth in order to shock and entice the reader, who is also witness to the prodigious event. The first page provides an initial physical description and illustration of the child—born with normal female genitalia, but also with a male penis in the middle of his/her face. Likewise, the baby has no eyes or nose but has three big teeth in his/her mouth, six fingers on each hand, and two holes in one ear, through which the child wheezes. Then, after discussing the shocking nature of monsters in general, the text relates certain details of the delivery. Like Juan Rana's experience in labor, the mother endures difficult pain, but unlike the comical male mother, she is assisted by an experienced midwife. As soon as the midwife declares, "Oh my child, look, you haven't delivered yet,"[70] the baby suddenly appears in the bedsheets and the midwife discards the afterbirth, saying "Thank God, we came through that victorious—the newborn is safe."[71] Then the real dramatic spectacle begins: "They discovered the child; those present were staring at it, and for a long while they remained stunned, in a deep silence, shocked, looking at each other—pondering such monstrosity."[72] Like watching a horror film, the reader waits with anticipation, enjoying the focalization on the witnesses'

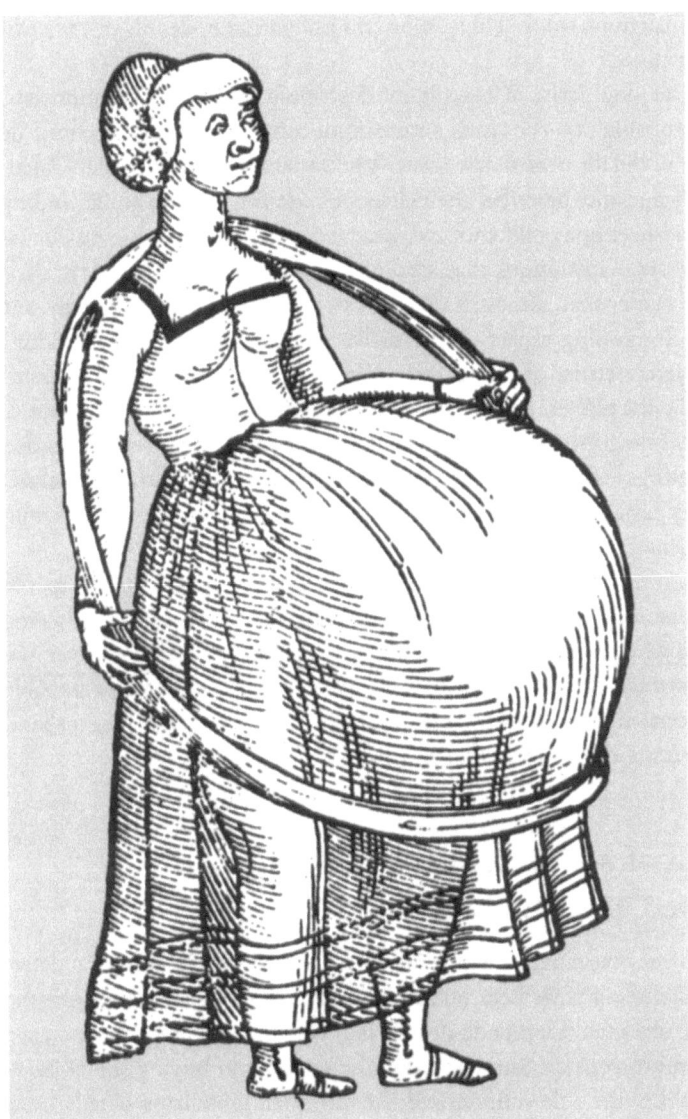

Figure 12: Illustration from Ambroise Paré's *On Monsters*: Dorothy pregnant with several fetuses. (Reproduced by permission from the British Library)

speechless reactions before being allowed to observe the details of the creature's deformities.

Given the popularity of news items describing the delivery of monsters, it is not surprising that the visual nature of monstrous births can become the focal point of the illustrated narratives. A news pamphlet published in Valencia in 1634 not only describes the delivery of conjoined twins (or according to the broadsheet one child with two heads), but its narrative is constructed around the two illustrations that accompany the news item. The text clarifies for the reader that, although there are two drawings, there was only one birth. The interesting aspect of the delivery narrative and the "shocking" physical characteristics of the "child" are evident through the need for multiple visual perspectives: a frontal view of the newborn, a view from behind, and a verbal description of the child's internal organs, which was recorded from the autopsy when the baby died.[73] Unlike most births during this time, the delivery took place in a hospital and was assisted by male doctors who later performed the autopsy.

The danger of monster gazing to the spectator can also apply to the child's mother. Núñez warns his readers of the fatal consequences of allowing the woman who gives birth to a monster to see her offspring: "However, the pregnant woman is warned not to look at the monster whenever possible because a certain woman from Toledo died of fright (and later her husband too) after seeing the monster that she had delivered" (8v-9).[74]

## "Portrait of a Monster Who was Conceived in the Body of a Man"

While "monster narratives" tend to involve maternity and a shocking delivery, one fascinating news item published in Barcelona in 1606 narrated the strange tale of a man (Hernando de la Haba) who became pregnant and gave birth to a monstrous creature. To hook the reader into buying the tabloid-style pamphlet, the title summarized the case with tantalizing details from the complete narrative: *Portrait of a Monster* [Retrato de un monstruo] *who was Conceived in the Body of a Man named Hernando de la Haba, (habitant of Fereyra, Marquisate of Cenete) due to an evil potion that was given to him. The midwife Francisca de León helped him deliver the newborn through his posterior part on June 1, 1606. Composed by Pedro Manchego, habitant of Granada.*[75]

The description of Hernando's delivery demonizes the birthing experience with details that shock and entertain the reader without inspiring the burlesque humor evoked in other male deliveries such as *El parto de Juan Rana*. We first find Hernando in labor, seated on a chair or birthing stool as a midwife coaches him through the painful delivery. The newborn not only emerges from the man's anus (as indicated in the title), but the demonic imagery is reinforced by the fact that the creature is no sooner born when it violently scratches the midwife's face (she cries out "Good God . . . without a doubt this is the Devil himself—he shows it through his arrogance" [2]).[76] The monstrous newborn (who survives less than two hours) is described as a hideous human-animal hybrid, including part man, goose, porcupine, tortoise, horse, and ox. Not surprisingly, this narrative has been compared to accounts of the birth of the Antichrist in tracing the creature's paternity to the Devil.[77]

The reader later discovers that Hernando's pregnancy has been caused by a vindictive ex-lover with whom he broke an engagement before marrying another woman. Convinced by a sorceress to ingest her special "medicine," the husband soon finds his belly swollen and confesses his condition to his wife: "I swear I must be pregnant because I can feel something jumping and kicking in my stomach" (3v).[78] When his wife touches his belly, she concurs: "My God, you're right; there is no doubt that the devil himself has impregnated you" (3v).[79]

After the shocking delivery, the authorities investigate the case and discover the old witch is to blame. Under torture, she confesses the contents of her evil potion, but the narrator will only state that "it is so dirty and disgusting I will not reveal it" (4).[80] Once she is paraded, ridiculed, and executed in public (while the ex-lover receives two-hundred lashes and is exiled from the city), the text reveals its misogynistic message to its male readers: "Men, open your eyes and do not trust evil women . . . They are little worms like leeches that suck your blood from your soul and your conscience. They are poisonous snakes . . . Take heed that they do not make you give birth like the witch did to this man. May you all learn from his mistake" (4v).[81]

As José González Alcantud argues, it is not by chance that this fantastic tale takes place among a community of *moriscos* during a conflictive period in Granada. And whether or not the news pamphlet was intended to further criminalize this marginalized group through its details of monstrosities and sorcery, the narrative reveals a much bigger fear, that of women's power to alter or manipulate reproductive issues that can impact men in dangerous and terrifying ways.

It is impossible to know exactly how these sensationalist *relaciones* were interpreted by seventeenth-century consumers. Lope de Vega, for example, refers to the 1606 news story of the man who gave birth to a monster in his play *La octava maravilla* (written in 1609, published in 1618) using the case to show the naivety of "uncivilized" Spaniards who are inclined to believe such tales (Morley and Bruerton, 40). When Motril praises the verses that narrate the story ("They are so good! They describe a man from Granada who suddenly gave birth"), Don Juan laments the gullibility of people like Motril: "Must we bear such ignorance! Yet this only confirms the barbarity of Spain" (Vega, *Octava*, 255).[82] Of course, the author of the news pamphlet (Pedro Manchego) addresses both the unbelievability of the story as well as the issue of barbarous nations when he exclaims: "Although it is true that there are some unbelievers who pride themselves on saying that these events are lies, but even so I hope that my account will be so clear that it shows the world its truth. This has not happened in the New World nor in the Canary Islands, nor in the land of Great Cayne nor even in Cyprus, Africa, and Asia" (1v).[83]

Interestingly, Lope de Vega had already incorporated the idea of male pregnancy (a few years before the 1606 news pamphlet) in the plot of another play that contrasts the "civilized" urban protagonists with barbarous Spaniards from an isolated region of Extremadura in *Las batuecas del Duque de Alba*.[84] When Brianda (disguised as a man named Celio) gives birth and is found nursing the newborn, she ("he") is able to convince some of the "uncivilized" inhabitants of the remote mountain village that men from the city are capable of getting pregnant and giving birth. The discussion that ensues reveals an interesting reaction to the possible consequences of male pregnancy. Taurina insists, "I tell you that Celio gave birth and I have seen the child sleeping in his lap and Geralda told me that she saw it yesterday hanging from his breast" (Vega, *Batuecas*, 398).[85] Giroto responds, "And if it is true that they have figured out such an incredible feat, they would be celebrated as the most intelligent men in the world! . . . Taurina, would you want to be the wife of a man who gives birth? How would you work things out? Who would have the children in the family?" (399).[86] Considering the hypothetical arrangement, Giroto suggests that male pregnancy could ennoble men while it would cause confusion for women's identity and gender roles, which is confirmed by Taurina when she echoes the paternity anxiety usually displayed by men: "Feel free to take revenge on my pregnant beloved. What a disgrace this has been; in marrying him I hoped to have his baby, when in fact he came to me already pregnant" (399).[87]

The male pregnancy narratives featured in the monster broadside as well as in Lope's plays display a marked class distinction that is likewise apparent in other early modern European representations of the same theme. Richard K. Reed, for example, notes a similar critique of uneducated rural inhabitants in dramatic works that alluded to the male matrix: "The seventeenth-century playwrights used male pregnancy to refer to the common life of the rural folk, contrasting the silliness of peasants with the rationality of the intellectual movement in society" (37). According to Aaron W. Kitch, the same can be said of the news pamphlets describing the birth of a monster: "One subtext of the monstrous offspring is the rural laboring class whose connection with deformity reveals a specific set of class dynamics" (232). Consequently, any analysis of these "pregnant man" narratives would be incomplete without questioning the role of class and ethnicity as well as the dynamics of gender and sexuality.

Like the 1606 news pamphlet recounting Hernando de la Haba's supernatural pregnancy, Paré also includes illustrated narratives that suggest the potential for engendering monsters through the male body. In his chapter titled "On Certain Monstrous Animals that are Born Abnormally in the Bodies of Men, Women, and Small Children," Paré describes various cases of men who "engendered" worms and other animal-like materials, which are presented visually in specimen form (53–56). On the other hand, in reference to monsters born from too great a quantity of seed, the accompanying illustrations could provoke an initial visual impact that might suggest male gestation, similar to the depictions of Christ healing the man with dropsy mentioned in Chapter 1. A monster born in Germany, for example, "having a head in the middle of its stomach, he lived to be an adult; and the head took nourishment just like the other" (21). Another figure portrays "a man from whose belly another man issued" (11). Not surprisingly, in her study of the masculine matrix in seventeenth-century scientific discourse, Ruth Gilbert rightly cites these cases as grotesque images of male reproduction:

> Underlying fantasies of male autogenesis was always the spectre of the monstrous birth . . . These images of male pregnancy, whilst ostensibly escaping 'the trivial and vulgar way of coition' with women . . . were placed in a more complex relation to the grotesque female body. By overspilling the boundaries of their own bodies and becoming associated with untidy reproduction, these men took on some of the grotesque characteristics of openness, excess and what has been termed 'leakiness' traditionally attributed to women in early modern culture. ("Masculine," 163, 165)

## Mothers' Imagination, Resemblance, and Paternity Anxiety

Both teratologists and reproductive theorists underscored the extraordinary importance of the impact of visual images when discussing maternity and monsters. In his section on monsters who are created through the imagination of the mother during conception, Paré cites cases of African parents who gave birth to a white baby because the mother was looking at a painting of the "beautiful" Andromeda "during the embraces from which she became pregnant." Likewise, a girl was born furry and therefore "deformed and hideous" because her mother had "looked too intensely at the image of Saint John dressed in skins, along with his body hair and beard, which picture was attached to the foot of her bed while she was conceiving" (38). Paré's solution to the potential danger of visual images during conception as well as during the first thirty to forty days when the embryo is still being formed in the womb requires that the mother "not be forced to look at or to imagine monstrous things; but once the formation of the child is complete, even though the woman should look at or imagine monstrous things with intensity, nevertheless the imagination will not then play any role, because no transformation occurs at all, since the child is completely formed" (40).

Cases documenting the perils of mothers' overactive imagination (both during conception as well as late in the pregnancy) abound. In his 1630 *Curiosa filosofia y tesoro de maravillas de la naturaleza* (Curious Philosophy and Treasure of the Marvels of Nature), Eusebio Nieremberg describes both hybrid monsters resulting from a sudden shock or fright to the mother as well as other rare births as a result of a mere suggestion or comment made to the mother during her pregnancy:

> The pregnant woman who had a very large belly and she was to give birth near Christmas so some people began to say jokingly that she had such a large belly because she was carrying the Three Kings. She responded: 'That would be wonderful!' It happened that she gave birth to three boys and one was black. That just one of the three changed color can only be attributed to her vivid imagination. (62)[88]

Confronted with the discrepancy of a child born with darker skin than that of its parents, the power of the woman's thoughts at times could be used to divert attention from the threat of adultery. Nonetheless, the monstrous child who did not resemble either parent undoubtedly sparked accusations of the woman's infidelity since in a pre-DNA paternity testing era, resemblance played a key role in linking fathers to their babies.[89] Of course, considering that the child is born to man alone in *El parto de Juan Rana*, when the issue of resemblance is raised by the father himself ("I still need to know if he is my son, since it's possible that another man created him in my absence"), it becomes both ironic and indicative of the paternity insecurities than could never truly be resolved during the seventeenth century.

In fact, some illustrated texts sought to justify the appearance of a child who did not resemble either parent by creating a reproduction narrative based on the mother's gaze. Paré cites and illustrates a case described by Hippocrates of a white princess accused of adultery when she gave birth to a black child; the woman "was absolved upon Hippocrates' persuasion that it was [caused by] the portrait of a Moor, similar to the child, which was customarily attached to her bed" (38–39). Similarly, a 1603 news pamphlet relates a complex story of a noblewoman (Doña María) from Seville who had given birth to a black baby. The apparent infidelity is clarified when the reader discovers in the married couple's bedchamber the presence of the daughter of one of the slaves in the household. While the couple engaged in sexual relations the two-year-old child was present in the bed and the wife became captivated by her beauty. Nine months later, when the black child is born, the husband expresses his doubts about the paternity of the newborn through sarcasm: "Perhaps there are people of this color in my family?" He then becomes so enraged that he grabs the child and throws him into the sea. Assuming that the boy (Vicente) had died, the crazed husband abandons his wife, country, and religion by marrying a Moorish woman in North Africa. In the meantime, Vicente is rescued by monks and is miraculously reunited with his mother years later. However, when Vicente's own doubts about his identity motivated him to find his father, eventually the renegade citizen, husband, and parent recognizes him as his true son. After the Moorish wife converts to Christianity, all infelicities appear to be resolved. Despite the restoration of imperial Spain's national and religious values, the family is captured and killed at the end. Henry Ettinghausen argues that since the author does not doubt the paternity of a black child born to white parents, the didactic nature of the text must involve the miraculous reunion between parents and child, which was facilitated by the mother's devotion to Mary (*Noticias*, 52).

In his 1575 medical treatise *Examen de ingenios para las ciencias* (*Examination of Wits for the Sciences*), Juan Huarte de San Juan uses classical theories of bodily humors to explain the contradictions of legitimacy, illegitimacy, and resemblance. The author addresses these issues by raising a few commonly asked questions: Why is it that bastard children resemble their fathers and ninety percent of legitimate children look and act like their mothers? Why do bastard children usually turn out to be courteous, positive, and smart people? Why is it that evil women get pregnant and even if they take potions or engage in bloodletting to abort the fetus they never miscarry while the married woman who gets pregnant by her own husband miscarries with the slightest provocation? (668). These commonly held beliefs incite Huarte (citing Plato) to discuss the relationship between sexual habits, state of mind, and physiology that can affect the physical appearance and character of the offspring (669).

Even when the child's appearance is not an issue, the anxiety of paternity and female adultery is a frequent leitmotiv in early modern Spanish texts (Vigil, 139). Like the well-known saying "*Pater semper incertus est, mater est certissima*," fathers could only hope they engendered the fetuses their partners carried and delivered (Finucci, "Maternal," 41). In this way, it is not surprising that Lanini Sagredo's interlude ends by confirming men's reticence to believe women's assurances about the father's identity. This fear led many early modern writers to express similar sentiments. Castiglione's *El libro del cortesano* (The Book of the Courtier), for example, explains that since the female sex is imperfect and not trustworthy, men must control women's chastity "in order for us to be certain of our offspring" (189).[90] Like the news pamphlet describing Vicente's father attempting infanticide because of his suspicions of marital infidelity, literary works abound with examples of unsure fathers who resort to violence. In María de Zayas's 1647 short story "Marriage Abroad: Portent of Doom" [Mal presagio casar lejos], Leonor's Italian husband becomes so jealous of his wife's praise of a Spanish captain that he murders both his wife and their four-year-old son: "While she was washing her hair, her husband came in through the dressing room door and with her own hair, which was very beautiful, he made a noose around her neck and strangled her. Then he poisoned the little boy, saying that he didn't want a child of questionable background to inherit his estate" (*Disenchantments*, 244).[91]

Economic concerns over inheritance undoubtedly played a role in the discussion and legislation of married women who gave birth to other men's children. Secular law described these children as *notos*: "These are such as are born in adultery. They are called by this name because they appear to be the acknowledged children of the husband who has them in his house, when they are not so"[92] (*Partidas*, 952, IV, XV, I). Likewise, Alonso de Andrade warns that "husbands believe that their children are theirs when they are not, which creates injustice with worldly goods and with issues of honor" (148).[93] Many ecclesiastics wrote about how adulterous mothers can compensate for the burden of a child fathered by another man. Both Pedro Galindo and Martín de Azilicueta maintain that the married woman who has a child with another man owes a debt to her family and consequently she must work extra to compensate for the illegitimate child and make sure that the child born from the infidelity must not inherit anything from her or the husband. Galindo also suggests that the *adulterino* or the biological father with whom the married woman had the affair should also make monetary reparations to the husband or should pay the expense of placing the baby in a hospital founded for poor children (455). Azpilicueta as well as Galindo advise married women who have a child from an adulterous relationship to convince the child to enter into the priesthood and leave the inheritance to the legitimate siblings. If this is not possible, then the woman should make up the difference to her husband and to the other children by working more than normally expected, spending less on clothing, food, and so forth (Galindo, 455–56, and Azpilicueta, 179–80).

On the other hand, Juan de Pineda minimizes the importance of the finances involved in inheritance issues. When considering how much men worry about their wives cheating on them, Pineda maintains that the issue at stake is not about property or inheritance but personal factors. As Pineda explains, "Poor people are just as jealous as the rich" (quoted in Vigil, 144).

While medieval and early modern civil law legislated the inheritance rights of children not fathered by the mother's husband, it did not always distinguish between those born to women who are not the legal wives of the biological father or the offspring resulting from female infidelity—in other words, the children fathered by another man but raised with the husband's natural children. Partida VI, Title XIII, Law X of Alfonso X's legal code, for example, states that "where a person is born in fornication, incest, or adultery, he cannot be called a natural son, and shall not inherit any of the estate of his father; and if his father should give such a son any of his property the legitimate children of the said father can revoke the donation or the bequest."[94] The next statute (Law XI), nonetheless, acknowledges the paternity anxiety at the crux of the efforts to control reproductive policies and authorizes economic compensation accordingly: "Mothers are always certain of the children born of them, and for this reason every child, together with the legitimate children born of her shall inherit the property of its mother, whether it is legitimate or not" ( 1273).[95] Of course, this concession would not affect many cases since most property was passed from male to male. However, in some cases a preference is made to male relatives on the mother's side of the family since they are "certain":

Where a natural son, not born of lawful marriage, dies intestate without children, grandchildren, or mother, his brothers on his mother's side shall inherit his entire estate, and if he has any brothers on his father's side they shall not inherit any of it. This is the case because the brothers on his mother's side are certain, and those on his father's are doubtful ... Moreover, we decree that natural sons have no right to inherit the property of legitimate ones or that of any other relatives on their father's side, but they can inherit from any relatives on their mother's side, who are their next of kin and die intestate. (1274)[96]

Although medieval Spanish civil law appeared to punish adulterous men more severely than unfaithful women (Partida VII, Title XVII, Law XV states that a man committed of adultery must be put to death but a woman convicted of adultery must be publicly scourged, sent to a convent, and forfeit the dowry and marriage gift), early modern culture supported a no-tolerance policy for adulterous wives. Mary Elizabeth Perry argues that early modern Spain revealed a marked gender bias regarding infidelity: "Married women who engaged in extramarital sexual activity were prosecuted for adultery under secular law, which provided that the wronged husband could execute his wife and her lover in a public square. Married men were not prosecuted for extramarital sex unless they could be accused of saying it was not a mortal sin" (*Gender*, 120). Therefore, by monsterizing both female sexuality and the womb, early modern society could justify the need to take over all aspects of reproduction: sexual, medical, legal, iconographic, and moral. While this chapter has attempted to explore the multiple dimensions of the male fantasy of appropriating control over reproduction, the next chapter will examine the other side of the male pregnancy image: the nightmare of a perceived feminization of men in terms of gender roles, sex assignment, and desire.

# 4
# The Fear of Effeminacy in Early Modern Spain

The other central feature of the pregnant man icon that also emerges in *El parto de Juan Rana* reveals an imagined dystopia enacting all the cultural anxieties related to issues of gender-blurring, homosexuality, and unstable identity based on sex assignment. Juan Rana's reputation for playing effeminate characters (not to mention his prior arrest for sodomy) undoubtedly prepared the audience to consider these issues even before seeing one of their favorite actors give birth on stage. How, then, could the spectators not relate what they were watching in the interlude to similar matters debated in society? In fact, like early twenty-first-century America, concerned over the sexuality of the metrosexual urban male (one who spends significant time and money on his appearance and style), sixteenth- and seventeenth-century Spain displayed a near panic over what was perceived as the growing trend of effeminate men, whose devotion to fashion and grooming was associated with criminal sexual practices as well as with the increasing economic and political calamities afflicting their country.[1]

When we examine early modern medical and social theories of sex assignment, gender, and sexuality, we first see a rigid system. However, we soon discover that the rigidity is just a thin layer of social norms and that underneath emerges a multiplicity of cross-currents dominated by transmutations and fluid ambiguities. Given the instability of what would have been perceived as ideal fixed binary oppositions, sixteenth- and seventeenth-century theologians, physicians, and policy-makers were preoccupied with monitoring and controlling the sensationalized yet troublesome bodies of hermaphrodites, pre- and postnatal sexual transmutations, transgressive gender-benders, and those who participated in homosexual practices through sodomy.

## Prenatal and Postnatal Sex Changes

Early modern scientific discourse argued that prenatal transmutations caused by a sudden change of temperature of the humors or fluids in the womb resulted in a reversal of sex assignment, thus changing the sex of the fetus from male to female or vise versa. Juan Huarte de San Juan explains that one can detect when this prenatal transmutation had occurred in the womb by observing the physical traits, gender behavior, and sexual practices that do not adhere to cultural expectations for men and women. As a result, Huarte explains the origin of the effeminate male by using a prenatal essentialist argument:

> If Nature, having made a perfect male, wants to change him into a woman, it merely has to turn his reproductive organs back inside the body ... Many times Nature has made a female and, having been in the mother's womb for one or two months, for some reason her genitals are overcome with heat and they come out and a male is created. To whom this transmutation occurs in the mother's womb, it is clearly recognizable later by certain movements he has that are indecent for men: woman-like, effeminate, soft and mild voice; and such men are inclined to behave like a woman and they frequently fall prey to the sin of sodomy. (608–9)[2]

In other words, men who transgressed both gender and sexuality proscriptions (such as effeminate men and/or men suspected of sodomy) were originally destined to be women, but the unstable nature of sex assignment in the womb created an opportunity for a prenatal sex change. Consequently, the idea that a male (still in the womb) could be changed anatomically into a female (validated by the medical community through the theory of prenatal sexual reversals) was part of the cultural imagination during the sixteenth and seventeenth centuries.

While this male-to-female transmutation (according to early modern medical wisdom) might occur before birth, it was generally believed that postnatal spontaneous sex changes could only happen to women who suddenly transformed into men. As Ambroise Paré explains in his treatise on monstrous births, "we ... never find ... that any man ever became a woman, because Nature tends always toward what is most perfect and not, on the contrary, to perform in such a way that what is perfect should become imperfect" (33). Paolo Zacchia's early modern medical jurisprudential text *Questionum medico-legalium* (Medical-Legal Inquiry) explains this in terms of thermodynamics, arguing that men cannot transform into women because the heat characteristic of men drives forward, it does not contract, and therefore the penis cannot retreat inward, whereas with an onset of heat in women, the sexual member may propel itself outward (Laquer, 140–42).[3]

While cases of men who were transformed anatomically into women were uncommon, this possibility was, in fact, discussed by various theorists during the seventeenth century. Fray Antonio de Fuentelapeña's 1676 *El ente dilucidado: Tratado de monstruos y fantasmas* (The Elucidated Being: Treatise on Monsters and Ghosts), for example, reveals fascinating analyses of men who transmuted into women and of men who gave birth (229–48). First, Fuentelapeña confirms the existence of men who were known to have given birth but explains this phenomenon through a "hidden hermaphroditism" argument. In other words, the men who became pregnant and gave birth without the participation of a woman actually had female reproductive organs hidden inside their bodies: "Having the masculine sex showing on the outside, they also had female organs hidden on the inside, so that they seemed to be "only" a man by what you can see, but because of what you can't see they were women too" (229–30).[4] Although the author does not explain how these previously unidentified androgynes were impregnated, his argument implies that potentially any man could have the capacity to procreate, given a hermaphroditic condition unbeknownst to him and to others. Fuentelapeña continues to discuss numerous examples of men who menstruate, lactate, and who had given birth. One case, for example, involves a man named Luis Roosel, who in 1354 suffered an unbearable pain in his right thigh. Believing it to be a tumor, he watched it grow everyday until (after nine months) a live child emerged from his thigh "to the astonishment of everyone" (230–31). However, the author also considers (and then denies) some of the theological consequences of male maternity, such as whether the child resulting from male autogenesis would be exempt from being born in original sin (234–35).

After discussing male pregnancy, Fuentelapeña goes on to describe how men can also transform into women. He again resorts to the hermaphrodite argument to justify all sex changes:

> Although it happens through an inversion of sexual members, it only happens to those who are actually hermaphrodites and have both sexes because although it is true that usually they have both parts, for some reason or hidden impediment, they are unable to show both at the same time and therefore when one is exposed, the other remains hidden. Therefore, when there is an increase or decrease in heat, women can easily change into men or the opposite, men can change into women. (247–48)[5]

Earlier in the century, in his treatise on marvels and prodigies (which was translated into Spanish in 1603), Pedro Bovistau distinguished between the *natural* spontaneous transmutations of women who mutate into men and the *unnatural* voluntarily-provoked transformations of men who turn into women by castrating themselves:

> Some women have become men and some men have castrated themselves to become women ... in the first case, Nature was the author without any human intervention and according to the opinion of many ancient philosophers, this could happen naturally ... but that a man (whose desire is to govern campaigns, to lead nations, and to die honorably for his country) become a woman (whose function is ... to love her children and husband, to sew, and to take care of her home) is not only a prodigious event but so is the telling and memory of it. (165–66)[6]

In a sense, then, Bovistau normalizes the female-to-male sex changes as logical while categorizing the male-to-female transformation as anomalous through its incredible and almost freakish nature. By the same token, the description of the dissimilarity between *natural* female-to-male sex mutations and the invasive techniques used by men to become women takes advantage of this offense by some men to reaffirm traditional gender expectations for all men and women. Moreover, the preoccupation with male gender roles and nationalism evident in Bovistau's comments also spills over into his discussion of the relationship between sodomy, effeminacy in men, anatomical alterations of men who become women, and social hierarchy.

The author uses Nero as an example of the dangers inherent in these transgressions, especially for men in positions of national leadership, since (unlike the common citizen) men in the public eye should serve as role models for other men. Bovistau describes in detail Nero's horrendous cruelty and perverse sodomitical practices. After killing his pregnant wife, Nero takes a young male lover and has him castrated, "using him as if he were a woman; he loved him very much. He was not satisfied with having committed such an evil act and, forgetting his high and important position and that he was emperor of the largest nation in the world, he married him publicly, gave him gifts, celebrated the wedding, and held him in the same esteem as if he were his legitimate wife" (167).[7] Having married three different men, Nero was reported to have entertained a number of male lovers in a special room in his palace designed especially for this purpose. According to Bovistau, he would use a soft and effeminate voice to invite men there and pay for their sexual services (168).

However, it is Bovistau's description of Nero's third husband Hierocle that best summarizes the fears inherent in the pregnant male figure. Initially, Hierocle's identity was categorized in terms of an early modern configuration of homosexuality or the criminal sexual activity between the two men. According to Bovistau, Hierocle also transgressed traditional gender expectations for men by doing women's work (such as spinning, sewing, and needlework), removing facial hair "in order to appear more soft and delicate like a woman," and by insisting that people call him a woman (168v).[8] Nonetheless, the adoption of traditional social roles for women was just part of his identity transformation. It was believed that he also found someone to "cut off what made him a man in order to achieve what he so desperately desired" (168v).[9] The message here warns that effeminacy in men is one of the first signs of homosexuality and that these men do not have to wait for Nature to spontaneously change their sex: they have the power to disregard sex assignment at birth by altering their bodies to eliminate the genital mark of male identity. Interestingly, Bovistau's text does not refer to the men in same-sex relationships who castrate themselves as eunuchs but rather as women. However, unlike the women who spontaneously acquire a penis and suddenly become men, these male-to-female transsexuals are not passive recipients of Nature's mutations but must actively seek their solution through surgery.

In contrast to the censured cases of men who willingly became women, accounts of women who unwittingly began to exhibit primary and secondary sex characteristics associated with maleness were frequently celebrated. In accordance with the medical opinion that seemed to normalize women who were anatomically transformed into men, numerous tales of such mutations were illustrated, circulated, and published during the early modern period. As Huarte de San Juan insists to his doubting reader, "that women have turned into men after birth should not shock anyone because besides having been related as true by many ancient writers, it has happened not long ago in Spain" (609).[10] Antonio de Torquemada's 1570 *Jardín de flores curiosas* (Garden of Curious Flowers) likewise cites ancient and modern cases of women who had been married (some had even given birth) before experiencing the spontaneous sex change, as does Paré in his chapter "Memorable Stories about Women who have Degenerated into Men" (31–33). Many of these early modern FTMs (female-to-male transsexuals) eventually married women after establishing their new identity as men: "There was another woman who, after having been married and given birth to a son, turned into a man and married a woman who had 'her' children" (Torquemada, 188).[11] Some cases involved adolescent girls who, instead of starting menstruation, discovered that a previously undetected internal penis had suddenly popped out: "This young woman, coming to the age when she should start menstruation, but instead a male member began to grow and came out from where it was hidden. Therefore being a woman she became a man and so they dressed her in men's clothing" (189).[12] In fact, Torquemada suggests that one case of female-to-male transsexuality was first preceded by infertility and marital problems and later attributable to the intense mental image of seeing herself dressed in men's clothing:

> As this woman had no children, her husband and she were not well suited for each other so she had a hard life. Out of envy or some other reason one night the woman stole the clothes of a boy who stayed in the house and put them on, left the house and traveled around pretending to be a man. She made a living that way until nature worked with such force to cause it or that her intense imagination from seeing herself dressed as a man was so powerful that it came true—she turned into a man and married another woman. (190)[13]

Again, just as visual or mental images during conception can affect the physical attributes of a child, transgressive gender roles (here through cross-dressing) can impact physiology through a change in sex assignment.

Citing Aristotle, Huarte explains the fertility of a female in terms of a cold and moist nature, "because if it weren't so, it would be impossible for her to menstruate or have enough milk to nourish the baby nine months in the womb" (610).[14] While anatomy dictates that "no man can be considered cold in comparison to women, nor a woman hot compared to a man," Huarte describes a flexible system that accounts for varying degrees of coolness or heat and moisture or dryness in both men and women (610).[15] Privileging the status and importance of men's testicles, Huarte argues that "eunuchism" or any other condition affecting the testicles causes tragic consequences: "How much damage is done to men by removing these members, however small, we wouldn't need much to prove it. We see from experience that his hair and beard fall out, his deep, strong voice becomes weak, and he loses strength and natural heat and has a worse and more miserable nature than if he were a woman" (619).[16] Similarly, hot but moist men "are happy, carefree, and given to leisure. They are simple-natured and agreeable, easily embarrassed and not much interested in women" (620).[17] A man who has low levels of heat and higher levels of moisture reveals a voice that is "soft and loving and very delicate" as well as a flabby physique, light complexion, little body hair, handsome, and humorous (620–21).

Moreover, these feminine men are not attracted to women nor are women drawn to them (622).

Despite the fact that these characteristics were considered innate, Huarte offers suggestions to help reverse the negative feminizing effects of moisture and coolness in men. First, he describes what worsens this tragic condition: excessive relaxation and too much leisure time, sleeping too much and in a soft bed, overindulging in food and drink, wearing too many and very elegant clothing, always traveling by horse, frequent indulgences, and playing recreational games and other things that give pleasure (674). So, for a child who is born effeminate (i.e., too cold and moist), Huarte recommends washing him in hot salty water but not in hot fresh water since the latter would make him "like a woman, with weak nerves, foolish, prepared for a flush of blood and fainting" (675). Regardless of the tendency to insist that men cannot transmute into women, medical wisdom demonstrated a preoccupation with preventing or reversing the physiological degeneration or feminization of men and thereby revealing an implied fear of the possibility of biological shadings of a male-to-female mutation.

## Intersexed Bodies: Hermaphrodites and Reproduction

The excess of coldness and moisture in men can also result in ambiguous sexual identities, such as those of eunuchs and hermaphrodites: "Because if there is more coldness and moisture than needed, according to Hippocrates, then men become eunuchs or hermaphrodites" (Huarte, 295).[18] This deficiency of heat, then, could "cause the male body to collapse back into a state of primary undifferentiation. No normal man might actually become a woman; but each man trembled forever on the brink of becoming 'womanish'" (Brown, 11). Perhaps the best example of the indeterminacy of sex assignment in certain cases is found in intersexed individuals. Covarrubias defines the hermaphrodite as one who "has both male and female sex organs, in other words androgynous," and paraphrases Pliny's claims that "certain people were called androgynes for being hermaphrodites and they were able to both engender and conceive, and so they have the right breast of a man and the left breast of a woman" (*Tesoro*, 531).[19]

Paré distinguishes between four different types of hermaphrodites: the male hermaphrodite (who can impregnate), the hermaphroditic woman (who has menstrual periods and a non-functioning penis), the hermaphrodites who are neither one nor the other and are "totally excluded from and void of reproduction," and those who have

> both sets of sexual organs well-formed, and they can help and be used in reproduction; and both the ancient and modern laws have obliged and still oblige these latter to choose which sex organ they wish to use, and they are forbidden on pain of death to use any but those they will have chosen, on account of the misfortunes that could result from such. For some of them have abused their situation, with the result that, through mutual and reciprocal use, they take their pleasure first with one set of sex organs and then with the other: first with those of a man, then with those of a woman, because they have the natures of man and of woman suitable to such an act. (27)

While early modern medical wisdom tended to insist that men can not acquire the female reproductive organs necessary to conceive and give birth, some individuals (such as eunuchs) were believed to have degenerated into a "womanish nature, by deficiency of heat" and thereby demonstrating the potential fluidity of sex assignment during the early modern period (Jones and Stallybrass, 86). Furthermore, given the sexual indeterminacy of the hermaphrodite, it may not be surprising to find a news item published in 1601 in *The Fugger Newsletters* relating the case of a married soldier named Daniel Burghammer who became pregnant after having extramarital relations with a Spanish soldier while serving in the Netherlands. After giving birth to a baby girl, he confesses to his wife that he was, in fact, "half man and half woman" and that he "only slept once with a Spaniard, and he became pregnant therefrom [ . . . ] The aforesaid soldier is able to suckle the child with his right breast only and not at all on the left side, where he is a man. He has also the natural organs of a man for passing water" (quoted in Río Parra, 149). This case not only suggests that an ambiguously sexed individual may have the capacity to reproduce, but that the pregnancy is necessarily the result of same-sex relations with a man. Moreover, since the veracity of this news item is not questioned in the narrative, the image of a pregnant man becomes less implausible in the minds of the early modern viewer and reader.

In Sebastián de Covarrubias's *Emblemas morales* (Moral Emblems) (1610), the pictorial image representing androgyny portrays the famous bearded lady of Peñaranda accompanied by the motto "Neither and Both." The text emphasizes a third possibility that is simultaneously neither and both male and female:

> I am masculine, and feminine, and neuter. I reveal myself,
> I am a man, I am a woman, I am a third,
> which is neither one nor the other, and it is not clear
> which of these things I am. I am a terror,
> one of those shown to be rare and horrendous.
> I am believed to be evil, an omen.
> Take heed all who have seen me,
> for you are like me if you are effeminate [male] (164).[20]

Although the illustration is based on a portrait of Brígida del Río painted by Juan Sánchez Cotán in 1590, the text in Spanish features gender markers that are masculine (*afeminado*, or "effeminate male"). In fact, Brígida became so well-known for her hirsutism that she and other women like her inspired the saying, "The Bearded Lady is best greeted from afar" [A la muger barbuda, de lexos la saluda] (Covarrubias, *Tesoro*, 193). Similarly, the famous portrait of "La mujer barbuda" (The Bearded Lady) Magdalena Ventura, painted by José de Ribera in 1631, reveals many of the strategies that promote and exploit people with sexual ambiguity. While the representation displays nontraditional secondary sex characteristics, the visual impact of seeing a masculine figure with full beard, receding hairline, and hairy chest, posed breastfeeding an infant and standing next to "his/her" husband clearly participates in a homoerotic male maternity imagery (Figure 13).

Although the apparent rigidity of an Aristotelian model placed male and female in fundamentally separate categories, the Hippocratic and Galenic traditions "admitted a certain indeterminacy and mutability in the construction of sexual difference" that is not present in the Aristotelian "two-sex" configuration for sexual definition (Gilbert, *Early*, 37). Despite the differing biological explanations for sex assignment, social and cultural norms insisted on gender conformity to only *one* of two sex categories, regardless of possible ambiguities. Accordingly, the cases of those sexually indeterminate individuals who attempted to move from one gender role to another were investigated and frequently criminalized by civil and ecclesiastical authorities.

Perhaps the most complex example of the policing of mutable gender, sex, and sexuality is found in the case of Elena/Eleno de Céspedes. Born female in the mid-sixteenth century to a Moorish slave (Francisca de Medina) and a Castilian peasant (Pero Hernández), Elena de Céspedes (named after the mistress of the household) transformed into a man during her adolescence (because of what she describes as a sudden onset of hermaphroditism while giving birth to her son), and thereafter adopted the name Eleno de Céspedes.[21] Although Céspedes transgressed traditional proscriptions for

102    Male Delivery

Figure 13: Bearded lady Magdalena Ventura painted by José de Ribera in 1631.
(Reproduced by permission from the Fundación Casa Ducal de Medinaceli)

gender behavior, sex reconstruction, and sexual attraction, the way in which her/his case was processed by the legal, medical, and religious authorities (as well as in the popular imagination) ultimately indicate the fear of male-to-female transmutations as well as of the transgressions of gender and sexual behaviors that inevitably accompany a change of sex assignment.[22]

The nature of Céspedes's anatomy was complex and controversial, not to mention elusive. According to her autobiographical testimony [*discurso de su vida*], she suddenly acquired a penis after giving birth at age sixteen to a son while she was briefly married to Christóval Lombardo. Her husband soon left town, and Céspedes later received word of his death. Because the masculine nature of her/his bisexed condition predominated after childbirth, s/he decided to follow suit and start living as a man. However, medical intervention was necessary to facilitate sexual relations with women, as his newly developed phallus was impeded from full erection by a layer of skin, which he had removed surgically. Céspedes eventually married María del Caño after receiving official medical confirmation of his male genitalia from the physician Francisco Díaz. In a 1586 deposition, Díaz determined Céspedes's identity as male, and not hermaphrodite:

> It is true that he has seen Eleno's genital member, and having touched all around it with his hands and seen it with his eyes, he made the following declaration: That he has his genital member, which is sufficient and perfect, with its testicles formed like any other man . . . And he thus said and declared that in his opinion Eleno does not bear any resemblance to a hermaphrodite or anything like it.[23] (Quoted in Burshatin, "Written," 433)

Despite this previous medical confirmation of Céspedes's exclusively male identity, in 1587, during the preliminary sodomy hearings in Ocaña, s/he was charged with having used an instrument during sexual intercourse ("with a stiff and smooth instrument, she committed the unspeakable crime of sodomy"),[24] and midwives testified that the defendant possessed only female genitalia and that her virginity had not been compromised (despite the fact that she had given birth to a son years earlier): "She stuck the candle up her female sex, and it entered a bit, with difficulty, and this witness was suspicious, so she also introduced her finger, and it entered with difficulty, and the witness, therefore, does not think that a man has ever been with her" (quoted in Burshatin, "Elena," 106). [25] After the charges were changed to bigamy, and the trial was transferred to the Inquisition courts in Toledo, Díaz changed his testimony, now believing that the defendant's male genitalia had been a deception, "an art so subtle that it sufficed to fool him by sight and by touch" (quoted in Burshatin, "Written," 433).[26] Céspedes nevertheless attributed the loss of his penis to cancer and insisted that his/her sexual identity as a hermaphrodite could not be monosexed or static, and therefore s/he was not guilty of sodomy, lesbianism, desecration of the sacrament of holy matrimony, or demonic involvement:

> I never made any pact, explicitly or tacit, with the devil, in order to pose as a man to marry a woman, as is attributed to me. What happens is that many times the world has seen androgynous beings or, in other words, hermaphrodites, who have both sexes. I, too, have been one of these, and at the time I arranged to be married the masculine sex was more prevalent in me; and I was naturally a man and had all that was necessary for a man to marry a woman. And I filed information and eyewitness proof by physicians and surgeons, experts in the art, who looked at me and touched me, and swore under oath that I was a man and could marry a woman, and with this judicial proof I married as a man. (447–48)[27]

The multiple and contradictory interpretations of Céspedes's anatomy reveal the inconsistencies and fluctuations in a binary model of sexual identity. In effect, the medical, legal, and religious authorities culturally transformed Céspedes's identity (through medical examinations and expert testimonies) from man to woman, thus demonstrating the possibility of an official transformation of sex assignment from male to female, which not surprisingly required a quick retraction of the previous medical confirmation of Céspedes's male anatomy. Interestingly, in his analysis of hermaphroditism, male pregnancy, and sex changes, Fuentelapeña mentions Céspedes's story as the example frequently cited by those who doubt nature's capacity to change one's sex assignment, insisting on Céspedes's ability to deceive specialists (245).

Like the precedent set for mutability in sex assignment, a similar instability in gender behavior and sexual activity is revealed in Céspedes's case (not unlike Juan Rana's reported sexual experiences with both sexes): Elena participated in a heterosexual marriage to a man, and he insisted that his marriage to María while living as Eleno was also heterosexual. Later, when Céspedes's identity was deemed unequivocally female, her desire was seen as transgressive (that is, lesbian), given her open sexual relations with other women: "And she remained with the wherewithal to have relations with women, and she returned to Ana de Albánchez and had sex with her many times as a man" (Burshatin, "Interrogating," 13).[28]

While Céspedes's case was fraught with controversy because of the slippery and mutable nature of his/her gender roles, sex assignment, and sexuality, most cases of postnatal female-to-male transmutations were interpreted as success stories. A news pamphlet published in Granada in 1617, for example, tells the "true story" of a thirty-four-year-old nun, María Muñoz, who suddenly possessed male genitals, dark facial hair, and a deep voice. This relation describes how her naturally masculine nature drew suspicions in the past, wherefore she had been examined by the prioress and found to be female. Nonetheless, when later involved in heavy physical labor, she discovered a swelling in her groin, and three days later male organs came forth through a small hole where her female genitalia had been located. A new examination revealed that she was now a man. Despite the scandal, the shocking case has a happy ending, thus underscoring the preference for male identity: "Her father is very pleased because he is rich and had no son to inherit his wealth. Now he has a very manly son who can marry; and she is also happy because after twelve years of incarceration she enjoys freedom. Having been transformed from woman to man, nature could not have bestowed upon her any better material blessing."[29] Of course, the official interpretation of the nun-turned-man story deems her case a success since there is no longer an issue of sex or gender ambiguity, despite the fact that the new man is still referred to as a "she" in the narrative. The assumption is that women would want to achieve the perfection of being male but no man should want to become a woman.

If the early modern sex-bias tended to privilege only female-to-male transmutations, then the numerous cultural narratives relating pre- and postnatal sex changes (as well as other cases of nonconforming sex characteristics) expose a system that is vulnerable to all sorts of mobility in sex assignment. The celebrated cases of female-to-male transsexuals not only demonstrate Nature's way of improving itself through the masculinization of women but imply a deep-seeded fear of a reverse flow from male to female. This anxiety is most poignant, in fact, when we consider the implications of the success story of María Muñoz as a "butch" nun who triumphantly becomes a man. Since the news pamphlet describes her pre-mutation identity in terms of female masculinity, we might assume that the medical theories expounded by Huarte de San Juan would explain this transgression in terms of a prenatal transmutation. In other words, Muñoz was originally destined to be a male but the prenatal humoral temperature change caused the genitals to retract and a female was born. In this way, her post-natal sex change thirty-four years later can be interpreted as Nature's way of correcting a previous error. Logically, then, the unspoken fear would indicate that feminine men could also expect a similar resolution to their infractions of gender norms, thus reversing the prenatal mutation that, according to Huarte, changed the would-be female into a male baby.

## The Feminization of Men in Early Modern Spain

Like the policing of sex assignment, the transgression of traditional gender expectations was a frequent topic of debate among moralists and humanists during the sixteenth and seventeenth centuries. In particular, the prevailing perception of the decay of conventional male gender roles during this time revealed a shift from masculine to feminine behavior, as the medieval warrior had become the urban courtier who perverted the values of the noble class. José Cartagena-Calderón argues that the rise of a new political order in early modern Spain was accompanied by the emergence of a different urban masculinity that threatened to cross the traditional gender boundaries imposed by the culture of that time. Of course, the backlash to this cultural transformation is evident in the dozens of protests against and harsh criticism of the feminine behavior of the courtiers (Cartagena-Calderón, "Rara," 141). As Federico Garza Carvajal argues, an analysis of the discourses on sodomy and the prosecution of sodomites demonstrates how early modern Spanish notions of manliness intertwined themselves with Spain's imperialist-colonialist politics.[30] In fact, the feminization of upper-class men involved a complex configuration of issues related to biology, nation, economics, race, and ethnicity, as well as nonconforming gender and sexual practices.

The appearance and demeanor of the more sophisticated yet effeminate gentleman are critiqued in Baldassare Castiglione's *El cortesano* (The Book of the Courtier), which was translated into Spanish by Juan Boscán in 1534:

> I would have our Courtier's face be such, not so soft and feminine as many attempt to have, who not only curl their hair and pluck their eyebrows, but preen themselves in all those ways that the most wanton and dissolute women in the world adopt; and in walking, in posture, and in every act, appear so tender and languid that their limbs seem to be on the verge of falling apart; and utter their words so limply that it seems they are about to expire on the spot; and the more they find themselves in the company of men of rank, the more they make a show of such manners. These, since nature did not make them women as they clearly wish to appear and be, should be treated not as good women, but as public harlots, and driven not only from the courts of great lords but from the society of all noble men. (36)[31]

Castiglione's lamentations regarding the feminine hair, face, voice and movements of these "female impersonators" are interesting insofar as they highlight a few key points about the effeminate courtiers: first, that they can be compared to women of ill-repute; secondly, that they use their womanly fashions and behavior to flirt with other more impressive men; and thirdly, that they experience a form of sexual dysphoria or the feeling of discomfort with one's sex-at-birth.

In his 1691 treatise on vices such as excessive interest in fashion, *Voces de dolor nacidas de la multitud de pecados . . . trajes profanos* (Voices of Pain Born of the Multitude of Sin . . . Profane Clothing), Fray Antonio de Ezcaray relates the recurrent anxiety over the feminization of men with economic concerns and Spanish nationalism. His analysis mourns the loss of a perceived masculine past, as the author describes the cultural shift in men's gender practices from male to female:

> Most of our sins are apparent in men nowadays with such evil in the Spanish nation. Separating from the original valor of this nation, men have shaved their beards and hair in favor of wigs that are expensive and make them look more like women, thus with the curls in their wigs, they inspire women, creating envy so that they too must curl their hair. Not long ago the Spanish nation inspired fear and respect: . . . Oh what times we live in! Poor Spain, who has bewitched you? Who has made you degenerate from your past brilliance? I myself am unable to respond. Ever since they brought chocolate to Spain men have become effeminate . . . and the affectation of men has come to such an extreme that when a doctor was visiting a patient, he found him with so many ribbons and daintiness in bed that he swore that he was a woman. I won't say more so as not to provoke laughter about something that should make us cry. (22)[32]

Detailed accounts of how much attention men devoted to their physical appearance emerge in Bartolomé Jiménez Patón's 1639 *Discurso de los tufos, copetes y calvas* (Discourse on Curls, Toupees, and Baldness). In particular, the author bemoans the focus on hair design by men, especially the popularity of wearing toupees instead of showing a balding head, like the "excellent bald men celebrated throughout history."[33] Conversely, he describes the men who try to cover their baldness with wigs as "dolls, womanish and effeminate men who are good for nothing" (18v).[34] Like Jiménez Patón, Fray Tomás de Trujillo (in his 1563 *Libro llamado reprobación de trajes* (Book on the Reform of Clothing)) laments how men focus so much of their time, money, and interest in clothing and fashion. He begins by denouncing men who wear women's clothing or multicolored shoes as scandalous, and continues by citing the specifics that occupy these men's attention: the design of their shoes and the height of their heels, the size of their collars, and the color and fabric selection for different articles of clothing, as well as other fashion details. Trujillo concludes by asking men "how much time, then, do you have left to run your own households?" again implying a connection between social and economic decadence.[35]

Unlike the censure of what was perceived as an epidemic of feminine men in early modern Spain, much of the twenty-first-century response to the metrosexual trend actually highlights the possible economic advantages of a "heightened aesthetic sense" for men. In *The Metrosexual Guide to Style. A Handbook for the Modern Man*, for example, Michael Flocker demonstrates how everyone can benefit from heterosexual men embracing their feminine side without fear of being accused of gay tendencies: "Secure in his masculinity, he no longer has to spend his life defending it. . . .More and more, young, urban, straight men are appropriating certain elements of style and culture from the gay community and marketing executives have been quick to catch on. A whole new range of cars, fashions, grooming products, restaurants and sports clubs have been launched to cater to the new man" (xiii). Not surprisingly, the December 2003 issue of the business magazine *Entrepreneur* ("What's Hot for 2004") included metrosexuality as a hot trend "and only getting hotter," especially if entrepreneurs can convince the man in middle America to take a risk by spending money on luxury grooming products, having a facial, or getting a manicure (Penttila, 91).

Both twenty-first-century metrosexuality and early modern male effeminacy imply a certain socioeconomic status that allow for these "indulgences" and "luxuries." However, unlike the recent capitalistic embrace of male "femininity," most early modern writers pointed to indulgence and effeminacy as the causes of the country's distressing economic crisis.[36] Sancho de Moncada (a priest and writer on the economy), for example, argued in 1619 that Spain was in grave danger because "all the people [are] so indulging and effeminate" (2).[37] In a 1635 sermon, Francisco de León also lamented the male-to-female gender transition during this time: "Men have converted into women, from soldiers into effeminates, covered with hair cascading over their ears, trailing locks in back, and frizzed up in front, and who knows if they aren't made up and dressed up in things resembling what women wear" (quoted in Maravall, 37). As Sidney Donnell concludes, "By the mid-1600s,

Spain had become an ailing empire, and its enemies ravenously singled out its 'feminine' vulnerabilities" (152).

Not surprisingly, motherhood also played a part in the feminization of Spanish men. In his 1618 treatise against idleness in Spain, Pedro de Valencia traces the economic crisis, infertility, and male effeminacy to a maternal biological defect that is affected by class and ethnicity:

> In conception the male and female come together but later the woman carries the fetus in her womb, where it is formed and nourished with her blood and fluids, and then from breast milk after birth. Therefore, when women are weak, indulgent, and delicate like a painting or playthings, they cannot give birth to strong males and these women often are raised with much idleness and indulgences. In this way they aren't very big, strong, healthy, or fertile but rather have a thousand female troubles and evil humours and become infertile. Consequently, there are no infertile slaves or gypsies and their children as well as those of laborers and workers are big, strong, and healthy while many noble and pampered women are sick or infertile. In general, princes and noblemen are born and raised effeminate. (55–56)[38]

In his study on the inherent connection between sodomy and notions of effeminacy in the peninsula and New Spain during the sixteenth and seventeenth centuries, Federico Garza Carvajal examines how the priest Pedro de León and other early modern Spanish writers embellish their discourses on sodomy by linking it to concepts of male femininity in order to police any "deviation from proper gentlemen attire and a display of womanly attributes" ("Silk," 8). By comparing the effeminate costume required of sodomites forced to parade publicly before execution with the similar attire of the male aristocracy in attendance at the spectacle, the priest used his sermon to instill fear of being accused of homosexual activity into anyone exhibiting nontraditional gender trends:

> Some of you do not partake of the vice . . . nonetheless some of you dress as if you do . . . you too could be mistaken for one of them . . . honourable men had no reason to dress, or to wear hosiery or shoes, or curl one's hair, in a manner that ventured outside the common ordinary dress of honourable men . . . If you are not one of them then don't dress like them . . . if you do not sell wine then do not exhibit a tavern bush on your door. (Quoted in Garza Carvajal, *Butterflies*, 62–63)

Literary accounts also seemed to confirm similar concerns espoused in the political, moral, and economic treatises. María de Zayas's best-selling 1647 collection of short stories, *Desengaños amorosos* (*Disenchantments of Love*), for example, chastises men for their decadence into femininity. Curiously, the protagonist Lisis's narrative has traditionally been described as feminist, her alleged feminism is based in part on a condemnation of men's refusal to adhere to traditional gender expectations. While defending women's right to formal education, the author laments the loss of the "good old days" when Spanish males were "real" men. Discussing male femininity in Zayas's work, Susan Paun de García summarizes, "She argues for a return to a social and political Golden Age, when men were men, acted like men, and dressed like men" (254). Relying on a nationalist argument that also defends traditional gender roles, Zayas's Lisis reprimands men for neglecting their country, class, and gender responsibilities in favor of fashion and idleness. Likewise embedded in this argument is Zayas's manipulation of the feminine male movement as a strategy to accuse men of what some have described as early modern antifeminism:

> What law human or divine enables you, noble gentlemen, to so hurl yourselves against women that you can hardly find a single man to defend them, that you see so many men persecute them? . . . I think you seek and desire nobility only as adornment like silk stockings and curly locks. Where do you think the lack of courage you all exhibit nowadays comes from? That lets you tolerate the enemy within Spanish borders, and while our king is doing battle you sit in the park and stroll along the river all dolled up in feminine frippery? . . . It comes from your low regard for women. I swear if you did love and cherish women as was the way in former times, you'd volunteer not just to go to war and fight but to die, . . . Aren't you ashamed to be here at court, donning your gala outfits and curling your hair, strolling through parks and gallivanting in carriages instead of defending us? . . . So this is Spanish valor! . . . Some clever writer has said that the French have stolen Spanish courage and you have stolen French fashion. (*Disenchantments*, 399–401)[39]

Echoing the social and moral proscriptions that value masculinity over femininity, Zayas praises masculine behavior in men and condemns excessive femininity in men (as we have just seen) as well as in women: "There can be no doubt that if women didn't devote themselves to their appearance, making themselves more feminine than nature intended, and if, instead of studying how to arrange their hair and make up their faces, they applied themselves to learning and to the art of bearing arms, it might well be that they would excel men in every way" (*Disenchantments*, 140). Not surprisingly, Zayas employs bellicose imagery to encourage women to rebel against misogyny: "Because all men are declared enemies of women, I have declared my war against all men . . . Courage, beautiful ladies, for we shall overcome!" (367–68).[40] Overall, in both sex assignment and gender roles, early modern society rewarded female-to-male inclinations but chastised male-to-female mutations.[41]

## Theater and Entertainment Contribute to Effeminacy in Men

Music, dance, spectacle, and popular theater (such as Juan Rana's performance in the interludes) were frequently linked to the feminization of men during the early modern period. Entertainment in general was believed to have softened men and made them useless. Fray José de Jesús María preached in 1600 about the moral and social dangers of theatrical festivities to the masculinity of the male spectator, performer, and participant, arguing that plays are evil, especially the erotic dances, and the fact that these performances and the concomitant partying "make men soft, effeminate and useless for any difficult or challenging task . . . so that they become in a short time so effeminate and cowardly in comparison to how they were once courageous and adventurous" (quoted in Cotarelo y Mori, *Bibliografía*, 375).[42] Again, this effeminacy was linked to Spain's political and economic woes: "The condemnation of specific 'un-masculine activities' in the entertainment industry partially stemmed from an urgent need to keep gender roles 'straight' so that Spain's able-bodied men would remain virile and war-ready" (Donnell, 67).[43]

The practice of blaming popular theater for the problem of men having degenerated into a womanish state continued throughout the seventeenth century. In 1689, Father Ignacio de Camargo associated the excess of the "pornographic" spectacle in theater with the womanly behavior observed in the men who attend public performances:

> Well who would have imagined seeing men who were born only for noble and masculine pursuits dejected to such low and effeminate activities, such that one can barely distinguish them from women? Completely dedicated to pagan parties, music, strolls in the park, lascivious affairs, idle conversations, games, and vain entertainment such as combing, braiding, and dyeing their hair, curling their wigs; polishing and adorning their

outfits with as much care and delicacy as the finest lady. Where do these vile and effeminate interests come from but the center of sensual delights: the theater stage—source of all sin . . . One cannot speak without blushing of the interludes and popular skits on stage because they are full of indecent filth, jokes and lewd stories from bars and taverns. (Quoted in Cotarelo y Mori, *Bibliografía*, 126–27)[44]

Suárez de Figueroa also spoke of the useless male adolescents at the court—the "current little sissies"—and their preference for idle and feminine pastimes, concluding with a reference to sodomy:

The vanity of songs and dances entertains the effeminate and makes them waste their time in skin care, curling their hair, raising the pitch of their voice, in feminine caresses and affectation, and in making themselves like women in the delicateness of their bodies . . . if we were to remove the veil covering them we would find the apple of Sodom: all beauty on the outside but nothing but ashes on the inside. (74v, 75v)[45]

The interludes, in particular, were a target of criticism, especially given the frequency (and obviously the popularity) of the effeminate figure on stage. For example, when discussing the theme of feminine men and same-sex desire on the early modern stage, Adrienne Martín mentions Quevedo's *El marión*, Benavente's *Los mariones*, and López Arnesto's *Los maricones galanteados*, as well as interludes featuring the homosexual *gracioso* Juan Rana (158).[46] As Donnell argues, "If transvestism is understood as female impersonation, and if female impersonation is a representation of essentialized feminine behavior, then men and boys who wear women's clothing (even on stage) could be sodomites promoting same-sex desire; therefore, the state should intervene and criminalize such behavior" (67). In this way, moralists were concerned with the impact that these transgressive characters had on the male audience as well as with the feminizing nature of theatrical and musical spectacles in general.

## Feminine Men and the Legislation of Sodomy in Early Modern Spain

Early modern terms commonly associated with male femininity and sodomy include

*pecado nefando* or *crimen contra naturam* (sodomy)[47]
*lindo* (described by Covarrubias as an unequivocal way of calling a man "effeminate" (*Tesoro*, 768))
*maricón* and *marimaricas* ("the effeminate man who is inclined to do women's activities, also known as a sissy" (*Tesoro*, 790))[48]
*afeminado* ("a man of female condition, inclined to do what women do, speak their language with a soft voice" (*Tesoro*, 46))[49]
*bujarrón* or *sodomita* (sodomite)[50]
*putillo* (sodomite (Navascués, 101))
*bugre* (sodomite (Navascués, 162))
*garzón* ("male passive sodomite" (Heiple, 222))
and *horadado* (bugger, or "something that has holes used derogatorily in reference to a man, as it means sodomite, and for a woman it connotes a lack of virginity, if not worse" (*Tesoro*, 698).[51]

José Cartagena-Calderón likewise notes that the caricaturized figure of the *lindo* or effeminate dandy was clearly associated with sodomy during the seventeenth century ("Rara," 142), and one of the definitions of effeminacy in early modern Spain discussed by Federico Garza Carvajal refers specifically "to men sodomites. It constituted notions of the 'loss of virile characteristics in one's aspect, dress and manners, decadence, degradation or corruption' " ("Silk," 20). As Ursula K. Heise concludes, "Obviously, there is an awareness that sodomy typically involves young boys, and that it is a vice linked to and possibly induced or helped by a particular kind of effeminate attire" (365).

Francisco de Quevedo also rails against men who entertain themselves with activities traditionally associated with women. In his *España defendida y los tiempos de ahora de las calumnias de los noveleros y sediciosos* (Spain Defended and the Insult of the Trendy and Subversive Men in Current Times), Quevedo refers to feminine men as if they are really women, and associates the gender transgression with sodomy:

> And even more lamentable is the way that men imitate women with their fancy outfits and effeminacy, such that a man is now no more appealing to women than another woman. And so much so that the fancy attire of some men reveals that they regret having been born men while other people try to teach nature how to turn a man into a woman. In the end their true sex becomes doubtful, which has caused more legislation for having introduced new crimes against nature not previously known. (371)[52]

Quevedo assumes that the recent feminization of men will not attract women, despite the frequently expressed desire of female characters on stage who are more attracted to the feminine nature of the deceptive woman disguised as a man (for example, the protagonist in Tirso's *Don Gil de las calzas verdes* and Estela in Ana Caro's *Valor, agravio y mujer*). Then the author comments on an implied sexual dysphoria, as the effeminate male regrets his anatomy, trying to teach nature how to convert a man into a woman. The result, Quevedo argues, is that society is in doubt about their "true" sex and must therefore create new legislation for the deviant sexual behavior associated with the man who feels trapped by his sex at birth.

Various scholars have noted that the sin and crime that caused the greatest "horror and scandal" during the sixteenth and seventeenth centuries in Spain was sodomy (Heise, 363). It is not surprising, then, that sodomy laws in Spain during that time reflected an increasing intolerance and fear of nonconforming sexual practices. While punishment for sodomy in medieval Spain had been castration and stoning to death, in the late fifteenth century, under Ferdinand and Isabella, the punishment was changed to burning alive and confiscation of property, emphasizing that the previous laws had not been effective enough to eliminate and punish the practice of sodomy:

> And because the penalties previously decreed have not sufficed to eradicate and definitively punish such an abominable crime, . . . and because the laws previously passed have not provided a sufficient remedy, we establish and order that any person of any estate, condition, preeminence, or dignity who commits the wicked crime against nature, being convicted by that manner of proof that according to the law is sufficient for proving the crime of heresy or treason, shall be burned at the stake in the place . . . and similarly shall lose his movable and landed property. (Quoted in Cowans, 202)[53]

The monarchy also facilitated Inquisitional involvement by mentioning the crime of heresy in their legislation of sodomy in the royal decrees of 1497 as well as relaxing the evidence needed for conviction: "And to better avoid said crime, we order that if it should happen that it is not possible to prove said crime with perfect and complete evidence, but if very close and related acts can be found out and proven . . . the delinquent shall be considered truly guilty of said crime, and shall be judged and sentenced and suffer the same penalty as those convicted by perfect evidence" (quoted in Cowans, 202).[54] Later, in a 1524 papal brief, Clement VII also gave the Inquisitional courts in Aragon jurisdiction over sodomy cases, regardless of the presence or absence of heresy (Kamen, 207–8). As a result, the last three decades of the sixteenth century and the first three of the seventeenth demonstrated a dramatic increase in the persecution of sodomites (Monter, 287). William Monter describes scenes of "miniature holocausts" in Seville, with fifteen men executed for sodomy in one day in 1588 and thereby "surpassing the Inquisition's peak of twelve (Saragossa 1572 and Valencia 1625)" (289–90). Through the royal decrees of Felipe II in 1598, sodomy laws made the burden of proof even easier by reducing the number of witnesses needed to convict the accused (Bennassar, 298).

While the number of sodomy investigations in both secular and Inquisitional courts increased during the early modern period, all accounts confirm that secular courts were much more severe than Inquisitional tribunals (Pérez Escohotado, 181). The Jesuit priest Pedro de León reported 54 sodomy cases among the prisoners he attended between 1578 and 1616 in Seville (Herrera Puga, 305). However, Mary Elizabeth Perry cites a total of seventy-one men convicted of sodomy and burned at the stake in Seville between 1567 and 1616, as Pedro de León's numbers do not account for other persecutions such as the fifteen executions in one day in 1600 when he was absent from the city (*Gender,* 124). Reviewing the prison chaplain's observations, Perry notes that "the far greater number of sodomy convictions implies that these offenses were reported more often than rape or adultery and that they were considered more serious" ("Nefarious," 72). Similarly, the statistics for sodomy cases tried by the Inquisition in Valencia demonstrate a marked increase after 1570, with two periods of severe persecution: between 1571 and 1590, there were 62 sodomy cases of which 14 resulted in death by burning, and from 1616 to 1630 there were 75 cases with 22 death sentences (Carrasco, 73–74).

As legislation of sodomy became increasingly harsher during the early modern period, representations of sexual practices between men in literary texts likewise criminalize those suspected of the forbidden crime. For example, María de Zayas's story "Mal presagio casar lejos" (Marriage Abroad: Portent of Doom) portrays the homosexual relationship between Doña Blanca's husband (who happens to be a foreign prince) and his sixteen-year-old page Arnesto as abominable and unspeakable. Their relationship, nonetheless, is not based only on the physical act of sodomy but also on an emotional commitment. Interestingly, unlike the recurrent images of effeminate same-sex partners, neither the husband nor his young lover raised suspicions based on a transgressive feminine appearance (despite the fact that the young lover was known to be handsome): "The prince loved him so dearly that he would have exchanged his wife's favors for the page's, and the page was so proud in his privilege that he seemed more the lord than the servant . . . The prince confided his most intimate secrets in his page and valued him above everything" (*Disenchantments*, 255–56).⁵⁵ When the wife entered his private bedroom unexpectedly, she discovered the two men in bed. However, the way in which the episode is narrated tells much about early modern attitudes toward same-sex practices:

> She found . . . What do you think she found? Beautiful ladies and discreet gentlemen, I wish I could be so subtle that you would understand what she found without my having to say point-blank because of its *hideousness* and *enormity*. In the bed she saw her husband and Arnesto engaged in such *gross* and *abominable* pleasures that it's *obscene* to think it, let alone say it. At the sight of such a *horrendous* and *dirty* spectacle, Doña Blanca was more stunned. (264–65; emphases mine)⁵⁶

Undoubtedly narrated to shock and entice the reader to consider such a sensational scene, the episode also reinforces a nationalistic message, as the homosexual partners were from Flanders.

As in Zayas's story, Quevedo's picaresque novel *El Buscón* also includes a scene that emphasizes the criminal nature of the alleged sodomite who does not display the typical effeminate characteristics associated with the sexual transgression. Unlike the serious version in Zayas, Quevedo's text uses humor and anal imagery, as the other characters express their own fears of homosexual violation in the jail cell:

> There was a man in prison who was tall and one-eyed. He was a mean-looking fellow with a moustache and broad shoulders covered with whip scars . . . he was in prison for something to do with wind . . . he said no; it was for posterior crimes. I thought that he meant old crimes, but at last I realized it was because he was a queer. . . .Sometimes the governor threatened him by saying: 'You poor fool, don't you know you can be burnt at the stake? I hope for your sake they'll strangle you first.' He had confessed, and we hated and feared him so much that we all wore protectors round our arses like dog-collars, and nobody dared fart in case they reminded him where their backside were. (*Swindler*, 172–73)⁵⁷

In addition to his critique of social transgressions through sexuality, Quevedo may be responding to previous picaresque novels that also engage homoeroticism. Some critics find implicit homosexual connotations in *Laz-*

*arillo de Tormes* in the cryptic fourth chapter dealing with the overactive friar. The best-selling picaresque novel *Guzmán de Alfarache* describes the protagonist's father as an effeminate man whose excessive primping raised suspicions about his sexual preferences: "These are actions of effeminate sissies, allowing others to gossip about them, suspecting all kinds of evil, seeing them all made-up and dressed up in things that only women can wear" (Alemán, 140).[58]

Like the early modern fictional autobiographical genre of the picaresque novel, some of the "non-fictional" life narratives of soldiers during the same period also reveal an unexpected frankness in their confessions of same-sex flirtations and innuendo. Don Diego Duque de Estrada, for example, admits that a Frenchman for whom he worked "was so taken with me that he showed it with many hugs. He was a sixteen-year-old nobleman, as beautiful as an angel with white skin and brown eyes and hair, good height and well proportioned, a gentleman, generous and good-natured. Above all, he was virtuous, devout, and not interested in sex ... at the same time people were surprised to see a Spaniard and a Frenchman hugging in public and to hear him call me 'my Spaniard' " (379).[59] Shortly after his time with his French admirer, he became close to a man from Italy who was equally smitten with the protagonist (380). Similarly, in Miguel de Castro's autobiography, he describes a friendship with another soldier named Quevedo, with whom he shared sleeping quarters. Not surprisingly, their close relationship inspired jokes: "I was displeased with Antonio Osorio, a comrade of the lieutenant's because of a stupid comment that he let slip. When Quevedo and I were walking together he said in front of him, the lieutenant, the sergeant, and everyone else: 'It's not a bad thing for bunk-mates to be affectionate with each other.' Quevedo heard this but didn't say anything but I told him that it was better not to say stupidities, that even though they are not true they can create suspicion and bad feelings" (Castro, 576).[60] These potentially incriminating details of homoerotic relationships were most likely included as part of the authors' strategies to generate interest in their life stories through the creation of personal myths based on a tabloid-style shock value. Of course, other accounts of heterosexual attraction also included in both narratives serve to neutralize the provocative episodes.[61]

Conversely, accusations of sodomy and other illicit homosexual activities were used to pathologize the minority group of the Moriscos (Spanish Muslims converted to Christianity). In Baltasar Gracián's allegorical work *El criticón*, Salastano associates the "poison" of Moriscos in Spain with problems of atheism, heresy, discord, paganism, treachery, sodomy, and "another thousand kinds of monstrocities" (186). Likewise, Diego de Haedo's 1612 publication of Antonio de Sosa's historical treatise on the cultural geography of Algiers, *Topographía e historia general de Argel* (Geography and General History of Algiers),characterizes the Muslims as perverse sodomites who esteem the young boys who provide sexual services to other men: "The corsair captains and the ship-soldiers are in the habit of dressing their lads—who are their bearded women—very lavishly and to show them off and compete over who has a greater number of lads, more beautiful and better dressed" (quoted in Garcés, 113). [62] Similarly, in his 1612 defense of the Morisco expulsion, *Expulsión justificada de los moriscos españoles* (Justified Expulsion of the Spanish Moors), Pedro Aznar Cardona blames the Koran for encouraging people to practice sodomy, thus necessitating stricter Christian laws against it, as this "unspeakable sin" was also prosecuted as heresy by the Inquisition in Aragon (Perry, "Politics," 41).

Rafael Carrasco also highlights the role of literary writers as well as moralists in the nationalist, racist, and homophobic movement to demonize the Morisco minority in defense of their expulsion beginning in 1609:

> The authors of the Golden Age ... spread the idea (even in the most minor references) of the double sin—that of having a false God and the violation of natural law—arguing that they practiced incest, bestiality and most of all sodomy. The theorists, hard-liner moralists, and learned literature in general, frequently used the argument of sexual aberration that was believed to have been permitted in Islamic culture. In this way, the writers could praise the superiority of Catholicism, which was used by the defenders of the 1609 expulsion. (212–13)[63]

Cervantes, among many others, employed the negative stereotypes of Muslims as predatory sodomites in his Algerian plays (*El trato de Argel* [Life in Algiers] and *Los baños de Argel* [The Dungeons of Algiers]). In her insightful study of these Cervantine plays, Adrienne Martín concludes that they "validate the perception of homosexuality as the ultimate threat to Spanish Christianity in the Algerian bagnios. There innocent Christian boys are inducted into the degradation of Moorish sodomy, either by force or by enticement" (12). One of Saint Teresa's confessors (Fray Jerónimo Gracián), for example, observes in his account of his first days of captivity in Tunis how some of the captives agreed to engage in sodomy with the Turks, especially some beardless young men, while in *El trato de Argel* (toward the end of the third act), a conversation between Francisco and Aurelio, describing the threat of sodomitic violations against Spanish prisoners in North Africa, was undoubtedly intended to stress the urgency for more generous ransom and rescue, as well as to provide another justification for the expulsion of the Moriscos that would soon be initiated in 1609.[64]

## The Spectacle of Punishing Sodomites

While the gender transgression of male femininity was already linked to homosexual activity in medical, economic, literary, and religious texts, the way in which the punitive practices publicly exhibited convicted sodomites served to reinforce the gender-sexuality conflation (i.e., effeminacy is one visible indication of private sodomitic activities). The published news items informing the public about important events recount the scandalous nature of sodomy executions and the spectators' responses. Mary Elizabeth Perry notes that, although attitudes about young men became more "puritanical" during the early modern period, the public spectacle of burning men convicted of sodomy attracted crowds of curious observers (*Crime*, 142). In December of 1622, "they burned five boys for sodomy. The first was Mendocilla, a buffoon. The second a personal servant of the Count of Villamediana. The third was a young mulatto slave. The fourth, another servant of Villamediana. The last was Don Gaspar de Terrazas, the page of the Duke of Alba. It was a case that was quite publicized in the capital" (quoted in González Palencia, 43).[65] On March 18, 1626, they tortured Diego Gaytán to gain a confession and on March 21, they "burned two boys for sodomy. One was one of those who accused Don Diego Gaytán . . . who denied it shouting in the streets when they took him away to be executed. The incident inspired much pity in the city" (quoted in González Palencia, 133).[66] Perry suggests that the descriptions of men accused of sodomy wearing makeup, jewels, and women's clothing might actually be part of a staged performance for punitive purposes:

> Pedro de León described Mayuca as wearing a wig, a large lace ruff, and facial cosmetics, although this may have been how he was sentenced to appear at the bonfire rather than how he usually adorned himself. It seems likely that criminal justice officials deliberately caricatured his appearance in order to humiliate him and better impress the public with his crimes. Pedro de León noted the assertions of many "honorable gentlemen" who attended his burning that wigs, hairpieces, and lace collars should also go into the fire. Not all men who wore these things were considered homo-

sexuals, but the moralists such as Francisco de León preached with vigor against "men converted into women" and "effeminate soldiers, full of airs, long locks, and plumes." (*Gender*, 126–27)

In fact, 1636 (the year that the star of *El parto de Juan Rana* was arrested for sodomy) was particularly eventful in terms of sodomy cases. News reports from October of 1636 describe a "swarm" of thirty-seven men accused of sodomy, thereby creating much publicity about the case in Madrid and, according to Deleito y Piñuela, became another reason for the legislation prohibiting men from appearing effeminate by wearing their hair long (*Mala*, 66; Martín, 157). One month later, in November of 1636, Cosme Pérez (famous for his crowd-pleasing persona as the effeminate Juan Rana) was arrested for sodomy but later released. Commentaries regarding the inconsistency in case procedures attribute the lack of punishment of certain individuals charged with "unnatural" sexual practices to the power of fame and wealth: "With regard to the business about them being incarcerated for sodomy, the authorities were not as rigorous as was expected, . . . perhaps because with power and money anything is possible. We see Don Nicolas, the page of the Count of Castrillo, free to walk down the street and they have released the famous actor Juan Rana from jail, but we haven't seen them burn any of the prisoners" (quoted in *Mala*, 66).[67] In fact, Deleito y Piñuela argues that Juan Rana's comic talent on stage ultimately is what spared the actor from execution.

Juan Rana's comic talent, then, translated into theater commerce. As P. David Marshall demonstrates in *Celebrity and Power*, popular actors have an economic value that is protected by the entertainment industry: "The everyday way to identify movies is through their stars. Indeed, the economic discourse has become an acceptable and popular way of referring to film stars, as box-office draws—a title rarely bestowed on a Hollywood director. The star acts as form of insurance in Hollywood, a kind of guaranteed return on investment for the production company" (13). Given that the revenue from performances in the public *corrales de comedia* or commercial playhouses in early modern Spain was distributed between the theater company and local confraternities (with the earnings earmarked for hospitals and charitable services), numerous people (including the audience) had good reasons for wanting to see the popular actor back on stage.

The sodomy charges, then, instead of having an adverse effect on Juan Rana's popularity, might have been perceived as complementary to the features used in the construction of his celebrity icon. Despite the fact that the effeminacy emphasized in his successful gender-bending roles was commonly associated with illicit same-sex desire (which could have meant disaster for the famous actor), the audience's tendency to conflate the identities of stars and their characters actually may have worked to Pérez's advantage. The potential shock value must have been mitigated by what Richard Dyer describes as the "extreme gullibility" of the audience: "The roles and/or the performance of a star in a film were taken as revealing of the personality of the star (which then was corroborated by the stories in the magazines, etc.)" (20). Furthermore, the fact that Juan Rana was famous for his comedic skills on stage also impacted the audience's relationship with his public personality and private life. As Aristotle outlined in his *Poetics*, spectators feel superior to the lowly characters in comedy while they look up to the noble characters in tragedy. In this way, the same criminal charges against another actor famous for more noble roles in the "cape and sword" plays, for example, could have had very different consequences, both legal and professional.

Given the enormous celebrity of Juan Rana during the seventeenth century, we might assume that the audience had certain information about the actor that would impact their experience while viewing his performances. The spectators most likely were aware, for example, that the famous thespian had been married to a woman (María de Acosta) and had fathered two children, a daughter (Francisca María Pérez) and a son who died shortly after birth in 1634 (Cotarelo y Mori, *Colección*, clviii). Likewise, his fans would certainly know that he had become a widower some time before 1636 (according to Hannah Bergman, either in 1632 or 1636) and had been involved in a potentially disastrous legal conflict when arrested for sodomy. Consequently, like the non-fixed nature of sex assignment and gender roles for certain individuals during that time, Juan Rana's very public "private" history reveals what appears to be mutable sexual practices that include both heterosexual marriage and homosexual liaisons. As a result, his case may have exemplified a reactionary stance on the "tragic" consequences of male effeminacy (i.e., sodomy), not unlike the humorous yet implicitly ominous suggestion in *El parto de Juan Rana* that these "perversions" of gender roles and sexual acts could eventually lead to male pregnancy. At the same time, however, we cannot ignore that Juan Rana as cultural icon (on and off the stage) also embodies an empowering model for the possibility of nonconformity *and* professional success during a time when both men and women were persecuted for nontraditional behavior.

# Epilogue
## "Who's Laughing Now"

When considering the decisive changes in women's reproductive health and cultural attitudes toward male effeminacy, sodomy, and biological sex assignment in early modern Spain, it is not surprising that a comedy about a pregnant man who gives birth on stage emerges from this particular sociohistorical context. Although the purpose of the interlude is to provoke laughter, this piece also dramatizes serious concerns about the impact that nonconformist behavior can have on the body—in particular, how women's autonomy in the bedroom and/or the birthing room can create insecurities about paternity, while the male body is vulnerable to feminine traits (both physiological and social) as well as to unstable sexual desire.

Of course, a seventeenth-century theatergoer would not be shocked that the spectacle of a pregnant man in labor appears in an *entremés*, a genre known for its outrageous humor and exaggerated inversions of societal norms. Therefore, while some critics emphasize the apparently frivolous nature of the pregnant man figure as "merely a stock feature of comedy but that it did not represent a serious concern"[1] or nothing more than "the butt of jokes in folklore and popular culture from ancient times,"[2] early modern moralists as well as scholars of humor theory would agree that the comedy in the interludes could have serious implications for the audience, which invites us to question what kind of laughter is provoked by the image of a pregnant man in labor and what does it mean for different spectators?

If we follow Frédéric Serralta's example by departing from the text to consider the actor's performance and his enormous talent for improvisation and hilarious gestures and movements, we might imagine the possibilities of a liberating laughter that reveals a Rabelaisian reversal of power led by an early modern "drag queen" who garnered more professional acclaim than any other actor during his time, despite well-publicized transgressions of gender and sexual expectations.[3] While the playwright penned a one-act play that uses humor to expose and punish those who attempt to escape society's mechanisms aimed to control nonconformity (subversives such as sodomites, feminine men, masculine women, and women who deceive men about paternity), it is also possible that Juan Rana's performance might have communicated a different message to some members of the audience (such as those who participated in secret sexual relations with the same sex but who were not protected by royal patronage). Even though the sociopolitical concept of queer identity has evolved in the last four hundred years (from a behavior-based indictment to identity-based politics), can we imagine a reversed laughter outside mainstream culture—perhaps an early attempt at camp humor?

A review of what makes something "camp" indicates some significant correlations with the seventeenth-century farce. Camp, as summarized by David Bergman, is characterized by four basic features: First, camp is a style that favors " 'exaggeration,' 'artifice,' and 'extremity.' Second, camp exists in tension with popular culture, commercial culture, or consumerist culture. Third, the person who can recognize camp, who sees things as campy, or who can camp, is a person outside the cultural mainstream. Fourth, camp is affiliated with homosexual culture, or at least with a self-conscious eroticism that throws into question the naturalization of desire" (5). Surely Juan Rana's performance in *El parto de Juan Rana* could be easily described in terms of hyperbole and tension, personified by one whose prior arrest for sodomy places him outside the cultural mainstream, thereby suggesting an eroticism that negates "compulsory heterosexuality."

In her comparison of camp and carnival, Dianna Niebylski argues that camp is about "nothing but spectacle, theater, and play-acting . . . camp keeps its audience at too great a distance from the reality of characters and plots to inspire real revolutionary impulses. It is not that camp does not desire change, but rather that it refuses to specify which shape change should take" (128), while carnivalesque humor has the potential for overturning status quo. So when we consider laughter's potential for the liberation and disruption expressed through Bakhtinian carnivalesque and grotesque humor, we find that as this laughter degrades through humiliation, it also offers the hope of renewal or "rebirth" for the future.[4] Like the grotesque humor in *El parto*, Bakhtin's carnival laughter forces attention on the belly and the body's reproductive functions:

> To degrade also means to concern oneself with the lower stratum of the body, the life of the belly and the reproductive organs; it therefore relates to acts of defecation and copulation, conception, pregnancy and birth.

Degradation digs a bodily grave for a new birth; it has not only a destructive, negative aspect, but also a regenerating one. To degrade an object does not imply merely hurling into the void of nonexistence, into absolute destruction but to hurl it down to the reproductive lower stratum, the zone in which conception and a new birth take place. Grotesque realism knows no other lower level; it is the fruitful earth and the womb. It is always conceiving. (21)

As Barry Sanders reminds us, in his study of laughter as subversive history, "the victim in hostile joke-telling always feels humiliated, as in *humus*—dirt or shit—but moves through that decayed state in his or her passage toward rebirth and . . . into the welcoming arms of forgiveness" (199). While Juan Rana is found guilty, his punishment never goes beyond an entertaining display of public humiliation through cross-dressing (and his timely labor). More importantly, by the end of the interlude all the mayors have put down their authorial staffs to join in and celebrate Juan Rana's "procreative triumph" by imitating his gestures and movements, implying both "if you can't beat 'em, join 'em" as well as the male solidarity that leads to the final indictment of women's reproductive practices.

This male solidarity, then, also allows for a much more conservative potential for the humor in *El parto*. Following Aristotle's theory of comedy as an imitation of men who are considered inferior, F. H. Buckley argues that "laughter signals our recognition of a comic vice in another person—the butt. We do not share in the vice, for we could not laugh if we did. Through laughter, the butt is made to feel inferior, and those who laugh reveal their sense of superiority over him" (4). The "Superiority Theory" of humor assumes that comedy has a moralizing and cathartic component employed to maintain the conformity of status quo. So if we consider laughter to reflect standards of "normal" conduct by targeting the person who falls through the crack of normalcy, we can easily see how the humor in *El parto de Juan Rana* points to the pregnant protagonist as the butt of the jokes, which are based primarily on his crimes of effeminacy, transgression of anatomical boundaries (which makes his pregnancy possible), and the implied sin/crime of sodomy. The audience, then, would identify with the Court Clerk and/or Berrueco (who, according to Buckley's description, would be the "wit"): "'The wit proposes a joke to the listener, who may either accept it by laughing or reject it by silence. By laughing the listener accepts a tie of solidarity—a *lien de rire*— with the wit. In this way laughter's superiority may coexist with a sense of sociability" (5). Simon Critchley describes this as reactionary humor, which "simply seeks to reinforce consensus and in no way seeks to criticize the established order" (11). Critchley also stresses the need for consensus in order for a joke to be successful: "humor is a form of *sensus communis* that requires intersubjective assent of some sort" (86). As a result of the bond between the audience and the wit, Juan Rana's performance of labor and childbirth in the interlude could also be interpreted in terms of a moralizing attempt to reinforce the model for ideal manhood in Spain's troubled empire.[5]

At the same time, however, it is not by chance that both slapstick and camp have been described in terms of their ambiguous nature. Steven Shaviro states that slapstick is potentially subversive, but also easily recuperable by the ruling power structure (108–9). David Bergman likewise notes that theorists of camp and the gay sensibility either argue for its disruptive potential or "for its ability to be coopted by and integrated with oppressive forces" (9).[6] For example, in his analysis of the negotiation between subversion and containment in the mainstream (yet queer) television program *Will & Grace*, James R. Keller argues that "camp is employed to appease homophobes by reinforcing negative stereotypes, but it simultaneously perpetuates gay culture through its articulation of gay sensibility . . . so the portion of the audience who might find the satire of the episode offensive are palliated by the fact the Jack is ridiculous and easy to dismiss" (124, 129). Despite possible accusations of perpetuating negative stereotypes of the effeminate male who desires other men, in the end Juan Rana has the last laugh in both diegetic and extradiegetic levels: the protagonist seduces his accusers into song and dance in the interlude while the actor is successful in avoiding any consequences for his alleged sodomitic activities in his personal life, and eventually secured a life-long stipend from royal authorities for his professional achievements.

As the primary focus on the societal expectations for men shifts by the end of the farce, the interlude concludes with an answer to the "what if men could give birth" question inherent in the pregnant man image. Juan Rana has the last word as he redirects the indictment away from his own transgressions, toward women's untrustworthy sexual practices and their reproductive vices. It would seem, then, that Juan Rana ceases to be the butt of the joke when he joins the other men as a wit to transform women into the new target of his biting humor. The effeminate, sex-morphing sodomite is no longer the inferior subject of the moralizing gaze but rather he becomes the superior judge of women's sexual vice through reproductive control. Ultimately, these criminally procreative women are literally and symbolically eliminated from the scenario, as there are no women present on stage who participate in the principal action. Despite the brief presence of a female town crier (who announces Juan Rana's crimes), this lone woman offers no apparent variation from what the men had already expressed, no particular female perspective to challenge the officials' conclusions. Similarly, Juan Rana's absent wife Aldonza has been excluded (physically) from the play, as are the criminal mothers referred to in the last joke ("There is no doubt that we've seen lots of women who give their kids to other fathers for feeding"), which ultimately serves as the perfect justification for patriarchal control over women's sexual practices as well as for the intervention in and appropriation of reproductive health in the early modern period.

And yet, regardless of the ambiguities regarding who is laughing at whom, what we do know is that since (female) mothers in early modern Spain are denied access to center stage, their laughter must remain behind the scenes: the silent snicker of one who knows that despite all efforts to appropriate reproductive practices, *pater semper incertus est, mater est certissima.*

# Appendix 1A

## John Frog Gives Birth: An Interlude

by Lanini Sagredo*

**Cast**
John Frog
A Doorman
Cosme Berrueco
Six Mayors
A Court Clerk
John Frog Jr.
A Woman

*Enter a court clerk and Cosme Berrueco, the latter wearing a mayor's tunic and staff.*

**Court Clerk:** Because you, Cosme Berrueco, the eminent mayor of the town of Meco,[1] are such a famous judge, the council members have appointed you to preside over this hearing in which Mayor John Frog will be called to account, after being jailed for the most lewd and heinous crime that a mayor has ever committed since mayors and town councils have been in existence. What he's charged with is enormously perverse.[2]

**Berrueco:** Clerk, don't you be so perverse. Control yourself! What makes it an even more incriminating, perverse, heinous, and grave crime (and let no one think I'm exaggerating) is that John Frog makes a better woman than a man.

**Court Clerk:** But is it not an offensive and inappropriate crime for a mayor to be pregnant?

**Berrueco:** It would be a greater crime for a mayor, having been fertile, now to be sterile.

**Court Clerk:** What strange nonsense! Do you want him to be fertile?

**Berrueco:** What good is a mayor's staff if it doesn't bear fruit?

**Court Clerk:** Now you're comparing his staff to his member?

---

*Translator's Note: In this adaptive translation, I decided not to imitate the dramatist's use of verse. Instead, I have used prose for readability. References to the *Diccionario de Autoridades* will be abbreviated as "Aut." and those to Covarrubias's *Tesoro de la lengua* will be abbreviated as "Cov." The translations of the definitions into English are my own.

**Berrueco:** Clerk, you don't understand. A staff conceives thousands of things and later can deliver them prodigious. Now read the charges.
**Court Clerk:** I will proceed once the other judges have arrived.
**Berrueco:** In the meantime, take a seat. Call the doorman here at once.
**Court Clerk:** Hello out there, John Potter! The mayor is calling you.

*(The doorman enters on stage)*

**Doorman:** How can I help you?
**Berrueco:** Let no one enter on his own without announcing him first.
**Doorman:** Yes, sir.

*(He exits)*

**Berrueco:** Such a courteous doorman!
**Court Clerk** *(aside)*: And this mayor is a big dope!
**Berrueco:** I wonder, have you seen a notary on this case?
**Court Clerk:** I've never gone bad,[3] nor would I dream of it.
**Berrueco:** Just as well, since man is like good wine: no matter how hard you force something, it will turn to vinegar if pressed the wrong way.

*(The doorman enters with the first mayor and then exits)*

**Doorman:** The mayor of "Little Well"[4] has arrived for the assembly.
**Berrueco:** Well, it's the famous fisherman![5] How come you're so late?
**First Mayor:** I came as fast as I could on my donkey.
**Berrueco:** I gather that you rode on yourself since it would be the same as riding a donkey. Just take a seat.
**First Mayor:** I will sit next to you to be near my "dumb ass."[6]

*(The doorman enters with the second mayor)*

**Doorman:** The mayor from "Blabberville."[7]
**Berrueco:** He must have come out of its swamps.[8]
**Second Mayor:** What are you implying?
**Berrueco:** Are you a big fish[9] in your small pond or just a tadpole?[10]
**Second Mayor:** I may not be much, but what little I have is from my own efforts, while in Meco you are just a barfly.[11]
**Berrueco:** Take your seat.
**Second Mayor:** Among the first.

*(The doorman enters with the third mayor)*

**Doorman:** The mayor from "Ballsville"[12] has arrived.
**Berrueco:** You mean, from "Eunuchtown,"[13] since that's what these "balls" really are.
**Third Mayor:** Oh, what brilliant Ciceros!
**Berrueco:** Sit down before your empty balls become completely useless.[14]

*(He [the third mayor] sits on the first mayor)*

**First Mayor:** Mayor, do you think you're a packsaddle?
**Third Mayor:** I don't, but if it fits, you must be the donkey.
**First Mayor:** And you are a real idiot![15]

*(The doorman enters with the fourth mayor)*

**Doorman:** The mayor from "Here and There"![16]
**Berrueco:** Just say from "Down There."[17]
**Fourth Mayor:** Here's a fine bunch of dumb mayors.[18]
**Second Mayor:** Is anyone missing from the assembly?
**Court Clerk:** Only one person is missing.

*(The doorman enters with the fifth mayor)*

**Doorman:** The mayor from Ambrosia.[19]
**First Mayor:** Make sure he doesn't jump ahead.
**Berrueco:** How are you the last one here?
**Fifth Mayor:** In the courts, Ambrosia was always first.[20]
**All five:** What do you mean by first?
**Berrueco:** Stop all the commotion. Now that we have enough for a vote, let the proceedings begin.

*(The mayors start to talk amongst themselves and Berrueco rings a bell)*

**Doorman:** Can I help you?
**Berrueco:** Clear the court.
**Doorman:** There's not even an ant in here.
**Berrueco:** These doormen have an answer for everything. Clear out these pests!
**Doorman:** Speak no more; there they go.
**Berrueco:** Can't you hear their buzzing?
**Doorman:** I'll shoo them out.

*(He uses his hat to fan the mayors)*

**Berrueco:** Clerk, read to us solemnly and in simple language the charges against John Frog.

*(The mayors start talking again)*

**Doorman:** Everyone listen.

*(The court clerk takes some papers as if reading from them)*

**Court Clerk:** First of all, being married to Aldonza, John Frog has never given any indication of being a man; he is but a plaything,[21] so Aldonza was the one who ordered him (the aforementioned) around; she scolded him and sometimes beat him. By fighting with him, she got him to do all the housework: the sweeping, scrubbing, cooking—and he even did her errands for her.
**Berrueco:** Proof of the pregnancy ascribed to John Frog is plain. For if he allowed his wife to wear the pants on occasion, then it's not so incredible that he got pregnant since he did what she should have done.

**First Mayor:** The consequence is clear, and since he wanted it, he should deliver it.
**Second Mayor:** Continue.
**Court Clerk:** It is public, well-known, and quite evident that recently John Frog's stomach has grown so much that he's as big as a barrel.
**Third Mayor:** Full of wine he used to be.
**Court Clerk:** And he no longer feels like eating, which is a sure sign of pregnancy.
**Fourth Mayor:** And for him, being a glutton, it's even more notable.
**Fifth Mayor:** That's clear proof of the crime.
**Berrueco:** Has the pregnant prisoner confessed?
**Court Clerk:** He pleads not guilty.
**Berrueco:** Well, torture him then.
**Court Clerk:** How? He's pregnant, so the law excuses him from torture.
**Berrueco:** There's a solution for everything. Let's torture his wife.
**First Mayor:** What kind of solution is it to bring charges against her too?
**Berrueco:** It would be torture to make someone else suffer; since she is aware that a wife is an extension of her husband, *she* can take the heat for him.
**Court Clerk:** Torture is unnecessary when the crime is proven and shown on paper in summary and plenary.
**Second Mayor:** If the crime has been verified in plenary, let's vote on it in the summary.

*(They talk amongst themselves in secret)*

**Berrueco:** I approve.
**Third Mayor:** That is also my opinion.
**Fourth Mayor:** And I agree.
**Fifth Mayor:** And I.
**Berrueco:** What corroboration! The judgment looks so elegant with everyone in agreement.
**First Mayor:** *Nemine discrepante*,[22] so let's move on to the sentence.
**Court Clerk:** Have you already come to the verdict?
**Second Mayor:** And with no regret.
**Berrueco:** Let it be known that we should and do condemn him and that the town crier will soon proclaim to the world that John Frog must be publicly shamed by being paraded in women's clothing (and a very profane woman) where everyone can see him and be faithful witnesses that his crime is beyond doubt. If he goes into labor right there, then let him deliver in front of all. This we decree should be carried out forthwith, but we cannot sign it since we don't know how.
**Court Clerk:** Likewise, I will leave immediately to deliver the orders.

*(He exits)*

**Third Mayor:** He bears the burden of the law.
**Fourth Mayor:** The verdict was reasonable.
**Fifth Mayor:** In these sentences he was always knowledgeable.

**Berrueco:** I've never made a serious mistake in the sentences. But from the sound of the crowd, they must be bringing John Frog out for the punishment.
**First Mayor:** Well, let's see if they carry out what we command.

*(They bring John Frog out wearing a woman's dress and with a very big stomach. John Frog Jr. is hiding underneath the skirts. In front of him enter the court clerk and a woman who sings in the style of a town crier)*

**Woman** (*singing*): Let it be known to all that, since John Frog is in no way a real man, he is publicly shamed in women's clothing. Yes, as is custom, Mother Nature wrote John Frog, but he missed the letters. He has shown his mistakes, and with nine missed menstrual periods, everything he says now are pregnant words.[23]

**John Frog** (*singing*): Ay! Wretched is anyone whose pregnancy is their disgrace. And since, oh judges, there is no reasoning against it, I must, perforce, give birth. Let it be said that I don't know if I was asleep or careless but I discovered my own image in my belly. May I also confess to you that I am not guilty of anything. This living bump didn't come from any fall. Finally, it's worth mentioning that if mares can conceive by the wind, then John Frogs can do the same.[24] Ay, woe is me!

**Second Mayor:** His lament makes me sad.
**Third Mayor:** But his face makes me laugh.
**John Frog:** The birth is near![25] Ay! My hips are coming out of their sockets; Good God, what suffering, what hardship, what anguish! This pain is killing me. Is there no one who can help me deliver? I am paralyzed with fear and it dumbfounds me. Gentlemen, have mercy, my water just broke! I can't believe that I'm about to give birth without a midwife, having known so many![26]

*(Two of the men hold him by the arms)*

**Court Clerk:** Let's help him deliver.
**John Frog:** Get a good grip on me.
**The two men:** He's killing us!
**John Frog:** Hold me, it's coming, the head is crowning, but after this hell I swear that I will never get pregnant again, ever!

*(John Frog Jr., wearing a tunic, comes out from under John Frog's skirts)*

**Everybody:** Heavens! He just gave birth!
**John Frog:** Why do you look so shocked?
**Berrueco:** The boy is the spitting image of his father, both in body and face.
**John Frog Jr.:** Mommy, won't you hug your Little John Frog?
**John Frog:** Oh, the fruit of my womb! My little darling!
**First Mayor:** He doesn't deny his father at all.
**John Frog:** I still need to know if he is my son, since it's possible that another man created him in my absence.
**Second Mayor:** How do you plan to find out?
**John Frog:** By seeing if he dances the *zarambeque*[27] as I do.

**John Frog Jr.:** Well, let's have some music then; someone play the guitar.

*(The musicians play and the two begin to dance)*

**Music:** In their appearance, as in their movements, sons always resemble their fathers. Cha-cha-cha!
**John Frog** (*singing*): How he takes after me, my little John Jr., in the *zarambeque!*
**Court Clerk:** Mayors, what are you doing?

*(As John Frog and John Frog Jr. dance one more time, the six mayors put down their staffs and dance with them)*

**First Mayor:** Today we want to be just like John Frog.
**John Frog:** Let's see those moves!
**John Frog Jr.:** Come on everyone!

*(The two show their moves and the court clerk imitates them)*

**Second Mayor:** Clerk, what are you doing?
**Court Clerk:** I'm trying to look like John Frog.
**John Frog:** I swear he takes after me in everything, without missing a beat!
**Everyone:** We celebrate the birth of John Frog Jr. from John Frog!
**Court Clerk:** How?
**John Frog:** With one last refrain to end this little comedy.
**Woman** (*singing*): If men gave birth, it would be a great thing—since they would be certain of all of their offspring.
**John Frog:** There is no doubt about it because we've seen lots of women who give their kids to other fathers for feeding.[28]

*Don Pedro Francisco Lanini Sagredo.*

# Appendix 1B

### Entremés de *El parto de Juan Rana*
De Lanini Sagredo[*]

**Personas**
Juan Rana
Un portero
Cosme Berrueco
Seis alcaldes
Un escribano
Juan Ranilla
Una mujer

*Salen, un escribano y Cosme Berrueco con sayo y vara de Alcalde.*

| | |
|---|---|
| **Escribano:** | A vos, Cosme Berrueco |
| | (insigne alcalde del lugar de Meco)[1] |
| | a vos os han nombrado |
| | los concejos, por juez tan afamado |
| | para que presidáis en esta audiencia, |
| | en que a tomar se viene residencia |
| | al alcalde Juan Rana, |
| | que preso tienen por la más liviana |
| | fea culpa que alcalde ha cometido |
| | después que alcaldes en consejo ha habido: |
| | su cargo es enormísimo.[2] |
| **Berrueco:** | Escribano, |
| | no seáis vos inormísimo:[3] a la mano |
| | os id;[4] ¿es mas la culpa encreminada[5] |
| | enormísima,[6] fea y ponderada |

---

[*] I would like to thank Peter Thompson for sharing with me his transcription of the eighteenth-century manuscript copy of the interlude housed in the Biblioteca Nacional, Madrid. I have made changes to Thompson's transcription, which was printed in *Comedia Performance* 1, no.1 (2004): 219–37. I have also modernized punctuation and spelling.

|  |  |
|---|---|
| | el que Juan Rana (porque a nadie asombre) |
| | para hembra es mejor que para hombre? |
| Escribano: | ¿Luego no es feo delito y mal notado |
| | que un alcalde en persona esté preñado? |
| Berrueco: | Alcalde siendo, aun más delito era, |
| | siendo fecundo, que hoy estéril fuera. |
| Escribano: | ¡Necedad es bien rara! |
| | ¿Fecundo queréis sea? |
| Berrueco: | Pues la vara |
| | a un alcalde absoluto, |
| | ¿de que provecho le es, si no da fruto? |
| Escribano: | ¿La vara comparáis agora al sexo? |
| Berrueco: | Vos, escribano, no entendéis bien de eso. |
| | Una vara concibe dos mil cosas |
| | luego puede parirlas prodigiosas. |
| | Mas haced relación. |
| Escribano: | La haré en llegando |
| | a la junta otros jueces. |
| Berrueco: | Pues sentando |
| | entre tanto me voy; pero al portero |
| | me llamad al instante. |
| Escribano: | ¡Ah, Juan Ollero! |
| | que os llama el se[ñ]or alcalde. |
| | (Sale el portero) |
| Portero: | ¿Qué me mandáis? |
| Berrueco: | Que nadie entrar en balde |
| | dejéis, sin que primero |
| | digáis quien es. |
| Portero: | Lo haré. *(Vase)* |
| Berrueco: | ¡Gentil portero! |
| Escribano: | El tal alcalde es gran simplón. *(Aparte)* |
| Berrueco: | Pregunto, |
| | ¿escribano en la causa habéis visto? |
| Escribano: | Nunca yo me torcí;[7] ni lo imagino. |
| Berrueco: | Hacéis bien, pues el hombre que es buen vino |
| | por más que se le fuerce |
| | se volverá vinagre si se tuerce. |

*(Sale el portero con el primer alcalde y luego se va)*

|  |  |
|---|---|
| Portero: | A la junta el alcalde de Pozuelo[8] |
| | es el que llega. |
| Berrueco: | ¡Qué famoso anzuelo |
| | de pescar! ¿Pues tan tarde? |
| Alcalde Primero: | Por la posta, |

|  |  |
|---|---|
|  | en mi burro he venido a toda costa. |
| Berrueco: | A correrla en vos mismo yo discurro, |
|  | que era lo propio que correrla en burro. |
|  | Pero tomad asiento. |
| Alcalde Primero: | Junto a vos por estar con mi jumento.[9] |

*(Sale el portero con el segundo alcalde)*

|  |  |
|---|---|
| Portero: | El alcalde de Parla.[10] |
| Berrueco: | Saldrá de sus lagunas. |
| Alcalde Segundo: | ¿Qué se guarda? |
| Berrueco: | Si allá sois renacuajo[11] |
|  | o alcalde en las lagunas. |
| Alcalde Segundo: | A destajo |
|  | allá soy muy poquito, |
|  | mas vos en Meco sólo sois mosquito.[12] |
| Berrueco: | Vuestro asiento ocupad. |
| Alcalde Segundo: | De los primeros. |

*(Sale el portero con el tercer alcalde)*

|  |  |
|---|---|
| Portero: | El alcalde ha llegado de los Güeros.[13] |
| Berrueco: | Decid de los capones[14] |
|  | que esos los güeros son. |
| Alcalde Tercero: | ¡Oh! ¡Cicerones |
|  | eruditos! |
| Berrueco: | Sentando |
|  | os id, que vendréis güero |
|  | y será en blando.[15] *(Siéntase sobre el primer alcalde)* |
| Alcalde Primero: | Alcalde ¿sois albarda? |
| Alcalde Tercero: | No imagino, |
|  | mas pues vos la sentís, seréis pollino. |
| Alcalde Primero: | Pero vos sois en todo albarda viva.[16] |

*(Sale el portero y el cuarto alcalde)*

|  |  |
|---|---|
| Portero: | ¿El alcalde de abajo y el de arriba?[17] |
| Berrueco: | Decid Caramancheles.[18] |
| Alcalde Cuarto: | Brava turba hay de alcaldes moscateles.[19] |
| Alcalde Segundo: | ¿Falta en la junta aun más? |
| Escribano: | Solo uno falta. |

*(Sale el portero con el quinto alcalde)*

|  |  |
|---|---|
| Portero: | ¡El alcalde de Ambroz![20] |
| Alcalde Primero: | Miren si salta. |
| Berrueco: | ¿Cómo a esta junta vos venís postrero? |
| Alcalde Quinto: | Ambroz en cortes,[21] siempre fue primero. |

| | |
|---|---|
| Los cinco: | ¿Qué es primero? |
| Berrueco: | Dejad los alborotos |
| | y pues estamos ya bastante votos, |
| | la audiencia se prosiga. |

*(Empiezan a hablar los alcaldes unos con otros y Berrueco toca la campanilla)*

| | |
|---|---|
| Portero: | ¿Qué mandáis? |
| Berrueco: | Despejad. |
| Portero: | Aquí una hormiga |
| | no hay siquiera. |
| Berrueco: | ¡Que sean respondones |
| | siempre aquestos porteros! Los moscones |
| | despejad. |
| Portero: | No discurra, |
| | que aquí los hay. |
| Berrueco: | ¿No oís este susurro? |
| Portero: | Ya los aviento. |

*(Con el sombrero avienta a los alcaldes)*

| | |
|---|---|
| Berrueco: | Empieza, escribano |
| | a hacernos relación en canto llano |
| | del cargo de Juan Rana, solemnemente. |

*(Están los alcaldes volviendo a hablar)*

| | |
|---|---|
| Portero: | Oíos pues hay. |

*(Tomando el escribano unos papeles como que por ellos hace relación)*

| | |
|---|---|
| Escribano: | Primeramente, |
| | el que siendo casado |
| | Juan Rana con Aldonza nunca ha dado |
| | indicios de ser hombre, pues Aldonza |
| | (al susodicho) siendo una peonza[22] |
| | era quien le mandaba, |
| | le reñía y a veces le pegaba, |
| | logrando en sus contiendas |
| | que él hiciera de casa las haciendas, |
| | que barriese, fregase y que pusiese |
| | la olla, y aun a sus mandados fuese. |
| Berrueco: | La probanza está llana |
| | del delito que imputan a Juan Rana |
| | del preñado, supuesto |
| | que si él permitió que los calzones |
| | su mujer se pusiese en ocasiones, |
| | ser el preñado él, no es demasía |
| | pues hizo lo que ella hacer debía. |

| | |
|---|---|
| Alcalde Primero: | La consecuencia es clara, |
| | mas pues él se lo quiso, que lo para. |
| Alcalde Segundo: | Pasad más adelante. |
| Escribano: | Es público, es notorio y muy constante |
| | que de tiempo a esta parte, al contraído |
| | Juan Rana, le ha crecido |
| | el vientre de manera |
| | que una cuba parece. |
| Alcalde Tercero: | Antes lo era |
| | de vino. |
| Escribano: | Y le han faltado |
| | las ganas de comer, que en un preñado |
| | son las señas fatales. |
| Alcalde Cuarto: | Y en él, que es un glotón, son más señales. |
| Alcalde Quinto: | Clara probanza del delito es ésa. |
| Berrueco: | Y reo del preñado, ¿él se confiesa? |
| Escribano: | Está en un juramento |
| | negativo. |
| Berrueco: | Pues désele tormento. |
| Escribano: | ¿Cómo, estando preñado? |
| | Que la ley de tormento le ha excusado. |
| Berrueco: | Para todo hay remedio, |
| | dese tormento a su mujer. |
| Alcalde Primero: | ¿Qué medio |
| | es ése que un juicio le condena? |
| Berrueco: | Tormento es darle en cabeza ajena, |
| | pues su parte contraria es advertida, |
| | es cualquier mujer propia del marido. |
| Escribano: | El tormento excusado |
| | es, cuando el delito está probado |
| | y consta por lo escrito |
| | en sumaria y plenaria. |
| Alcalde Segundo: | Sí el delito |
| | se comprueba en plenaria |
| | votémosle nosotros en sumaria. |

*(Hablan unos con otros como en secreto)*

| | |
|---|---|
| Berrueco: | Eso apruebo. |
| Alcalde Tercero: | Mi parecer es éste. |
| Alcalde Cuarto: | Y éste el mío. |
| Alcalde Quinto: | Y el mío. |
| Berrueco: | Muy conteste |
| | el juicio se ve en todos elegante. |
| Alcalde Primero: | *Nemine discrepante,* |
| | se mira la sentencia. |

| | |
|---|---|
| Escribano: | ¿Habéis ya sentenciado? |
| Alcalde Segundo: | Y en conciencia. |
| Berrueco: | Decid pues que fallamos, |
| | debemos condenar y condenamos, |
| | que a voz de pregonero, |
| | que cantado lo expresa al mundo entero, |
| | que a la vergüenza saquen a Juan Rana |
| | vestido de mujer (y muy profana) |
| | donde todos le vean |
| | y públicos, testigos fieles sean |
| | de que es su culpa clara |
| | y si la da allí el parto, que allí para, |
| | y que aquesto mandamos |
| | que se ejecute luego y no firmamos |
| | por no saberlo hacer. |
| Escribano: | Del mismo modo, |
| | al punto a ejecutarlo, parto, todo. *(Vase)* |
| Alcalde Tercero: | La ley se le echó a cuestas. |
| Alcalde Cuarto: | En razón se ha votado. |
| Alcalde Quinto: | Siempre en estas |
| | sentencias fue muy dicho. |
| Berrueco: | En mi vida, jamás las erré mucho; |
| | mas según el bullicio |
| | a Juan Rana le sacan al suplicio. |
| Alcalde Primero: | Pues desde aquí veamos |
| | si se ejecuta bien lo que mandamos. |

*(Sacan a Juan Rana vestido de mujer y con una barriga muy grande y a Juan Ranilla debajo de las faldas y delante salen el escribano y una mujer que viene cantando en tono de pregón)*

| | |
|---|---|
| **Cantando Mujer:** | Venga a noticia de todos |
| | como por no ser Juan Rana |
| | hombre en nada, de mujer |
| | a la vergüenza le sacan. |
| | Pues si por el ordinario |
| | la naturaleza humana |
| | escribió a Juan Rana antes, |
| | ya le faltaron las cartas. |
| | Sus faltas ha descubierto, |
| | y viéndose en nueve faltas,[23] |
| | cuantas palabras pronuncia |
| | son ya palabras preñadas. |
| Canta Juan Rana: | ¡Ay! desdichada |
| | de quien es su embarazo |
| | su desgracia. |

|  |  |
|---|---|
|  | Y pues no vale, ¡oh jueces! |
|  | razón a la fuerza valga |
|  | razón, para que a la fuerza |
|  | lo que he concebido, para. |
|  | Valga decir que no sé |
|  | si dormida ni descuidada |
|  | sonando en mí, halle en mi propio |
|  | vientre, con mi semejanza. |
|  | Valga también confesaros |
|  | que no soy culpada en nada, |
|  | pues este chichón viviente |
|  | ningún tropezón le causa. |
|  | Y por fin, valga advertiros |
|  | que si en las yeguas se halla |
|  | concebir del viento, pueden |
|  | lo mismo hacer los Juan Ranas. |
|  | ¡Ay! desdichada. |
| Alcalde Segundo: | Su lamento a dolor mueve. |
| Alcalde Tercero: | Y a risa mueve su cara. |
| Juan Rana: | Mas aquí que ha llevado el parto. |
|  | ¡Ay! Que se me desencajan |
|  | las caderas. ¡Qué dolores |
|  | qué penas, cielos, qué ansias! |
|  | ¿No hay quien me ayude siquiera |
|  | a parir, que muero en tanta |
|  | fatiga? Mas un temblor |
|  | me hiela toda, y me pasma. |
|  | Señores, piedad, ¡que rota |
|  | tengo ya la fuente! ¡Que haya |
|  | de parir yo sin comadre |
|  | habiendo tenido tantas.[24] |

*(Tienen de los brazos dos de ellos)*

| | |
|---|---|
| Escribano: | Ayudémosle a parir. |
| Juan Rana: | Ténganme bien. |
| Los dos: | Que nos mata. |
| Juan Rana: | Tengan, que del parto está |
|  | la cabeza coronada. |
|  | Mas ya parir con mil diablos; |
|  | no me haré otra vez preñada |
|  | no más en mi vida. |

*(Sale por debajo de las faldas Juan Ranilla con sayo)*

| | |
|---|---|
| **Todos:** | ¡Cielos, que ha parido! |

| | |
|---|---|
| Juan Rana: | ¿Qué se pasman? |
| Berrueco: | Su retrato es el muchacho en talle y en rostro. |
| Juan Ranilla: | Mamá, ¿no abraza a su Juan Ranilla? |
| Juan Rana: | ¡Ay, parto de mis entrañas! ¡Ay, prenda mía! |
| Alcalde Primero: | No niega en nada a su padre. |
| Juan Rana: | Aún falta el saber si es mi hijo, pues puede ser que otro lo haya hecho en mi ausencia. |
| Alcalde Segundo: | Pues ¿cómo hacer la experiencia tratas? |
| Juan Rana: | Viendo si es que un zarambeque[25] también como yo le baila. |
| Juan Ranilla: | Pues la música le anime, y tóquele la guitarra. |

*(Canta la música y los dos bailan el zarambeque)*

| | |
|---|---|
| Música: | Los hijos al padre en las semejanzas, como en las mudanzas, se retratan siempre. Teque, teque, teque. |
| Cantando Juan Rana: | ¡Que se me parece, Ay, mi Juan Ranilla, en el zarambeque! |
| Escribano: | ¿Qué hacéis, alcaldes? |

*(Vuelven a hacer otra mudanza, y los seis alcaldes dejan las varas y bailan también)*

| | |
|---|---|
| Alcalde Primero: | ¡Querer parecer hoy de Juan Rana también retratos al vivo! |
| Juan Rana: | Vayan unas muecas. |
| Juan Ranilla: | Vayan. |

*(Hacen los dos las muecas y el escribano los imita)*

| | |
|---|---|
| Alcalde Segundo: | ¿Qué hacéis, escribano? |
| Escribano: | Ser de Juan Rana semejanza. |
| Juan Rana: | Digo que en todo es mi hijo, sin faltarle una migaja. |
| **Todos:** | Pues el natal se celebre de Juan Ranilla en Juan Rana. |

| | |
|---|---|
| **Escribano:** | ¿Con qué? |
| **Juan Rana:** | Con la conterilla |
| | con que un entremés se acaba. |
| **Cantando Mujer:** | Si los hombres parieran |
| | fuera gran cosa |
| | pues tuvieran por ciertas |
| | todas sus obras. |
| **Juan Rana:** | No hay duda pues que muchas |
| | mujeres vimos, que a mamar a otros padres |
| | los dan los hijos. |

*Don Pedro Francisco Lanini Sagredo.*

# Appendix 2A
## "Portrait of a Monster"

*Portrait of a Monster who was Conceived in the Body of a Man named Hernando de la Haba (habitant of Fereyra, Marquisate of Cenete) due to an evil potion that was given to him. The midwife Francisca de León helped him deliver the newborn through his posterior part on June 1, 1606. Composed by Pedro Manchego, habitant of Granada.* Printed with License in Barcelona by Sebastián de Cormellas al Call. 1606.

If you grant me silence and lend me your ear, I will describe such a case that will shock the world. Unlike vain orators, I will not tell flattery or fictions but rather a remarkable true story and one that has been proven to be true.

It is something never before seen and well worth telling and remembering for being so strange. It is true that there are some unbelievers who pride themselves on saying that these events are lies. Even so, I hope that my account will be so clear that it shows the world its truth. This has not happened in the New World nor in the Canary Islands, nor in the land of the Great Cayne nor even in Cyprus, Africa, and Asia.

In the heroic circle that encloses the Hispanic peninsula, near the illustrious city of Granada—in this city, there resides a merchant who, within Moorish quarters, is called Bartolomé de Mestança. This man typically comes each year to the Alpuxarras region to collect payments for debts made on credit. On the 21st of June of this year (1606), the above-mentioned merchant left to collect his payments and in the place that I will reveal, this same day he was doing business, walking along with a bailiff and a notary going to homes to carry out his tasks.

While walking down a street, they heard such frightful and pitiful shouts, enough to disturb Nature herself. They went there and asked what was happening and a young girl answered: "Sirs, it's my father; he is giving birth." "Little girl, are you saying that your father is in labor?" And to find out for himself he entered the house. They saw a man seated on a chair and a woman at his feet to help him with the delivery. The old, distressed woman coached him: "Push, sir, for if we wait, the baby will suffocate." They were all anxiously watching when, with a big moan, a diabolical creature was yanked out from the bowels of the poor fellow.

It had barely fallen into the basin when it scratched the midwife's face with its nails. "Good God," said the upset and confused old woman, "without a doubt, this is the devil himself—he shows it through his arrogance." They put the fierce monster in a bowl of water in order to better examine his body. And, after observing his shape and appearance, they certified what I am about to write.

It had the leg and calf of a man, and in one foot it had four long nails; in the other, no one could figure it out, because there was nothing. Half its body was that of a goose, and it had the back of a porcupine, the tail of a tortoise, and its sex, only the devil knows.

It had the neck and ears of a horse, and the big eyes of an ox; it had a snout, and its tongue hung out. It had the looks and condition of a rabid dog. If I have missed anything in my description, someone else can examine it as well.

After having stared at it, everyone was scandalized and amazed by such a frightful spectacle. Some said it was a demon; others, that it was so evil that everyone was horrified by its demonic figure. It didn't live more than an hour and a half, and during that time it squawked like a sucking pig swishing water with its tail. They took sworn statements and the midwife, when pressed, declared that the man had delivered it through his posterior part. The merchant testified to this and then drew a picture of the monster in order to verify this case in Granada. And if you are not too weary you can learn other details of this pregnant man (or pregnant woman) in the next ballad.

## SECOND BALLAD

In the kingdom of Granada, in the famous bishopric of the city of Guadix in the rich marquisate that they call Cenete of the Duke of the Infantazgo, an event took place which I shall tell if you lend me your ear for just a moment. In this area there is a place called Pites de Fereya and it was there that this strange case occurred. There lived (and still lives) a pleasant, peaceful bachelor of little pretension. In his youth (blinded by his lust) he had a relationship for a few years with a woman from the village. He promised to marry her and they got engaged, so the landlady where she lived let him enter the house to visit her whenever he desired.

During this lengthy period he began to get bored and he changed his affections (since poor taste is tiresome). He (who once had been a prisoner of possessive love stronger than a rock) now repaid her with ingratitude. In the end he became ardently enamored of a woman from his neighborhood and quickly entered into marriage with her. The other woman found out and became crazy with jealousy, swearing to take revenge on her hostile enemy. The deceived woman lamented having been fooled by a man who had once been the very image of true love. A few days passed and the above-mentioned man became ill and sought a cure.

The other woman found out that he was sick and sought to take revenge for the past grudge. She revealed her bad intentions to an old sorceress and the old woman responded to her worries with great concern: "Don't be troubled, my child, I promise to avenge this betrayal since it is not right that affairs of dishonor go unaddressed. Decide what you can pay me and I promise to help you. I will even do it in a way such that he will always live in shame." "Mother, if you do this, I promise to pay you well for your efforts—so make sure that you don't miss the mark. For now, I will give you enough for a skirt and cloak, and if it seems too little, there is more where that came from." Seeing the incentive for her promises within her grasp, with much enthusiasm the old woman jumped at the offer, saying: "Well, that seems fine, but the most important part you will need to do, and then just leave the rest to me. Quickly bring me this errand and I promise to do something that will be much talked about. Secrecy is of the utmost importance, so seal your lips, for if anyone finds out, we will pay dearly. Now go in peace." The other woman responded, "Believe me, even if they rip me to shreds no one will learn anything from me; you need not worry."

The following day, all dressed up, the old woman went with a small gift to visit the sick man. "How are you, my neighbor?" He answered: "Very ill—only God knows what pain my soul has suffered." She spent a few hours talking to him, using loving words cloaked in deceit. She said: "I know of a potion that many others have taken and they have felt much better, and it is very easy to take. May God bless you and tomorrow I will return to see you, and what I bring will give you much relief." The old woman then made an evil potion and put it in a small glass which she brought carefully to the sick man.

The patient drank it like a man anxious to feel healthy again, not noticing whether it was sweet or bitter. Eventually, he got up, and although he could walk, he was upset, sad, pale, and weak. His belly swelled out and he walked around slowly and heavily. Some said he had a tropical fever, and others said it was his spleen. One day he told his wife: "I swear I must be pregnant because I can feel something jumping and kicking in my stomach." When his wife touched his belly, she said: "My God, you're right; there is no doubt that the devil himself has impregnated you." She told him to drink the juice from esparto grass for three days so it would move whatever he had, and he agreed it was a good idea. He drank it and then one day he felt very fatigued; he grabbed his chest and nearly passed out. They called a midwife, who verified the pregnancy. He sat down and gave birth to what is described below.

## THIRD BALLAD

You will hear the end of the case if you listen carefully to the third part of this story. As I mentioned before, the man gave birth to a fierce monster, whose prodigious case shocked everyone.

They gave the new father some bread with honey and eggs, which he ate but later made him sick. The local authorities arrested the new father, taking him to Granada, as was required by law. The officers in Granada conducted an investigation expected of such a case. They took his confession and he explained how such a bewildering thing had happened. "It is true that I have given birth and since I delivered, I must have been pregnant, but by whom I do not understand. Don't ask me any more questions, I am resolved not to say more—even if I wanted to, I could not." They tightened the straps on him and he continued to say it was true "that even if you kill me I won't say more on the subject." Eventually they found out that at one time he had had a lover, so they sent for her.

Once she arrived, they questioned her under torture, and she confessed the truth about the pregnancy in detail, implicating the old lady as the real author of the crime. Now knowing the truth, they immediately went for the old woman. When she arrived, she was confused and frightened, and even without force, she confessed more than they asked. She said that she made an evil potion and gave it to the sick man, having been persuaded by his ex-girlfriend (as I explained earlier). She revealed what was in the potion, but since it is so dirty and repulsive, I will not mention it (though God knows I could). They let the man go free because the officials saw that, since he was innocent, he did not deserve to be punished.

## FOURTH BALLAD

Take note of the punishment of the women described in the fourth ballad, which you will soon learn if you pay attention. Having investigated and obtained a confession, they punished the guilty parties accordingly.

Saturday, the 19th of August, they charged the two women, who accepted and confirmed the sentence without appeal. On the 21st day of the same month, on Monday at 10:30, the Inquisition paraded out the old witch, riding on a donkey and wearing a *coroza* (mitre) on her head, sitting proud and tall while the crowd applauded and cheered. Accompanied by many onlookers, they arrived to the Vivarambla, where all the young men were involved in wild celebrations.

So many yellow peppers, eggplants, and melon rinds were thrown that you couldn't recognize the old woman. Some were tossed at her face, others at her head, but her ribs (which were riper than a fig) caught the rest. She told them, swearing to God: "Only scoundrels would do this; if I could get down I would teach you some respect and some shame." They crossed the Zacatín and arrived at the new square, moving toward the Elvira entrance on the right side of the street. They arrived at the site for the burning, where the executioner lowered the old woman and tied her to a stake in the ground. She soon choked, and when the wood got closer and hit her, it burned with a violent fury.

And so they turned the fraudulent old woman into ashes, since it is only right that whoever sins must pay. On another day, they gave the other woman a deserved lashing,[1] and with a payment of two hundred[2] they exiled her from the city.

Men, open your eyes and do not trust evil women since what they have to offer is bought at a high price. They are little worms like leeches that suck the blood from your soul and your conscience. They are poisonous snakes; they are false and full of flattery, and the more attractive woman is but a basilisk. Take heed that they do not make you give birth like the witch did to this man. May you all learn from his mistake.

# Appendix 2B

*Retrato de un monstruo, que se engendró en un cuerpo de un hombre, que se dice Hernando de la Haba, vecino del lugar de Freyra, Marquesado de Cenete, de unos hechizos que le dieron. Parteole Francisca de León, comadre de parir, en veinte y uno de Junio, de 1606 por la parte tras ordinaria compuestas por Pedro Manchego, vecino de Granada. Impresas con Licencia, en Barcelona en casa Sebastián de Cormellas al Call. Año MDCVI.*

Oy si me prestan silencio
y auditorio a mis palabras
pienso declarar un caso
que es caso que al mundo espanta.
No quan vanos oradores
diré lisonjas, ni fábulas,
sino una verdad notable,
y por verdad aprovada.
Una cosa nunca vista
digna de ser memorada,
y de tener en memoria
por ser una cosa estraña.
Aunque es verdad que ay algunos
incrédulos que se jatan
de dezir, que son mentiras
estos sucesos que pasan.
Pero con todo pretendo
será de tanta eficacia
mi obra, que dará al mundo
crédito por ser tan clara.
No ha sucedido en las Indias,
ni en las islas de Canaria,
ni en la tierra del gran Cayre,
ni en Chipre Africa y Asia.
En el cercuyto heroyco,
que encierra la Isla Hispana
junto a una insigne ciudad,
que se intitula Granada.
En esta ciudad reside
un mercader que se llama
dentro del Alcayzería
Bartolomé de Mestança.
Este acude de ordinario
cada año a las Alpuxarras,
a cobrar algunas deudas
de muchas cosas fiadas.
A veynte y uno de Junio
deste año que se halla,
por cuenta mil y seys cientos
y seys, según se declara.
Salió el dicho mercader
para hazer sus cobranças
y en el lugar que diré
este propio día estava.
Ocupado en sus negocios
con un Alguazil andava,
y un escrivano haziendo
execución por las casas.
Pasando por una calle
oyen vozes temerarias,

que rompen los elementos
con grandes lástimas dadas.
Llegan preguntas ques esto,
y responde una muchacha,
mi padre es que esta pariendo
señores, que es lo que mandan.
Pues tu padre ha de parir
que es lo que dizes rapaza,
y por informarse bien
mas adelante se lança.
Vieron a un hombre sentado
en una silla, y sentada
una mujer a sus pies,
que en tal trance le ayudava.
Empuge señor le dize
la vieja muy angustiada,
no ahogue la criatura,
que el peligro es la tardança.
Estando atentos mirando
con un gemido se arranca,
de las entrañas del triste
esta figura endiablada.
Apenas huvo caydo
quando del barreño falta,
y a la comadre le asió
con las uñas en la cara.
Santo Dios dize la vieja
confusa y atribulada,
este sin duda es diablo
bien lo muestra en su arrogancia.
Pusieron al monstruo fiero
en un librillo de agua
para conocer mejor
sus partes proporcionadas.
Y desque huvieron mirado
su figura y semejança,
certificaron ser esta
que ya mi pluma relata.
Pierna y pantorrilla de hombre,
y en el pie quatro uñas largas,
y el otro nadie puede
juzgarle, porque no es nada.
El medio cuerpo de ganso
de puerco espino la espalda,
de galápago la cola,

la natura entienda Bargas.
El pescueço de cavallo
y orejas la misma traça,
los ojos grandes de buey
hozico y lengua sacada.
De traça y suerte de un perro
quando de corage rabia,
si yerro en algo, otro puede
juzgarlo si en ello ay falta.
Después que hubieron mirado
la gente escandalizada,
deste espectáculo fiero,
se estava maravillada.
Unos dizen es demonio,
otros es cosa tan mala,
que a todos nos pone espanto
su figura endemoniada.
No vivió mas de hora y media
y en este tiempo graznava,
a modo de un lechoncillo
dando al agua coleadas.
Tomaron le juramento
y la comadre apremiada,
declaró, que le parió
por la parte extraordinaria.
Pidió testimonio desto
el mercader y retrata,
en un papel este monstruo
por dar dello fe en Granada.
Lo demás que sucedió
deste preñado, o preñada,
en el segundo Romance
lo verán sino se cansan.

### SEGUNDO ROMANCE

En el Reyno de Granada
en el famoso Obispado
de la Ciudad de Guadix
en el rico Marquesado,
que le llaman de Cenete
del Duque del Infantazgo
sucedió lo que dire,
si atención prestan un rato.
En esta tierra que digo

ay un lugar ques llamado
Pites de Fereyra, allí
sucedió este caso estraño.
Vivió y vive en el lugar
que al presente he declarado,
un hombre apacible, afable
de trato senzillo y llano.
Estando en su juventud
tuvo amistad ciertos años
con una muger del pueblo
ciego del amor liviano.
Prometióle casamiento,
dándole palabra y mano,
y la muger en su casa
le dio entrada y paso franco.
En este tiempo prolixo
causó molestia este estado,
y el hombre mudo de gusto
porque el mal gusto es enfado.
Pagó con la ingratitud
el que antes avia estado,
con mas firmeza que un risco,
preso del amor tyrano.
Al fin le cobro afición
a una muger de su barrio,
y el casamiento se hizo
con fervor y no despacio.
Vino a oydos del amiga,
y ella de zelos rabiando,
juró de tomar vengança
de su enemigo contrario.
Sintió la burlada dama
el averla ansí burlado,
el que primero avia sido
de su amor vivo retrato.
Pasaronse algunos días
y el hombre que aquí he nombrado,
de una enfermedad estuvo
de salud necesitado.
El amiga que lo supo
que estaba de salud falto,
procuró tomar vengança
de los enojos pasados.
A una vieja hechizera
le descubrió el pecho falso,

y la vieja le responde
solicita de sus cuydados.
No os aflijáis hija mía,
que prometo de vengaros,
porque un negocio de honra
no es bien que se pase en blanco.
No es razón que vuestro honor
ansí quede ultrajado,
y que aquel que mal pago os dio
es bien se le de mal pago.
Mirad que me quereys dar
y prometo de ayudaros,
que yo haré de manera
que viva siempre afrentado.
Si lo hazeys madre mía
prometo gratificaros,
vuestro trabajo, y afe,
que no echeys el lance en vano.
Desde aquí os prometo dar
para una saya y un manto
y si os pareciere poco
no faltara mas que daros.
Viendo el cebo entre las uñas
a la promesa aplicado,
con grande liberaleza
la vieja acude al reclamo.
Diziendo: Pues eso basta,
mas falta lo necesario,
y esto vos lo aveys de hazer,
lo de mas quede a mi cargo.
Andad con Dios, y traedme
en breve aqueste recado,
y prometo de hazer
un hecho que sea sonado.
El secreto es la importancia
pone a la boca un candado,
que si se viene a saber
hemos de pagar el pato.
Creedme señora dixo,
que aunque me hagan pedaços,
nadie lo sabrá de mi,
en eso perded cuydado.
Llegando el día siguiente
la vieja tocada a papos
fue a visitar al enfermo

con un pequeño regalo.
Como esta señor vezino?
el le respondió: Muy malo,
sabe Dios si lo he sentido,
en el alma me ha pesado.
Estuvo algunas horas
con el enfermo hablando,
con palabras amorosas
doradas con el engaño.
Dixo, Yo se un bevedizo
que otros muchos lo han tomado,
y se han sentido mejores
y es muy fácil de tomarlo.
Quedad con Dios que mañana
yo bolveré a visitaros,
y os traeré, que pretendo,
que sentireys gran descanso.
La vieja hizo un hechizo
y en un pequeñuelo vaso,
al enfermo lo llevo
otro día con recato.
El dicho enfermo lo beve
como el que esta deseando
la salud, que no repara,
en lo que es dulce o amargo.
Pero al fin se levantó,
y aunque andava levantado
andava triste, afligido
sin color pálido y flaco.
Hinchósele la barriga,
andava lerdo y pesado,
unos le dizen que es trópico,
otros dizen, que del baço.
Dixo un día a su muger
vive Dios que estoy preñado,
porque en la barriga siento
que me dan brincos y saltos.
Tentóle pues la muger
y dixo, por Dios hermano,
que teneys razón, no ay duda,
qual diablo os ha empreñado.
Aconsejóle que tome
tres días aguas de esparto,
porque mueva lo que tiene,
y el dixo, será acertado.

Tomólas y un cierto día
sintiéndose muy fatigado,
cubriósele el coraçon,
dieronle grandes desmayos.
Llamaron a la comadre,
y certificó ser parto,
sentóse y parió con el
lo que aquí esta retratado.

## TERCER ROMANCE

El fin de toda esta historia
oyrán si prestan silencio
adelante en el discurso
deste Romance tercero.
Parió como tengo dicho
el hombre este monstruo fiero
de cuyo prodigioso caso
quedaron todos suspensos.
Hizieronle a este parido
torrijas con miel y huevos,
comiólos, pero después
le hizieron mal provecho.
La justicia del lugar
pone al parido hombre preso,
remetiéndolo a Granada,
como es razón de derecho.
Los señores de Granada
guardando justicia hizieron
las diligencias cumplidas,
que requiere tal exceso.
Tomáronle confesión
y respondió al pedimento,
que no sabe de que suerte
sucedió este desconcierto.
Es verdad que yo he parido,
y pues que parí pretendo,
que devía estar preñado:
pero de quien no lo entiendo.
No me pidan otra cosa
en aquesto me resuelvo,
no piense declarar mas
porque aunque quiera no puedo.
Apriétanle los cordeles
y dixo lo dicho es cierto,

aunque me maten señores
no he de dezir mas, ni menos.
Al fin fueron informados,
que tuvo el hombre en un tiempo
una amiga, y siendo así
embiaron por ella al pueblo.
Siendo venida el amiga
la pusieron a tormento,
y en su dicho declaró
el preñado por estenso.
Y a la vieja condenó
que fue autor deste enredo,
y sabiendo la verdad
van por la vieja al momento.
Siendo la vieja venida
confusa llena de miedo,
sin apremiarla declara
mucho mas que le pidieron.
Dixo, que hizo un hechizo
y se lo dio estando enfermo,
persuadida de su amiga
como atrás dixe primero.
Declaróles el hechizo
mas por ser tan suzio y feo,
lo dexo pasar en blanco,
que sabe Dios mi deseo.
Al hombre dieron por libre,
porque los señores vieron,
que no merece castigo
por ser innocente desto.

## QUARTO ROMANCE

El castigo que se dio
a las mugeres se advierta,
que en este quarto Romance,
lo sabrán si atención prestan.
Hecha pues la información
y la confesión ya hecha,
de los dichos delinquentes
retificados en ella.
El Sábado es diez y nueve
de Agosto, a las dos condenan
y ellas consienten y otorgan
sin apelar la sentencia.

A veynte y uno del dicho,
Lunes a las diez y media,
de la Inquisición sacaron
a la vieja hechizera.
Cavallera en un borrico,
con una coroça puesta,
con grande aplauso y trofeo
bien repatingada y tiesa.
Acompañada de muchos
a la Vivarambla llegan,
donde todos los mochachos
tuvieron alarde y fiesta.
Tanto pepino amarillo
tanto de berengenas,
de cortezas de melón
no se parece la vieja.
Qual le sacude en la cara,
qual le da en la cabeça,
paráronle las costillas
mas maduras que una breva.
Dize jurando la Cruz,
bellacos pues para esta,
que si me apeo que os haga
tener respeto y verguença.
Traviesan el Zacatín,
llegan a la plaça nueva,
van azia la puerta de Elvira
toda la calle derecha.
Llegaron al quemadero
adonde la vieja apea
el verdugo y la arrimó
a un palo que estava en tierra.
Ahógala en breve espacio,
y acercándole la leña
le pego y ardió
con una furia violenta.
Y así hizieron ceniza
a la vieja fraudalenta,
que quien haze mal que pague
que es muy justo que así sea.
A la amiga a otro día
danle un jubón para cuenta,
y con dozientos cruzados
de la ciudad la destierran.
Abrid los ojos señores

no os fieys de malas hembras
la que mejor cara os haze
os vende en buena almoneda.
Mirad que son gusanillos
del alma y de la conciencia,
que os van chupando la sangre
qual haze la sanguijuela.
Son víboras ponçoñosas

son falsas y lisongeras,
es basilisco en los ojos
la que mejor rostro os muestra.
Guardad no os hagan parir
como hizo esta alcagüeta
a este hombre, escarmentad
todos en cabeça agena.

**FIN**

# Notes

## INTRODUCTION

1. For a fascinating study of Cosme Pérez and the queer factor in various interludes, see Thompson, *The Triumphant Juan Rana*. For a more general yet thorough study of Juan Rana, see Sáez Raposo.

2. Sáez Raposo dates *El parto de Juan Rana* between 1653 and 1658 (68). While early modern conceptions of same-sex desire between men tended to focus more on behavior and specific acts such as sodomy (compared to a post-nineteenth-century "identity-based" definition of homosexuality), there are many cultural references during the sixteenth and seventeenth centuries that imply more than just criminal sexual activity when referring to men who desire other men (such as attraction, intimacy, flirtation, and so forth). Various early modern terms and associations related to desire between men are discussed in Chapter 4.

3. This text is reproduced and translated in Appendix II.

4. See Riddle.

5. See Ibero, 103–5, and Perry, *Gender,* 40–42.

6. "It's Still a Man's World on the Idiot Box," a telling editorial published in the *New York Times* on December 2, 2004, reveals how pervasive the issues invoked by male pregnancy are today. When Maureen Dowd protests the race and sex discrimination in news coverage (the "white guy anchor" tradition), she cites a comment made by her mother: " 'If men could figure out how to have babies, they'd get rid of us altogether.' " Furthermore, Dowd's editorial also considers the impact of women's reproductive issues on their professional successes: "And then there's biology. Asked why there couldn't be an anchorette as we enter 2005, Brokaw, the father of three accomplished daughters and the husband of one strong, cool wife replied: 'You know, honestly, what happens is career interruptus by childbirth and a couple of other things. It's unfair to women that they have to juggle all this stuff, but it plays some role, I think.' "

## CHAPTER 1

1. Even in the age of paternity tests that can confirm or refute the mother's "word" about the biological father's identity, paternity-related anxieties are still cited among the fears of "expectant fathers." In Jerrold Lee Shapiro's 1993 *When Men are*

*Pregnant*, for example, one of the "seven major fears of expectant fathers" involves questions of paternity (18–22). Shapiro divides this concern into two parts, "irrational fears" and "realistic issues," noting that "more than 50 percent of the men surveyed had acknowledged fleeting thoughts, fantasies, or nagging doubts that they might not really be the biological father of the child (18). The author attributes these "irrational fears" to insecurities and feelings of inadequacy, concluding that "the expectant father with paternity fears needs a generous portion of reassurance that he is loved, and that there is no other man in the picture" (20). Likewise, Shapiro explains the "realistic" concern of false paternity resulting from an extramarital affair in terms of the wife's anger at her husband "from a feeling of being rejected" (22). It might also be noted that "surprise" paternity testing has become a popular topic on certain "shock" television programs in the early twenty-first century.

2. See also Finucci, *Manly*, 39.
3. See Bynum, 147; Zapperi, 3–32; and Surtz, *Guitar*, 7, 45–46.
4. See also Finucci, *Manly*, 65–67.
5. Rael, 360–62, 761–62.
6. For an interesting study on the image of pregnant male poets and their brain-wombs in works written by men in the seventeenth and eighteenth centuries, see Stephanson.
7. See Huarte de San Juan.
8. "Desocupado lector: sin juramento me podrás creer que quisiera que este libro, como hijo del entendimiento, fuera el más hermoso, el más gallardo y más discreto que pudiera imaginarse. Pero no he podido yo contravenir al orden de naturaleza; que en ella cada cosa engendra su semejante. Y así ¿qué podrá engendrar el estéril y mal cultivado ingenio mío sino la historia de un hijo seco, avellanado, antojadizo y lleno de pensamientos varios y nunca imaginados de otro alguno" (50). Even the apocryphal version of the second part of *Don Quijote*, written by Alonso Fernández de Avellaneda (1614), concludes with a curious scene in which Don Quijote hires a young squire who suddenly gives birth in the middle of the street while the famous knight looks on with amazement at what he must initially assume to be a miraculous male delivery. Of course, the reader knows that the squire is actually a pregnant woman disguised in men's clothing:

> He took as his squire a 'working girl' . . . dressed like a man and was fleeing from her master because in his house she became, or they made her become pregnant unwittingly, although not because she didn't give plenty of cause for it. She was roaming around in fear, and the good knight took her without knowing she was a woman until she gave birth in the middle of the road and in his presence, leaving him highly astonished at the birth and imagining the wildest fancies about it (346).

> [Llevando por escudero a una moza de soldada . . . vestida de hombre, las cual iba huyendo de su amo porque en su casa se hizo o la hicieron preñada, sin pensarlo ella, si bien no sin dar cumplida causa para ello; y con el temor se iba por el

mundo. Llevóla el buen caballero sin saber que fuese mujer, hasta que vino a parir en medio de un camino, en presencia suya, dejándole sumamente maravillado el parto; y haciendo grandísimas quieras sobre él (462)].

While there is no doubt about the female identity of the childbearing squire, the visual impact (on the unsuspecting observer) of a male-attired individual suddenly giving birth may be even more shocking than the initial appearance of a man dressed as a woman in labor. Despite its comical intent, the passage also provides a glimpse into the fear and isolation that an unmarried pregnant woman with limited economic and social resources might have experienced during that time.

9. "¡ . . . Por lo que os toca de su humor y de su caballería! En mal punto os empreñastes de sus promesas, y en mal hora se os entró en los cascos la ínsula que tanto deseáis" (563). See also Ziomek, 115, and Río Parra, 149.

10. "He who easily believes what people tell him seems to be impregnated with words because he learns them and conceives them to the point that he completely ignores anything else" [El que fácilmente cree lo que le dizen parece empreñarse de palabras, porque las aprehende y concibe de manera que totalmente excluye lo contrario] (Covarrubias, *Tesoro*, 509). See also Velasco, "Reading."

11. "—Yo no estoy preñado de nadie—respondió Sancho—, ni soy hombre que me dejaría empreñar, del rey que fuese" (563).

12. For an interesting discussion of "procreative sodomy" see Knight.

13. " 'No, por cierto, señor; no tengo tal, ni aun me pasa por pensamiento.' Respondió: 'No os pregunto si habéis parido' " (210–11).

14. Some critics suggest that Pelling's story inspired both Dryden's plot and a passage in Alexander Pope's *Rape of the Lock* in which Belinda dreams of pregnant men (Cody, 91).

15. Even Angelo symbolically appropriates images of pregnancy: "Angelo finds the overwhelming presence of his bodily parents in 'the strong and swelling evil/ of [his] conception'; swollen with this conception, he replicates the swelling both of phallic potency and of pregnancy, hence reproduces within himself the downright way he was conceived . . . as he becomes equivalent to Juliet, female and soiled, pregnant with his own sexuality" (Adelman, 93).

16. James Joyce in *Ulysses* seems to take male maternity as literary metaphor one step further, as Leopold Bloom appears to experience pregnancy and childbirth through his role in the mystical rebirth of Stephen. Jeanne Perreault describes this miraculous event in terms of Joyce's own creative power, which consequently "dispenses with the need for a female participant in what he sees as the quintessential creative act" (304).

Writers have continued to use the pregnancy metaphor for linguistic and literary efforts and at times staging elaborate birthing scenes to represent the climatic moment when their writing comes together. In Robert S. Phillips's 1978 collection of poetry titled *The Pregnant Man*, for example, the poet ("the world's first pregnant man!" [32]) uses images of labor pain and delivery to express the discomfort, suffering, and eventual release from "birthing" a poem. Documenting the hours that pass during all stages of childbirth, the poet employs the typical stereotypes of the chaos surrounding the period when the water breaks until the actual birth, which is described in the following verses:

> [ . . . ] clutching
> the bedpost, screaming
> between gold inlays,
> a duck squeezing out
> a Macy's Thanksgiving Day
> parade balloon, gave birth
> to an eight-pound blue
> -eyed bouncing baby
> poem. Spanked it to life,
> lay back and had a drink. (32–34)

17. See also Gassier and Wilson, 339, and Río Parra, 149.

18. Needless to say, Freudians have been interpreting mock male birthing desires and rituals in numerous ways. For example, Theodor Reik (one of Freud's early students) "suggested that the process of 'pseudo-maternal' couvades could be understood in terms of unconscious sadistic urges against the mother . . . Thus, a man imposes on himself the pain he wishes for his partner, who in turn symbolizes his mother" (Reed, 51).

19. See "A Gallery of Pregnant Men" (www.sscnet.ucla.edu/ioa/arnold/arnold-webpages/pregmen.htm), and Mathews and Wexler, 206.

20. See Emery.

21. See also Gilbert, "Masculine," 171.

22. See Sawday.

23. I would like to thank the co-writer and director Joan Lipkin for sharing the script and videotape of the performance.

24. I would like to thank my colleague Susan Larson for bringing this short to my attention.

25. See www.haymotivo.com/en/shorts.html.

26. "Dames at Sea," September 25, 2003 [Season 6].

27. "The Unsinkable Mommy Adler," February 9, 1999 [Season 1].

28. "Moveable Feast," November 22, 2001 [Season 4].

29. "William, Tell," November 9, 1998 [Season 1]. In "Hey La, Hey La, My Ex-boyfriend's Back" (March 14, 2000 [Season 2]), Will reprimands Grace for not protecting him from his ex-boyfriend, joking, "Nice job of protection, Grace. If you were a condom, I'd be pregnant." Likewise, in "Cop to It" (aired on January 26, 2006 [Season 8]) when Will runs into his ex-boyfriend (and after a discussion of their friend's possible pregnancy) Grace jokes: "I think Will's water just broke."

30. "Seeds of Discontent," January 25, 2000 [Season 2]; "Marry Me a Little," November 21, 2002 [Season 5].

31. See Greer and www.leighboweryfilm.com/productionnotes.

32. I would like to thank José Cartagena-Calderón for this reference. See also

www.leighbowery.com.br/portal/default.asp. For photographs of Bowery's designs that imply male pregnancy, see Greer, 40–41 and 93–95.

CHAPTER 2

1. For a look at the frequency of the biological metaphor to describe an author and his work as father and son, see Montauban, 12–13.

2. "Se empeña y pare y tiene hijos y nietos . . . se llaman genios por ser fecundos en producir y engendrar conceptos tocantes a ciencia y sabiduría" (Huarte, 188–89).

3. For a discussion of the political symbolism of the *vara* see Martínez Repoll.

4. Given the sexual indeterminacy of the hermaphrodite in general and the confusion created by heterobiased assumptions, it may not be surprising that the 1651 Inquisitional case against Francisco Roca involved a dozen conflicting testimonies regarding the defendant's anatomical identity and consequent sexual practices. Like the confused legalities related to Juan Rana's case in *El parto*, some witnesses testified that Roca was a man who slept with other men; others claimed he was a woman who dressed as a man and had clandestine sexual relations with men; and yet others swore that he was a hermaphrodite with functioning genitals of both sexes. It was eventually determined that Roca was a man with no genital irregularities and that, while the medical examination showed that his anus concaved inward a bit more than normal, the muscles were firm and tight as expected (Carrasco, 146–48).

5. For the *marimacho* (masculine woman) association with the name Aldonza, see Gossy and Redondo.

6. I would like to thank Luis Corteguera and Marta Vicente for this reference.

7. "Cansada cosa es haber de andar siempre con la vara, o el azote en la mano, para que el siervo, o el criado haga lo que la razón pide y su amo le manda" (Covarrubias, *Emblemas*, 176v). See also Martínez Ripoll, 67, 78.

8. See note 9 from the English translation, "John Frog Gives Birth," in the Appendix. It should also be mentioned that the figure of the small-town mayor (with authorial staff in hand) on the early modern Spanish stage frequently was designed for comic effect: "More often than not, when a mayor appears on stage, it is to evoke laughter" [Las más veces, cuando aparece el alcalde sobre el escenario, lo hace para provocar la risa] (Salomon, 91).

9. See Zapperi and Finnucci, *Manly*.

10. See also Rodríguez-Cuadros, 273.

11. See Fraenger, 335.

12. "Recordemos que rana es nombre genérico de prostitutas, mujeres libres y dueñas" (153).

13. See also Delpech, 576.

14. "Con su cuerpo tan redondo e hinchado, la cabezota grande, hasta una vaga sugestión de joroba, realmente tiene figura de rana" (67).

15. See Thompson, *Triumphant*. In fact, Vélez-Quiñones has suggested that perhaps the "best translation for Juan Rana is John Fag or John Faggot" (comment to the author, June 22, 2004).

16. "La sexualidad 'nefanda' de don Diego queda todavía más patente cuando en

medio de una discusión éste le reprocha a su rival, don Juan: '[u]sted me tiene por rana,' . . . alusión que en el contexto de esta pieza el público de entonces no hubiera tenido la menor dificultad de asociarla con la figura teatral de Juan Rana" (Cartagena-Calderón, "Rara," 166). Harry Vélez-Quiñones, on the other hand, argues that "Don Diego is actually saying: 'Do you think I am lame?' but also in the context of his identity as a 'lindo': 'Do you take me for a faggot?' He predicates his masculinity on having the accoutrements of a 'caballero': a sword, a gun, and two able hands ready for combat. It does not seem to me that 'rana' here is first and foremost an allusion to Juan Rana. However, it is pretty clear that the 'rana' in Juan Rana is synonymous with irregular sexuality, homoerotic practices, sodomy, queerness, etc." (comment to the author, June 22, 2004).

17. See Rossi, 61, and Martin, 156.

18. See Canavaggio.

19. "Dicen que no deben representar mugeres, porque en actos tan públicos con su desenvoltura provocan a pecado, y que si en lugar de ellas entraren muchachos en hábito de muger, no vayan con afeite o compostura deshonesta, parece al Consejo que es de mucho menos inconveniente, que mugeres representen, que muchachos en hábito de mugeres aunque no se afeiten" (cited in Cotarelo y Mori, *Bibliografía*, 164). See also Restrepo.

20. "Ay algunos hombres tan deshonestos y mal disciplinados que han dado en otro desuario: vistiendose y disfrazandose con ropas de mugeres. No conociendo el bien que de Dios han recebido, por aver los hecho varones: cosa en la humana naturaleza tan señalada y aventajada . . . mas aun havias de considerar, quantas mugeres havrá en lel mundo, que darian cuanto tuviesen por ser hombre como tu, y tener la libertad que tienes?" (Trujillo, 92–93)

21. "Dexa hermano por tu vida tales trajes, averguénzate de tales vestidos: que son muestra de poca honra y de gran liviandad y aun son insignias y reclamo de torpedades y vicios" (94).

22. See Lobato, 187–88. Interestingly, Lobato excludes any mention of Pérez's arrest for sodomy from her otherwise inclusive description of the actor's life.

23. "El hundimiento del cuello, los perfiles gruesos de toda la fisonomía que se acentúa en la curvatura del vientre, la cortedad de miembros, la mirada caída, los belfos insinuados" (Rodríguez Cuadros, 273). See also Bass.

24. See Restrepo.

25. "Ajustar determinadas desventajas físicas para una habilísima construcción de una máscara" (Rodríguez Cuadros, 273).

26. "Suelen estos que se precisan aquí de lindos, y relindos juntar a estas mujeriles afeminaciones, otra no menos digna, no sé si diga de risa, o escarnio; esto es hablar afeminado con voz y tono fingido, alternando las dicciones, trocando la s en z, y la z en s, y la j en h, y otras afectaciones culpables . . . Eres (dize) boquimuelle, tienes la lengua afeminada, quien lo oye así hablar dirá que es muger sin duda" (Jiménez Patón, *Discurso*, 32–32v).

27. "En ningún lugar se puede más bien conocer los hombres envanecidos, que en las barberías mirando los Ganímedes, y Narcisos, que teniendo paciencia para ponerse dos horas en manos de un barbero, con tan exquisita diligencia quieren

ser afeitados, y gastan más tiempo en hacerse la barba, torcerse el bigote, levantar el copete, y peinar las guedexas, ampollar los cogotes, que la más hermosa dama en componer la cabeza ... cualquiera pelillo, que sobrepuje a salga desmandado de entre los otros o que esté un poco torcido juzgan que les haze parecer feos demonios" (26v–27). See also Terrón González.

28. See also Martín's discussion of *El amante liberal*; Heiple, "Góngora"; and De Armas.

29. See Cartagena-Calderón, Stroud, and Heiple, "*Lindo*"

30. See also Rodríguez Cuadros,468.

31. Peter Thompson also dates *El parto* to sometime around the 1660s (*Triumphant*).

32. "La mujer enojada, y aun sin enojarse, no sabe guardar secreto" (Covarrubias, *Tesoro*, 340).

33. "El hombre que anda metido con mujeres y gusta sólo de la conversación de unas y de otras, por entretenerse, es mucho de viejos o de hombres fríos y maricones" (340). Covarrubias defines *maricón* as "el hombre afeminado que se inclina a hazer cosas de muger, que llaman por otro nombre marimaricas" (the effeminate man who tends to do womanly activities and who is also called a sissy) (790).

34. "La mujer fría y húmeda en el primer grado, cuyas señales dijimos que eran ser avisada, de mala condición, con voz abultada, de pocas carnes, verdinegra, vellosa y fea. Esta se empreñará fácilmente de un hombre nescio, bien acondicionado, que tuviere la voz blanda y melosa, muchas carnes, blancas y blandas, con poco vello" (Huarte, 624).

35. "Inhábil para engendrar. Estos no son muy amigos de las mujeres ni las mujeres de ellos" (622).

36. Interestingly, there is a joke based on "male" vs. "mail" delivery in the feature film *Rabbit Test* when a postage stamp is created in the likeness of the world's first pregnant man.

37. See also Pomata, 113, 120–21.

38. Like Juan Rana's reference to "wind eggs" (*hupenemia*) that are produced without male involvement, Aristotle, Virgil, and Pliny wrote of mares who were impregnated by the wind (Finucci, *Manly*, 51–52; Laquer, 58; and Saintyves, 74).

39. When discussing the political-sexual caricatures explicit in prints during the French Revolution, Vivian Cameron shows how "when reproduction is depicted, the imagery is that of the immaculate conception" (98). In a political image curiously similar to Juan Rana's birthing scene, a very masculine woman (perhaps a man in women's clothing) "standing up and effortlessly giving birth to an immediately ambulant child" (98), who emerges from his mother's skirt. Cameron also analyzes other imagery of the Revolution, in which the reproductive capabilities of women are appropriated by men as a way of emasculating the constitution and its founders (96–100).

40. "Las mismas ansias y náuseas que sienten las mugeres preñadas ... se sintió con dolores de parto, a cuya fuerça parió de un muslo un infante perfecto y verdadero" (Rivilla Bonet y Pueyo,78). See also Río Parra, 149.

41. For a study of dance in early modern Spain, see Brooks. For a study of music in theatre of the same time, see Stein.

42. Interestingly, Juan Rana is also holding a frog in his hand in his portrait (see Figure 6).

43. "También se cuenta por ahí que una señora parió un hijo más moreno de lo que convenía por estar imaginando en un rostro negro que estaba en un guadamecil, lo cual tengo por gran burla; y si por ventura fue verdad que lo parió, yo digo que el padre que lo engendró tenía el mesmo color que la figura del guadamecil" (Huarte, 653).

44. "Si la simiente del padre vence del todo, saca el hijo su figura y costumbres; y cuando la simiente de la madre es más poderosa, corre la mesma razón. Por donde el padre que quisiere que su hijo se haga de su propia simiente, se ha de ausentar algunos días de su mujer y aguardar que se cueza y madure, y entonces es cierto que él hará la generación y la simiente de su mujer servirá de alimento" (669).

45. "Para que al adultero corra dicha obligación de restituir, ha de tener certeza moral, de que la criatura es suya; y si hay duda igual de qual de dos sea, siendo ciertos moralmente, que de uno de los dos, entrambos deben restituir por iguales partes, y si la duda es con el marido, debe pagar la mitad" (Galindo, 457).

46. "No estar el hijo adulterino obligado a creer a la madre, que le descubre su adulterio, salvo si le convencieren las razones que le diere, o circunstancias que concurriesen, como si recibidos los Sacramentos a la hora de la muerte lo jurasse, o fuese convencido de testigos fidedignos aver estado su padre putativo ausente al tiempo de su concepción" (457).

47. "Y a éstos, cuando se fueron, les di a entender que quedaba preñada, que soy gran mujer de fingir vómitos, que me toman desmayos, y quitárseme la gana de comer, antojárseme de lo uno y de lo otro" (Quevedo, 20). See also Huerta Calvo, 70.

## CHAPTER 3

1. The issue of how artists could or should represent the origin of Mary's pregnancy is treated in Alfonso X's Cantiga 306. The miracle tells what happened to a heretic who, upon seeing a painting of a visibly pregnant Mary, expressed disbelief in the Immaculate Conception (since "the painter who painted it was such a good artist that he made it seem that when the angel saluted Her, She became pregnant at once. Therefore, he made Her abdomen look enlarged" [371]. "E tan bon maestre era o pintor que a pintou, / que fezo que semellasse que quando a saudou / o angeo, como logo atan toste s'enprennou; / e poren lle fez o ventre mui creçudo parecer" [109]).

2. In Cantiga 86 of Alfonso X's *Cantigas*, for example, the artists depict a pregnant woman who is forced to give birth under water (after being trapped by the rising tide when crossing over to pray at a shrine). Here Mary performs the role of midwife to prevent both mother and newborn from drowning. This miracle is also treated in Gonzalo de Berceo's *Milagros de Nuestra Señora* number 19. See also Scarborough, "Virgin."

3. "Mas mal conorto dun fillo prendeu/ que del avia, que a fez prennada" (Alfonso X, *Cantigas*, 102).

4. "Mas depois pariu / un fill,' e u a nenguu non viu / mató-o dentr' en sa cas' ensserrada" (102).

5. Medieval civil law condemned incest and punished those guilty of the crime:

when a man knowingly commits the sin of licentiousness with one of his female relatives . . . and the fact is proved in court by credible witnesses, or by the confession of the party; he must suffer the penalty for adultery. The women must also suffer the same penalty who knowingly commits this offense. (Alfonso X, *Partidas* [1931], page 1421, Partida VII, Title XVIII, Law III)

[Con su parienta o con su cuñada faciendo home pecado de luxuria a sabiendas . . . sil fuere probado en juicio por testigos que sean de creer o por su conoscimiento, debe haber pena de adulterio: et esa misma pena debe haber la muger que a sabiendas ficiese este pecado. (*Partidas* [1972], 660)]

Assuming that the son with whom she had sexual relations was over fourteen years of age (as stipulated by Partida VII, XVIII, II), both mother and son would receive the death penalty if the crime were discovered (*Partidas* [1931], 1421). Likewise, anyone guilty of infanticide

should be publicly scourged in the presence of all, and besides should be enclosed in a leather sack, along with a dog, a cock, a serpent, and an ape; and after he had been placed in it with these four animals the mouth of the sack should be sewed up, and they should all be thrown into the sea or into the river nearest to the place where this occurred. (*Partidas* [1931], 1349, VII, VIII, XII)

[Sea azotado ante todos publicamente, et desi que lo metan en un saco de cuero, et que encierren con él un can, et un gallo, et una coluebra et un ximio: et despues que él fuere en el saco con estas quarto bestias, cosan o aten la boca del saco, et échenlo en la mar o en el rio que fuere mas cerca de aquel lugar do esto acaesciere. (Partidas [1972], 571)]

Given the severe punishments for both crimes, it is interesting to discover that the murderous, incestuous mother in Cantiga 17 is not punished but protected by Mary, as the text redirects blame to the devil.

6. In this book, all English quotations from Alfonso X's *Las Siete Partidas* are from the 1931 Scott translation, and all Spanish quotations from the 1972 Real Academia de la Historia edition.

7. "Esa misma pena [muerte] decimos que debe haber el home que firiese a su muger a sabiendas seyendo ella preñada, de manera que se perdiese lo que tenie en el vientre por la ferida: et si otro home extraño lo ficiese, debe haber pena de homecida, si era via la criatura quando murió por culpa dél: et si non era aun viva, debe seer desterrado en alguna isla por cinco años" (570, VII, VIII, VIII).

8. Other Cantigas that treat pregnancy, childbirth, abortion, birth control, infant mortality, and infanticide include 306, 7, 55, 17, 201, 21, 43, and 184, as well as

Gonzalo de Berceo's *Milagro*, 21. See also Scarborough, "Virgin," "Verbalization," and *Women*, Diz, and Fidalgo Francisco.

9. In their study of the *Cantigas de Santa María*, John Esten Keller and Annette Grant Cash also comment on Alfonso's apparent benevolence toward women who would be judged sinful and criminal by both Church and State. In reference to incest in Cantiga 17, Keller and Cash argue that the "Church would have punished such a sin by execution, and the law of the land would have done the same; however, the Virgin forgives the sinful mother and saves her." Keller and Cash add that this attitude of forgiveness "strengthened the populace's concept that Alfonso, through his divine patroness, superseded the often harsh influence of the ecclesiastical hierarchy" (46). The authors also note Alfonso's own personal experience with reproduction and paternity: "The learned king fathered eleven legitimate and four attested illegitimate offspring. Quite probably there were others of the latter category from his youth spent in Galicia and in the army" (34).

10. "No sólo se halla sin el Niño en los brazos, mas aún sin haberle parido" (Pacheco, 576). See also Perry, *Gender*, 41.

11. While actual birthing scenes seemed to have diminished in early modern Spain, Renaissance Italy continued to depict childbirth in illustrations as well as in childbirth objects such as birthing trays and bowls. See Musacchio.

12. See also D'Ancona.

13. "Suélese poner en lo alto del cuadro Dios Padre, o el Espíritu Santo" (Pacheco, 577).

14. See Katz.

15. Joseph's metamorphosis in Counter-Reformation art is evident in seventeenth-century Spanish paintings such as Murillo's *Marriage of the Virgin* (Warner, 293).

16. The self-justification behind the fatalist tone explaining the need for male physicians to invade the female space of childbirth is also reflected in Núñez's complete title: "Book of Human Delivery which Contains very Useful Remedies for Women's Difficult Deliveries and Many other Secrets Relevant to this and to Children's Illnesses."

17. "Fue necessario por honestidad de dexar estas cosas en poder de muger" (7r).

18. For example, see Carbón, 32r, and Núñez ,17.

19. Bicks, 7.

20. In his study of Damián Carbón's text, Antonio Hernández Alcántara insists that the autor wrote his manual to "serve in the education of midwives" [servir a la educación de las 'comadres'] (312).

21. "Dícese tiene la Reina sospechas de preñada. Dios lo haga, y si ha de ser hija, ¿para qué la queremos? Mejor será que no lo esté, que mujeres hay hartas" (Barrionuevo, 1:61).

22. "Desde el domingo duerme el Rey con la Reina Dios les dé hijos de bendición para la quietud de España y defensa de la fe, y sobre todo paz, que es lo que por ahora nos conviene" (1:238).

23. "El domingo le vino el mes a la Reina, con que se anubló el preñado. No debe de estar de Dios que tenga hijos" (1:310).

24. "Hay ha entrado la Reina en nueve meses, y todo el preñado le ha pasado sin ansias, congojas ni bascas, como los pasados, de donde quieren inferir, por adular, los médicos y comadres, que tiene varón. Presto saldremos de este preñado" (2:108).

25. "La Reina tiene dieciocho días de falta. Paréceme que, según va, parirá cada año." (2:162).

26. "Hase hecho a posta para que vean todos que es hombre" (2:127).

27. Cabre, Montserrat, trans. "Public Record of the Labour of Isabel de la Cavalleria." Online Reference Book for Medieval Studies: www.the-orb.net/birthrecord.html.

28. Ibid.

29. See also López Terrada, 111–12.

30. "El arte de partear es la parte de la Cirugía que enseña los medicos conocidos con que se puede ayudar a la naturaleza para facilitar la expulsión de la criatura" (1).

31. "Fue instrumento de subordinación o sumisión más que de liberación, ya que lo utilizaron los cirujanos para su propia definición y ascenso profesionales y acabó expropiando a las matronas de su saber, de su lenguaje, de su culturas/s y, en definitivo, de gran parte de su poder social" (Ortiz, "Educación," 156). For a less sympathetic interpretation of early modern midwives, see Lanning, 298–303.

32. For a concise summary of ancient, medieval, and early modern theories on reproduction circulated in Spain, see Montauban, 22–46.

33. See Tuttle, 47, and Zoja, 122.

34. See Finucci, *Manly*.

35. "Las partes carnosas que se forman de la menstrual sangre, se perfeccionan en el varón al tercero mes, y en las hembras al quarto: y estando el feto perficionado, se anima, y empieza a moverse" (quoted in Granjel, 145).

36. "Avicena, cuya es esta doctrina, como Galeno, llama embrión a la criatura después de animada, porque si se formó a los treinta y cinco días muévese a los setenta de su concepción; . . . Si la criatura se formare a los cuarenta y cinco días, moveráse otros noventa días después y nacerá a los docientos y setenta y tanto días, que son los nueve meses ordinarios. . . . Galeno dice que en estando bien formada la criatura y que ni antes de los treinta días se puede causar aborto del varón entero, ni antes de cuarenta de la hembra, y esto cierto es, supuesto lo que él dice que antes de aquellos días no están enteros ni bien formados; . . . dice que el macho se mueve después de tres meses de su concebimiento y la hembra después de cuatro. . . . Dicen Aristóteles y S. Tomás, no ser el niño a los cuarenta días de su concebimiento, cuando se le infunde el anima racional, . . . mas de la niña dice que hasta entrar en el cuarto mes no tiene tal delineación, ni se le infunde hasta entonces el alma (y comunmente se tiene que a los ochenta días), y de las almas humanas concede en otra parte, conforme a la doctrina católica, no ser solamente engendradas por los padres, sino también entrar de fuera, que es por criación de solo Dios" (Pineda, 73).

37. "El feto tiene alma racional en el vientre de la madre, pues condena como homicidario al que haze abortar el feto *animado*" (Fuentelapeña, 226; italics mine).

38. See Pinto-Correia and Brockliss.

39. See also Stephanson, 102–5, and Sawday, *Body*, 230–70.

40. See Newman, *Fetal*, 7–27, and Petchesky. Georges and Mitchell also describe the photographs and illustrations in two popular books for expectant mothers (*Nine Months for Life* and *What to Expect When You're Expecting*): "Although it includes several pictures of the fetus and one of a newborn, *Nine Months for Life* does not include a single image of a woman. Nilsson completely erases women's bodies from his images; he pictures the fetus against an opaque and dark background. The illustrations in *What to Expect* do not so much erase the woman from pregnancy as they reduce her to a fetal environment or transparent fetal container. In this guide, descriptions of each month of pregnancy begin with a drawing of a headless, armless woman, her breast bared and her transparent torso containing only vagina, rectum, bladder, uterus, and fetus" (189).

41. Although the illustrations reproduced in the *Rosengarten* were widely distributed, Wendy Arons reminds us that they "did not reflect a contemporary understanding of anatomy." Both Leonardo da Vinci's detailed depictions of fetuses in the womb and Jane Sharp's illustrations depict more accurate portrayals of gestation (Arons, 17–18).

42. These early representations of the disembodied fetus are similar to how some anti-abortion activists today manipulate ultrasound images (visually disconnected from the woman's body) to establish the embryo with separate rights equal to if not greater than those of the woman. Less politically charged but no less controversial (due to health concerns) is the booming business of photographing unborn babies. Ultrasound images are no longer used exclusively as a diagnostic tool by doctors, as mall shops such as "Fetal Fotos," "A Peek in the Pod," and "Womb with a View" sell souvenir albums of ultrasound images to expectant parents (Schindehette and Finan, 111–13).

43. Finucci, *Manly*, 44–45.

44. Pérez Escohotado, 97.

45. See also Ríos Izquierdo, 34

46. P. Y si la muger, por ser ilicito su preñado, solicitase que la matrona le procure por qualquier medio el aborto, pretextando el escandalo, el dishonor, y otras gravisimas causas, qué deberá esta hacer?

R. Deben todas la matronas seguramente creer, que por quantas causas sean capaces ponderarse, no les es lícito dar consejo ni arbitrio, que sea dirigido a inferir el aborto; y que por sólo este hecho están con las mayores Censuras excomulgadas por los Sumos Pontifices, y por los Jueces Seculares hechas reos de pena capital: sin que para la minoracion de la culpa les pueda servir el vano pretexto de que el aborto se procuró en tiempo que la criatura aun no estaba animada; pues fuera de que nadie es capaz de asegurarlo, aunque no lo estuviese, es cierto, que desde el instante que se concibe, goza el embrión de aptitud o potencia para poseer el Alma racional. (Medina, 34–36)

47. While midwives were imprisoned or executed for facilitating abortions, an

interesting case of a male doctor in a 1674 court proceeding reveals the complexity of the morality issues behind the abortion debate (Perry, *Crime*, 67, 92). Doctor Juan López Batanero reportedly gave women patients prescriptions to terminate pregnancies. He had reportedly given various women an herb from the Jabalón River, which resulted in an abortion for a woman from Solana. Ironically, the doctor was ultimately convicted, not for performing an abortion, but for supporting the idea that extramarital sex between two consenting adults was not a sin (Pérez Escohotado, 96–97).

48. See also McLaren and Gélis.

49. "Se teme más la difusión popular de una práctica como la del aborto que las consecuencias derivadas de la ignorancia de un riesgo en la aplicación de un remedio médico" (Pardo Tomás, 218).

50. "Una mujercilla deshonesta dar tantos saltos recién preñada, que vino a expeler el concepto en muestra de clara de huevo en un telilla delgada, con muchas puntillas sanguíneas y hebras bermejas, y un puntillo en medio que le pareció ser el omligo" (Pineda, 78).

51. See also Casey, 31.

52. "Escusado me sería hablar en este caso, pues soy religioso y no he sido casado, . . . porque muchas vezes da mejor cuenta un sabio de una cosa que ha leydo que no la da un simple aunque la haya experimentado" (Guevara, 392).

53. "Todo esto procede por culpa dellas, en querer ser homicidas de sí mismas . . . por su culpa malparen las criaturas" (401).

54. "Deve el marido quitar a la muger de ocuparla en mucho trabajo, y la muger dévese guarder del demasiado regalo; porque en las preñadas es ya regla general que el mucho trabajo las haze malparir y el mucho regalo las haze peligrar. . . .Porque la ociosidad no sólo es ocasión de no merecer el cielo, pero aun es causa de las mugeres tener mal parto" (402–3).

55. "Admite mucho aire y frialdad, que envía al utero donde se fragua el cuerpo humano . . . es totalmente inepto para la generacion" (Carranza, 20–20v).

56. "Estos ornatos y composturas acarrean muchos males e impedimientos contra la salud, pues muchas se esterilizan, y enferman, ya porque andan con el potro de una ballena y continuo tormento de su apretura" (Ezcaray, 39).

57. "Gran culpa tuviste en eso. Por cierto es así por dos cosas tan livianas, como apretarte el cuerpo y tomar un enojo de no nada por ventura, mataste a la criatura que engendraste, y pusiste en peligro tu vida. . . .Por dos causas de la parte agente puede venir aborto, a mi ver (lo que comúnmente acaece), la una por causa de la mujer y la otra del marido. Pues agora no estamos sino mujeres, quierote contar las de las mujeres; . . . Bien me pueden decir que cómo oso hablar en mal que no he probado, y digo que el medico tampoco ha probado todas las enfermedades, y por las letras que tiene, y por lo que ha visto y curado, las curan; así yo hablaré en esto según lo que he visto, oído, y aun leído" (Luján, 178).

58. "Porque en ley de buen marido cabe que emplee los ojos en mirarla, las manos en servirla, la hacienda en regalarla, y el corazón en contentarla" (187).

59. The dangers for both the pregnant woman and the fetus commented in various circulated and published letters again show the experiences of those impacted by

high-risk pregnancies and unwanted miscarriages. A letter written by Felipe IV to his spiritual advisor and friend Sor María de Agreda, relating his pain upon seeing his wife Mariana on the verge of dying while giving birth, reveals just one aspect of the realities of reproductive health (Ríos Izquierdo, 28). Likewise, the response to the miscarriage of the popular actress Francisca Bezón ("La Bezona") hints at both the emotional and economic impact of reproduction: "Bezona miscarried two days before Corpus Christi and to encourage her to perform in the religious plays, José González sent her 400 *reales* since he was the commissioner of those performances" ["Mal parió la Bezona dos días antes del Corpus, y para que se animase a representar los autos, le envió José González 400 reales como comisario que era de ellos."] (Barrionuevo, 2: 201).

60. When the popular and then pregnant seventeenth-century actress Ana Muñoz was forced by theater director Andrés de Claramonte to ride out toward stage on horseback, the wild cheers and whistles of the male spectators caused the horse to throw Muñoz to the ground. The accident led to a miscarriage. Two centuries after the episode, the critic Ricardo Sepúlveda interprets the incident in terms of loss, not for the actress (and her lineage) but for her husband: "As a result, she had a miscarriage, from which the future generations of Villegas (Ana Muñoz's husband) were lost forever" ["vino ésta a malparir de las resultas, dejando perdida para la posteridad la sucesión de Villegas, marido de la Ana Muñoz"] (cited in Díaz de Escovar, 734). See also Rodríguez Cuadros, 591.

61. "Es avito escandaloso y que fácilmente provoca a lujuria porque conociendo los ombres que es trage acomodado para encubrir el preñado, se atreben con unas desenvoltura a requerirlas de amores a tales hembras" (quoted in Jiménez Patón, *Reforma*, 46).

62. For a comprehensive study of the relationship between discourses of poverty and the picaresque genre, see Cruz.

63. "Entró Serafina . . . y que tragándose unos gemidos sordos, llamando a Dios y a muchos santos que le ayudasen, parió una criatura, . . . Pues, como Serafina se vio libre de tal embarazo, recogiéndose un faldellín, se volvió a su casa, dejándose aquella inocencia a lo que le sucediese" (Zayas, *Novelas*, 298).

64. "Confusa y cuidadosa de lo que le había sucedido, y más del desalumbramiento que tuvo en dejar allí aquella criatura, viendo que si se había muerto o la habían comido perros, que cargaba su conciencia tal delito" (300).

65. For an intriguing pregnancy plot that involves maternity and paternity (with a zealous preference for having a male child), see Tirso de Molina's play *Todo es dar en una cosa* (especially the first act).

66. The second publication was Francisco Núñez's *Libro del parto humano en el cual se contienen remedios muy útiles y usuales para el parto dificultoso de las mujeres* . . . (Alcalá, 1580). For a discussion on midwives in early modern Spain, see Ortiz.

67. "Falta de virtud informativa en el humor espermático y también por corrupción de la materia . . . la muchedumbre de la materia cuando la corresponde qualidad y sequedad de la matriz, por la qual dicha material es condenada. . . . Y por eso dezía Aristoteles . . . la dicha monstruosidad cuando no concorre la simiente

del varón cuando la muger en sueños esta en su vaso sin concurso de varón, se sigue semejante monstruo ser engendrado" (Carbón, 12v).

68. "Aver nacido un cuerpo con dos cabezas, y no ha mucho que en otro pueblo nació un monstruo con cuernos y dientes y cola. Otra muger en Sevilla, la qual era de mi patria, despues de largo y dificultoso parto parió un monstruo como lagarto, el qual repentimamente se vio huir, y según Plinio dize, una muger llamada Alcipe parió un elefante, y una esclava una serpiente, y que en Monviedro un niño nacido se tornó al vientre" (Núñez, 8v-9).

69. "En la calle Mayor, enfrente de las casas de mi madre, . . . tiene preñada su muger con tan grande exceso que es monstruosidad, que parece trae una razonable tinaja en lugar de barriga. Admiréme mucho de verla, y me dijeron ella y su marido y todos los demás vecinos que el año pasado había parido cuatro muchachos, todos varones uno tras otro, y que hogaño sentía otros tantos y más, señalando las cabezas en el vientre. A los cuatro meses se le mueren todos. Está ya en ocho meses . . . Hela hablado y visto y lo cuento por cosa rara" (Barrionuevo, 1:265).

70. "Ea hija, mira que no has parido." All references to this news pamphlet are from Ettinghausen, *Noticias*.

71. "Gracias a Dios, que salimos con vitoria, que lo nacido ya está seguro."

72. "Descubrieron la criatura, que viendola los que se hallaron presentes, por mucho rato quedaron en un profundo silencio atonitos, y pasmados, mirandose los unos a los otros, por ver tal monstrusidad."

73. See Ettinghausen, "Illustrated."

74. "Empero adviertase a la parida no vea el monstruo en quanto ser pueda, porque cierta muger Toledana viendo un horrible monstruo que pario, dende a pocos dias murio de espanto, y luego su marido" (Núñez, 8v-9).

75. *Retrato de un monstruo, que se engendró en un cuerpo de un hombre, que se dice Hernando de la Haba, vecino del lugar de Freyra, Marquesado de Cenete, de unos hechizos que le dieron. Parteole Francisca de León, comadre de parir, en veinte y uno de Junio, de 1606 por la parte tras ordinaria compuestas por Pedro Manchego, vecino de Granada* (Manchego). This news pamphlet is reproduced in Cordoba, 308–17. See also González Alcantud and Río Parra, 148–49. See Appendix II for a complete translation in English and the news pamphlet in Spanish.

76. "Santo Dios dize la vieja/ confusa y atribulada, / este sin duda es Diablo/ bié lo muestra en su arrogacia" (Manchego, 2r).

77. See Cordoba, 320–27. See also Delpech, 563.

78. "Vive Dios que estoy preñado, / porque en la barriga siento / que me dan brincos y saltos" (Manchego, 3v). Given the belief that witches were known to intervene in reproductive issues (repeated in texts such as Heinrich Kramer and James Sprenger's widely translated *Malleus Maleficarum* [The Witches Hammer]), it might not surprise us to see a twenty-first-century reference to witchcraft and male pregnancy in the 2005 feature film *Bewitched*. When an actor (played by Will Ferrell) discovers that his costar (played by Nicole Kidman) *is* actually a witch (in other words, a real witch who is playing a witch on television), he panics and asks her: "Am I going to get pregnant? Because I can't get pregnant right now!"

79. "Por Dios hermano, / que teneys razón, no ay duda, / qual diablo os ha empreñado" (3v).

80. "Mas por ser tan suzio y feo, / le dexo passar en blanco" (4). Given the anal imagery, demonic involvement, and the need for silence, Pierre Cordoba supposes the presence of sperm in the concoction (325).

81. "Abrid los ojos señores / no os fiéys de malas hembras / . . . Mirad que son gusanillos / . . . que os van chupando la sangre / . . . Son víboras ponçoñosas / . . . Guardad no os hagan parir / como hizo esta alcahueta / a este hombre" (Manchego, 4v).

82. "¡Y qué tan buenos! / de un hombre que cuando menos / dicen que parió en Granada." . . ."¡Qué se sufre tanto error!/ mas concreto se confirma/ la barbaridad de España" (Vega, *Octava*, 255) See also Cordoba, 308, and Caro Baroja, 51–53.

83. "Aunque es verdad que ay algunos / incrédulos que se jatan/ de decir, que son mentiras / estos sucesos que pasan. / Pero con todo pretendo / será de tanta eficacia / mi obra, que dará al mundo/ crédito por ser tan clara. / No ha sucedido en las Indias, / ni en las islas de Canarias, / ni en la tierra del gran Cayne, ni en Chipre Africa y Asia" (Manchego, 1v).

84. *Las batuecas del Duque de Alba* was believed to have been written between 1598 and 1600 and was published in 1638 (Morley and Bruerton, 173, 362). See also Delpech, 579.

85. "Digo que Celio parió / y que el niño he visto yo / en su regazo dormido: / y Geralda me ha contado / que le vio colgado ayer / del su pecho" (Vega, *Batuecas*, 398).

86. "Y si es verdad que ellos saben / facer tan alta invención, de que los más sabios son / de todo el mundo se alaben . . . ¿querrás tú, Taurina, ser / mujer de un home parido? ¿Cómo os pensáis concertar? / ¿Quién ha de parir en casa?" (399).

87. "Bien podéis tomar venganza / de ver a mi amor preñado. /Notable desgracia ha sido; / pues, casándome con él, / cuando pienso parir dél, / viene a mi poder parido" (399).

88. "Aquella que trayendo el vientre muy grande, y haziendo la quanta que venia a parir por la Epiphania, la dixeron por burla que pariría los tres Reyes, ella respondió, ojala: y parió tres muchachos, moreno el uno. Aquí solo pudo hazer la imaginación que el uno mudase el color" (Nieremberg, 62).

89. See Finucci, "Maternal," 42, and Huet, 34.

90. "Y esto porque no estemos en duda de nuestros mismos hijos, si son nuestros o ajenos" (330).

91. "Estándose lavando la cabeza, entró el marido por una puerta excusada de un retrete, y con sus propios cabellos, que los tenía muy hermosos, le hizo lazo a la garganta, con que la ahogó, y después mató al niño con un veneno, diciendo que no había de heredar su estado hijo dudoso" (338–39).

92. "Otra manera hi ha de fijos que son llamados notos, et estos son los que nascen de adulterio: et son llamados notos, porque semeja que son fijos conoscidos del marido que la tiene en casa, et non lo son" (*Partidas*, 88).

93. "Los hijos, suponiendo los que no son legítimos por legitimos, ocasionando muchoas injusticias en los bienes temporales" (Andrade,148).

94. "Nascido seyendo alguno de fornicio, o de incesto o de adulterio, este atal non puede ser llamado fijo natural ni debe heredar ninguna cosa de los bienes de su padre. Et si a tal fijo como este diese el padre alguna cosa de lo suyo, los otros fijos legítimos que fueren de aquel padre mesmo pueden rovocar la donacion o la manda quel dexase, fueras ende si el rey le confirmase la donacion o la manda por su previllejo" (*Partidas*, 483).

95. "Las madres siempre son ciertas de los fijos que nascen dellas, et por esta razon todo fijo debe heredar en los bienes de su madre en uno con los otros fijos legítimos que nascen della, quier sean legítimos o non" (483).

96. "Fijo natural que non es nascido de legítimo matrimonio, si moriese sin testamento non habiendo ijos, nin nietos nin madre, entonce sus hermanos quel pertenescen de parte de su madre son ciertos et los de parte del padre son en dubda. . . .Otrosi decimos que los fijos naturales non han que les pertenecen de parte de su padre; mas a los otros parientes que les pertenecen de parte de su madre que mueren sin testamento, bien los pueden heredar seyendo ellos los mas propincos parientes" (484).

## CHAPTER 4

1. For more on metrosexuality, see Flocker.

2. "Si acabando Naturaleza de fabricar un hombre perfecto, le quisiese converter en mujer, no tenía otro trabajo más que tornarle adentro los instrumentos de la generación . . . muchas veces ha hecho Naturaleza una hembra y lo ha sido uno y dos meses en el vientre de su madre, y sobreviniéndoles a los miembros genitales copia de calor por alguna ocasión, salir afuera y quedar hecho varón. A quien esta transmutación le acontesciere en el vientre de su madre, se conoce después claramente en ciertos movimientos que tiene, indecentes al sexo viril: mujeriles, mariosos, la voz blanda y melosa; son los tales inclinados a hacer obras de mujeres, y caen ordinariamente en el pecado nefando" (Huarte, 608–9).

3. See also Paré, 32.

4. "Que teniendo descubierto el sexo masculino, interiormente tienen el femineo oculto, de modo, que siendo en lo que se ve solo varones, en lo que no se ve son tambien hembras" (Fuentelapeña, 229–30).

5. "Aunque se haze por inversion de instrumentos, no sucede sino en solos aquellos que son en la realida Hermafroditas, y tienen de su naturaleza ambos sexos: porque aunque es verdad, que por la mayor parte suelen tener los ambos patentes, puede con todo esso suceder, que por alguna causa, o impedimento oculto, no puedan a un mismo tiempo manifestarse ambos, y por consiguiente, que quando el uno se manifiesta, el otro se aya de ocultar necesariamente, de donde se sigue, que creciendo o disminuyendose el calor natural, puedan fácilmente convertirse de mugeres en hombres, o al contrario, de hombres en mugeres" (247–48).

6. "Algunas mugeres han hecho en hombres y de algunos hombres que se han castrado para hazerse mugeres . . . porque de lo uno fue autora la misma naturaleza, sin que en ello interviniese ninguna industria humana; y según la opinion de muchos filosofos antiguos, naturalmente pudo acaecer, . . . mas que el hombre, cuyo deseo

es governar exercicios, regir republicas, y morir honrosamente por su patria, se haga muger, cuyo oficio es . . . Amar a sus hijos y marido, hilar y tener cuidado de su casa, es cosa no solo prodigiosa mas aun lo es la historia y memoria dello" (Bovistau, 165–66).

7. "Se servia del como si fuera muger, y le amava sumamente. Y no satisfecho de aver cometido tan grande maldad, pospuesta su magestad y grandeza, y de que era Emperador de la mayor Republica del mundo, públicamente se casó con el, y le dotó y solenizó la boda y le tenía en el mismo grado como si fuera su legítima muger" (167).

8. "Para parecer blando y delicado como muger" (168v).

9. "Se puso en manos de quien le cortó lo que tenía de varon, para ver si podia conseguir lo que tanto deseava" (168v).

10. "Y que se hayan vuelto mujeres en hombres después de nacidas, y no se espanta el vulgo de oírlo; porque fuera de lo que cuentan por verdad muchos antiguos, es cosa que ha acontecido en España muy pocos años ha" (Huarte, 609).

11. "Hubo otra mujer que, después de haber estado casado y parido un hijo, se convirtió en hombre, y se casó otra vez con otra mujer y tuvo hijos de ella" (Torquemada, 188).

12. "Esta doncella, viniendo a la edad en que le había de bajar su costumbre, en lugar de ella le nació, o salió de dentro si estaba escondido, el miembro viril, y así, de hembra se convirtió en varón, y le vistieron luego en hábito de hombre" (189).

13. "Y como esta mujer no tuviese hijos, el marido y ella estaban mal avenidos, y así le daba tan áspera vida, fuese de celos o por otra causa que la mujer, una noche, hurtando los vestidos de un mozo que en casa estaba, vestida con ellos, se fue y anduvo por algunas partes fingiendo ser hombre, y así, vivió y ganaba para sustentarse; y estando así, o que la naturaleza obrase en ella con tal pujante virtud que bastase para ello, o que la imaginación intensa de verse en el hábito de hombre tuviese tanto poder que viniese a hacer el efecto, ella se convirtió en varon y se casó con otra mujer" (190).

14. "Porque, si no lo fuese, era imposible venirle la regal ni tener leche para sustentar mueve meses la criatura en el vientre" (Huarte, 610).

15. "No hay hombre que se pueda llamar frío respecto a la mujer, ni mujer caliente respecto al hombre" (610).

16. "Cuánto daño haga al hombre privarle de estas partes, aunque pequeñas, no serán menester muchas rezones para probarlo. Pues vemos por experiencia que luego se le cae el vello y la barba; y la voz gruesa y abultada se le vuelve delgada; y con esto pierde las fuerzas y el calor natural, y queda de peor condición y más mísera que si fuera mujer" (619).

17. "Son alegres, risueños, amigos de pasatiempos; son sencillos de condición y muy afables, son vergonzosos y no mucho dados a mujeres" (620).

18. "Porque, si es fría y húmida más de lo que es menester, dice Hipócrates que salen los hombres eunucos o hermafroditas" (295).

19. "Tiene ambos sexos de hombre y muger, dicho por otro término andrógyno . . . Escrive Plinio . . . avía cierta gente a la qual llamavan andrógenos, por ser todos hermaphroditos, y usavan igual e indistintamente el acto de engendrar y el de con-

cebir, y assí tienen las tetas derechas como hombres y las izquierdas como mugeres" (Covarrubias, *Tesoro*, 531).

20. Soy hic, & haec, & hoc. Yo me declaro,
soy varon, soy muger, soy un tercero,
que no es uno ni otro, ni está claro
qual destas cosas sea. Soy terrero
de los que como a monstro horrendo y raro.
Me tienen por siniestro, y mal agüero,
advierta cada qual que me ha mirado,
que es otro yo, si vive afeminado (164).

See also Vélez-Quiñones, *Monstrous,* 18, and Smith, 16–17.

21. Manuscript documents related to Elena de Cépedes's case are housed in the Archivo Histórico Nacional, Madrid (Sección Inquisición, Tribunal de Toledo: Legajo 234, Expediente 24). To facilitate reading the Spanish, I have modernized the spelling and punctuation. See also Kagan and Dyer.

22. See Velasco, "Interracial."

23. "Verdad que él le ha visto sus miembros genitales, y las manos puso vecinas [y] ha vista de ojos, y tocadole con las manos. Y que declarábase de él así: que él tiene su miembro genital, el cual es bastante y perfecto, con sus testículos formados, como cual quiera hombre . . . Y ansí dicho y declare que a su parecer no tiene semejanza de hermafrodita ni cosa dello" (Céspedes).

24. My translation ["con un instrumento tieso y liso . . . cometió el delito nefando de sodomía"] (Céspedes).

25. "La cual le metió por su natura de mujer la dicha vela, la cual entró preiosa y poco, y esta testigo no se confió y también le metió el dedo . . . y entró premioso, y con esto esta testigo no entiende que haya llegado varón a ella" (Céspedes).

26. "Algún arte tan sutil que bastó para engañar a éste así en la vista como en el tacto" (Céspedes).

27. "Porque yo con pacto expreso ni tácito del demonio nunca me fingí hombre para casarme con mujer como se me pretende imputar. Y lo que pasa es que como en este mundo muchas veces se han visto personas que son andróginos, que por otro nombre se llaman hermafroditos, que tienen entramos sexos, yo también he sido uno de éstos. Y al tiempo que me pretendí casar incalecía y prevalescía más en el sexo masculino, y naturalmente era hombre y tenía todo lo necesario de hombre para poder casar. Y de que lo era hice información y probanza ocular de medicos y cirujanos perito en el arte, los cuales me vieron y tentaron y testificaron con juramento que era tal hombre y me podia casar con mujer. Y con la dicha probanza hecha judicialmente me case por hombre" (Céspedes).

28. "Y ésta quedó con aptitud de poder tener cuenta con mujer y volvió a la dicha Ana de Albánchez, y con ella tuvo muchas veces cuenta y actos como hombre" (Céspedes).

29. "El padre está muy contento porque es hombre rico y no tenía heredero, y agora se halla con un hijo muy hombre, y que se puede casar, ella tambien va contenta porque despues de doze años de carcel sabe muy bien la libertad, y se halla de

muger varon, que en las cosas y bienes temporales, ninguna merced mayor le pudo hazer naturaleza." Cited in Ettinghausen, *Noticias*, n.p. See also Garza Carvajal, *Butterflies*, 56–57.

30. See Garza Carvajal, *Vir* and *Butterflies*.

31. "Es tal cual yo la querría para nuestro cortesano; no regalada ni muy blanda, ni mujeril como la desean algunos, que no sólo se encrespan los cabellos y, si a mano viene, se hacen las cejas, mas aféitanse y cúranse el rostro con todas aquellas artes y diligencias que usan las más vanas y deshonestas mujeres del mundo. Estos son los que en el andar y en el estar y en todos los otros ademanes son tan blandos y tan quebrados que la cabeza se les cae a una parte y los brazos a otra; y si hablan, son sus palabras tan afligidas que en aquel punto diréis que se les sale el alma. Y las veces que se hallan entre hombres principales, entonces se precian de usar con todas sus fuerzas estas, tales blanduras o (por mejor hablar) deshonestidades. Estos, pues la natura no los hizo mujeres, como ellos (según muestran) quisieran parecer y ser, no debrían como buenas mujeres ser estimados, sino echados como públicas rameras, no solamente de donde hubiese conversación y trato de señores, mas aún de otra cualquier parte donde hombres de bien tratasen" (Castiglione,133).

32. "Por nuestros pecados lo mas de esto se halla ya en los hombres, pues con tanta vileza de la nacion Española, y de su nativo valor se han quitado los vigotes, y el pelo, poniendose cabelleras postizas, que cuestan muchos reales y parecen mas mugeres que hombrese, provocando con los rizos de la cabellera postiza a las mujeres, y causandoles embidia, para que ellas se rizen el pelo. En otros tiempos (no ha muchos años) la nacion española no dexarse ver, se hazia temer, y respetar: se daba un hombre una buelta con el vigotes a la oreja, . . . y mas miedo causaban con echar la mano a la barba, . . . O tiempos! O nacion española! Quien te ha fascinado? Quien ha hecho que degeneres de tu antiguo lustre, y valor? No sé que responda. Desde que ay chocolate en España se afeminaron los hombres . . . y ha llegado a tan exorbitante estremo la compostura en los hombres, que yo sé, que visitando un Medico a un enfermo, le halló con tantas cintas, y compostura en la cama, que juzgó era muger. No digo más, porque no cause risa lo que quisiera se llorasse" (Escaray, 22).

33. "Muchos varones excelentes calvos celebrados en las Historias" (Jiménez Patón, *Discurso*,18v).

34. "Muñecos, afeminados, mugeriles, para nada buenos" (18v).

35. See Vigil,184.

36. During his reading of the manuscript of this book, Harry Vélez-Quiñones reminded me that, unlike the seventeenth century in Spain, current interest in metrosexuality is not associated with the military or with national security (despite concern over the impact of openly allowing gays in the military): "The cultural panic about masculinity on account of the perceived crisis of empire is what feeds the negative depiction of *lindos* and their association with sodomites. One can argue that the metrosexual phenomenon could have a different cultural resonance if our current political/military self perception were compromised. Indeed, during the 1970s similar anxieties about long hair in males, unisex clothing, sexual mores, etc. characterized the national perception of masculinity in the USA."

37. "La gente toda tan regalada y afeminada" (Moncada, 2).

38. "Porque en la concepción, el varón y la mujer concurren, pero después ella tiene en su vientre y forma y alimenta con su sangre y humores la criatura, y nacida, la cría a sus pechos. Así siendo las mujeres flacas, regaladas y delicadas como pinturas o juguetes, no pueden parir varones fuerte, y ellas en criándose siempre la sobrea en ocio y regalo perpetuo, no suelen ser grandes ni fuertes, ni aun estar bien sanas, ni ser fecundas, sino tener mil opilaciones y humores viciosos y hacerse estériles. De aquí que no hay esclava ni gitana estéril, y que los hijos de éstas y de los labradores y trabajadores son grandes y fuertes y sanos y muchas señoras y mujeres nobles y regaladas viven enfermas o son estériles, y los príncipes y nobles en general nacen y se crían afeminados" (Valencia, 55–56).

39. "¿Pues qué ley humana ni divina halláis, nobles caballeros, para precipitaros tanto contra las mujeres, que apenas se halla uno que las defienda, cuando veis tantos que las persiguen? . . . ¿De qué pensáis que procede el poco ánimo que hoy todos tenéis, que sufrís que estén los enemigos dentro de España, y nuestro Rey en campaña, y vosotros en el Prado y en el río, llenos de galas y trajes femeniles, . . . De la poca estimación que hacéis de las mujeres, que a fe que, si las estimarais y amárades, como en otros tiempos se hacía, . . . ¿Es posible que nos veis ya casi en poder de los contrarios, pues desde donde están adonde estamos no hay más defense que vuestros heroicos corazones y valerosos brazos, y que no os corréis de estaros en la Corte, ajando galas y criando cabellos, hollando coches y paseando prados, y que en lugar de defendernos, nos quitéis la opinión y el honor. . . . . . todos efecto de la ociosidad en que gastáis el tiempo en ofensa de Dios y de vuestra nobleza? !Qué esto sufran ánimos casellanos! Bien dice un héroe bien entendido que los franceses os han hurtado el valor, y vosotros a ellos, los trajes" (Zayas, *Desengaños*, 505–6).

40. "Porque como todos están ya declarados por enemigos de las mujeres, contra todos he publicado la Guerra . . . ¡Ánimo, hermosas damas, que hemos de salir vencedoras!" (*Desengaños*, 470).

41. Perhaps the best example of the victory of female masculinity is embodied by Catalina de Erauso ("the Lieutenant Nun"). See Velasco, *Lieutenant*.

42. "Decir que sean útiles las comedias y representaciones de los teatros es contra la doctrina y sentimiento de los santos . . . y con la zarabanda y otros bailes deshonestos, con fiestas, banquetes y comedias, se hacen los hombres muelles, afeminados e inútiles para todas las empresas arduas y dificultosas . . . con los cual se hicieron en poco tiempo tan afeminados y cobardes, cuanto primero habían sido valientes y animosos" (Cotarelo y Mori, *Bibliografía*, 374–75).

43. See also Cartagena-Calderón, "Retablo," 27–28.

44. "Mas ¿quién jamás pensara ver a los hombres nacidos sólo para nobles y varoniles empresas abatidos a tan bajos y afeminados empleos, que apenas se distinguen de las mugeres? ¿Entregados totalmente a fiestas profanas, a músicas, a paseos, a los amores lascivos, a conversaciones ociosas, a juegos y divertimientos vanos, a peinar, trenzar y teñir el pelo, a rizar la cabellera postiza, a pulir y componer el vestido con tanta poligidad y melindre como la dama más delicada? ¿De dónde pueden nacer estos viles y afeminados afectos sino del centro de las delicias sensuales, que son los patios de las comedias, fuente universal de todos los vicios? . . . De los entremeses y burlas aplaudidas en los teatros no se puede hablar sin rubor, porque todos están

llenos de indecentes porquerías, de chistes y cuentos indignos de tabernas y bodegones; y lo que tienen" (Cotarelo y Mori, *Bibliografía*, 126–27).

45. "La vanidad de musicas y bayles entretiene los efeminados, y los haze vacar al afeyte del rostro, al enrizo de los cabellos, al adelgazar la voz, a los melindres, y caricias femeniles y al hazerse iguales a las mugeres en delicadezas del cuerpo . . . mas si por dicha queremos correr el velo a cada una, vendra a ser conocida por manzana de Sodoma, toda hermosura por defuera toda ceniza por dedentro" (Suárez de Figueroa, 74v, 75v).

46. For further study of the same-sex attraction and gender inversion in the entremés, see Restrepo.

47. See Garza Carvajal, *Vir*, 62.

48. "El hombre afeminado que se inclina a hazer cosas de muger, que llaman por otro nombre marimaricas" (Covarrubias, 790).

49. "El hombre de condición mugeril, inclinado a ocuparse en lo que ellas tratan y hablar su language y en su tono delicado" (46).

50. Accordingly, the soldier Jerónimo de Pasamonte defines *bujarrón* in his autobiography as a man "who had attempted sodomy" [había intentado el pecado nefando] (55). See also Chamorro, 183.

51. "La cosa que está agugerada, y suélese tomar en mala parte, quando se dize a uno horadado, porque vale bujarrón, y a la muger la nota de no virgen por lo menos" (Covarrubias, *Tesoro*, 698).

52. "Y lo que es más de sentir es la manera que los hombres las imitan en las galas y lo afeminado, pues es de suerte, que no es un hombre ahora más apetecible a una mujer que una mujer a otra. Y esto de suerte, que las galas en algunos parecen arrepentimiento de haber nacido hombres, y otros pretenden enseñar a la Naturaleza cómo sepa hacer de un hombre una mujer. Al fin hacen dudoso el sexo, lo cual ha dado ocasión a nuevas pragmáticas, por haber introducido vicios desconocidos de Naturaleza" (Quevedo, "España," 371).

53. See also Kamen, 207.

54. See also Bennassar, 299.

55. "Tenía el príncipe un paje, mozo, galán, . . . tan querido suyo, que tocara su esposa el agasajo suyo por el del paje, . . . con él comunicaba sus más íntimos secretos" (Zayas, *Desengaños*, 351).

56. "Halló . . . ¿Qué hallaría? Quisiera, hermosas damas y discretos caballeros, ser tan entendida que, sin darme a entender me entendiérades, por ser cosa tan enorme y fea lo que halló. Vio acostados en la cama a su esposo y a Arnesto, en deleites tan torpes y abominables, que es bajeza, no sólo decirlo, mas pensarlo. Que doña Blanca, a la vista de tan horrendo y sucio espectáculo, . . . .Quedando ellos, no vergonzosos ni pesarosos de que los hubiese visto, sino más descompuestos de alegría, pues con gran risa dijeron: 'Mosca lleva la española' " (360).

57. "Había en el calabozo un mozo tuerto, alto, abigotado, mohino de cara, cargado de espaldas y de azotes en ellas. . . .Decía que estaba preso por cosas de aire, . . . Respondía que no, que eran cosas de atrás. Yo pensé que pecados viejos quería decir. Y averigüé que por puto. . . .era tan maldito, que traíamos todos con carlancas, como mastines, las traseras, y no había quien se osase ventosear, de miedo de acordarle dónde tenía las asentaderas" (Quevedo, *Buscón*, 225–26).

58. "Son actos de afeminados maricas, dan ocasión para que dellos murmuren y se sospeche toda vileza, viéndolos embarrados y compuestos con las cosas tan solamente a mujeres permitidas" (Alemán, 140).

59. "Quedó tan aficionado a mí, que lo mostraba con muchos abrazos. Era este caballero de dieciséis años, hermoso como un angel, blanco, cabellos y ojos negros, de buena estatura y muy bien proporcionado, galán, liberal y risueño, y, sobre todo, virtuoso, devoto y no inclinado al acto venéreo . . . y al mismo paso la admiración de ver un español y un francés abrazados por la calle, a usanza de Francia, y que no me llamaba sino 'español mío' " (Duque de Estrada, 379).

60. "Yo me disgustase con Antonio Osorio, que era camarada del alférez, por una necedad que se dejó decir, y fue que yendo Quevedo conmigo, dijo delante de él y del alférez y sargento y los demás: 'No es malo que se hagan caricias entre cuarteros.' Lo cual oyó Quevedo y no respondió nada; pero yo le dije que era harto mejor no dejarse decir impertinencias, que aunque no son verdaderas, pueden concebir sospecha y causar disgustos" (Castro, 576).

61. See also Vélez Quiñones, "Deficient." For a discussion of sodomy in early modern poetry, see Díez Fernández.

62. "Acostumbran los arraeces y leventes vestir muy ricamente a sus garzones— que son sus mujeres barbadas- y presumir y contender de quien más número de garzones tiene, más hermosos y más bien vestidos" (quoted in Garcés, 113). See also Martín, 8.

63. "Los autores de los Siglos de Oro . . . difundieron hasta la más absoluta banalización el tópico del doble error de los moros, que veneraban a un falso profeta y violaban la ley natural, siendo incestuosos, bestiales y grandísimos sodomitas. Los tratadistas, los austeros moralistas, la literatura sabia en general, no poca veces utilizaron el argumento de las aberraciones sexuales según ellos permitidas en las tierras del Islam para exaltar la superioridad de la religión católica, argumento que no olvidarían los apologistas de la expulsión de 1609" (Carrasco, 212–13).

64. See Garcés, 148.

65. "Quemaron por el pecado nefando a cinco mozos. El primero fue Mendocilla, un bufón. El segundo, un mozo de cámara del Conde de Villamediana. El tercero, un esclavillo mulato. El cuarto, otro criado de Villamediana. El último fue don Gaspar de Terrazas, paje del Duque de Alba. Fue una justicia que hizo mucho ruido en la Corte" (quoted in González Palencia, 43). See also Deleito y Piñuela, *La mala*, 65.

66. "Quemaron dos mozuelos por el pecado nefando; y el uno era de los que culpaban a don Diego Gaytán . . . el cual se desdijo a voces por las calles cuando le llevaban a quemar. Hizo mucha lástima en toda la Corte." See also Deleito y Piñuela, *Mala*, 65.

67. "En cuanto al negocio de los que están presos por el pecado nefando, no se usa del rigor que se esperaba, . . . o sea que verdaderamente el poder y el dinero alcanzan lo que quieren. A don Nicolás, el paje del Conde del Castrillo, vemos que anda por la calle, y a Juan Rana, famoso representante, han soltado, y no vemos quemar a ninguno de cuantos presos hay" (*Mala*, 66).

## EPILOGUE

1. Finucci, *Manly*, 65.
2. See Emery.
3. See Serralta, "Risa."
4. Pablo Restrepo, in his study of humor, transgenderism, and the *entremés* in early modern Spain, also questions whether the laughter produced by sexual inversion jokes is conservative or subversive (201).
5. We might also consider other theories of laughter and humor when analyzing the comic elements in *El parto de Juan Rana*. According to the "Incongruity Theory," for example, we laugh when we experience something that violates our normal expectations for occurrences and conditions in life. In this way, the topsy-turvy carnivalesque features inherent in the *entremés* genre (male pregnancy, for example) would be explained by followers of the "incongruity theory" (such as Kant and Schopenhauer) as a "mismatch between our concepts and the real things that are supposed to be instantiations of these concepts" (Morreall, 130). By the same token, we could also relate elements of the "Relief Theory" of laughter by analyzing what kind of nervous energy is released with the interlude's jokes. The "Relief Theory" goes back to Aristotle's observations on catharsis in comedy and is later developed in Freud's theory of laughter as a release of psychic energy (such as repressed feelings and desires) in his *Jokes and Their Relation to the Unconscious*. Accordingly, *El parto de Juan Rana* would indulge normally suppressed feelings about transgressing traditional gender roles in marriage as well as sexual behavior considered suitable in early modern society. See Morreall, 128–32, and Stott, 131–40.
6. This gay sensibility is defined by Jack Babuscio as "a creative energy reflecting a consciousness that is different from the mainstream; a heightened awareness of certain human complications of feeling that spring from the fact of social oppression; in short, a perception of the world which is colored, shaped, directed, and defined by the fact of one's gayness" (19).

## APPENDIX IA

1. Meco is a small town located on the outskirts of Madrid.
2. *Aut.* defines *enormissimo* as "very enormous. This and much more vice, evil, and enormous and atrocious sins are brought by the nefarious sect of the evil Mohammad" (2:483).
3. *Torcer* (to twist or bend): "Metaphorically, it means to deviate from the path of virtue and reason . . . it also refers to judges who tend to make decisions of little justice . . . *Torcerse* also refers to wine that, once made or almost finished, turns to vinegar" (*Aut.*, 3:300).
4. "Little Well" = "Pozuelo." This most likely refers to one of two small towns on the outskirts of Madrid, either Pozuelo de Alarcón or Pozuelo del Rey.
5. Literally, "fish-hook."
6. *Jumento*: "ass or donkey, and to describe one who knows very little" (Cov., 722).

7. "Blabberville" = "Parla." Parla is a small town located south of Madrid. *Aut.* defines *parla* as "rapid speech" or "one who talks too much" (3:131).
8. Literally, "lagoons."
9. Literally, "mayor."
10. Cov. defines *renacuajo* as a tadpole as well as "a deformed and annoying boy" (904).
11. Cov.: *mosquito* is a "small fly, like those that breed in the wine cellars, attracted to the wine. Therefore, one who is fond of liquor is also called a mosquito" (815).
12. "Ballsville" = "los Güeros." According to Covarrubias, *güero* means "egg" (668). It can also mean "sterile, empty, without substance" (Chamorro, 471). In *Aut.*, "huero" is defined as an empty or rotten egg, and "by analogy it refers to a sickly man who doesn't leave the house due to his fear of the elements, which bother and tire him" (2:186). Interestingly, Delpech discusses images of the "huevo huero" in relation to impotence, sterility, and cuckoldry in his study on male pregnancy in Spanish folklore (560–67). "Los Güeros" is also most likely a play on "Los Hueros," a small town on the outskirts of Madrid, near Pozuelo del Rey.
13. "Eunuchtown" = "los capones." Pun on *capón*, meaning both "capon" and "eunuch" (a reference to castration and sterility) (Cov., 294–96).
14. In *Aut.*, "the man who is *blando* is effeminate" as well as "useless" (1:618). The joke in Spanish plays suggestively with his "eggs" going soft (i.e., effeminate) as well as being infertile or sickly. *Blando*: "coward," "penis," "cuckold," "effeminate" (Chamorro, 154).
15. A pun: *albarda* means both packsaddle and "a man considered to be stupid" (Cov., 66–67).
16. "Here and There" = "de abajo y el de arriba." According to Covarrubias, "many peasants on the road, when asked where they are from, respond *de allá arriba, de allá abaxo* when they don't want to say where they are from" (151). [Literally, "from above and from below" but here means "from here and there."] Since the mayor is sitting on another, the joke most likely refers suggestively to one man being on top of the other: "the mayor on top and the one on the bottom."
17. "Down There" = "Caramancheles." Another lower-body and possibly sexual reference. According to the *Diccionario etimológico de la lengua castellana*, "*Caramanchel* is most likely *camaranchel*, from *cámara* [room]"(480). "*Cámara* . . . in the plural means diarrhea . . . [or] the doubled-over, twisted, spastic movements and cramps resulting from diarrhea" (469). It can also refer to illicit sexual relations or prostitution (Chamorro, 209), and is most likely a pun on a small town near Madrid during the seventeenth century, *Caramanchel de abajo*, mentioned by Alonso de Castillo Solórzano in his 1631 *Las harpías en Madrid y coche de las Estafas* (cited in Simón Díaz, 229).
18. *Moscateles* literally means "muscatel wine," but also refers to an ignorant man who is annoying because of his lack of knowledge (*Aut.*, 2:614).
19. Possibly a reference to a small town just west of Granada called Ambroz.
20. As a noun, *cortes* refers to the capital or the residence of the royal court. As an adjective, it means "courteous." It can also mean *cornudo* or "cuckold" (Chamorro,

275). It may also play with a rural usage of *corte*, indicating the stable used to keep the livestock at night (*Dicc. Etimológico*, 544).

21. Literally, a "spinning top" or *peonza*. According to *Aut.*, *peonza* can also mean "one who is small and restless or boisterous" (3:209).

22. *Nemine contradicente*: "with no one speaking in opposition," or *nemine dissentiente*: "with no one disagreeing" (Morwood, 121).

23. These lines play on *faltar* ("to miss"): he missed Mother Nature's letters (*le faltaron las cartas*), his mistakes (*faltas*) were discovered, and his nine missed periods (*nueve faltas*).

24. Aristotle, Virgil, and Pliny wrote of mares that were impregnated by the wind: "wind eggs" (*hupenemia*).

25. Literally, "So this is where the delivery has brought us!"

26. *Comadre* means both midwife and, according to Covarrubias, "the angry woman, who even without getting mad, cannot keep a secret" (340). The line may also play on *comadrero*, "the man who is always with women and only enjoys their company. Typical of old, effeminate, or womanish men" (340). Therefore, John Frog's joke about having known so many midwives probably refers to women like his aggressive, domineering wife and perhaps to other male lovers.

27. The *zarambeque* is a joyful and lively African dance (*Aut.*, 3:562).

28. This last line implies that many women take advantage of men by telling them that they are the father of their children and thereby are required to provide support.

## APPENDIX I B

1. Meco is a small town located on the outskirts of Madrid.

2. *Aut.*: "Enormissimo. Mui enorme. Esso y mucho mas de vicios, maldades, pecados enormíssimos y atrocíssimos trahe consigo la nefanda secta del malvado Mahóma" (2:483). "Enorme. En lo moral vale perserso, lleno de fealdad y maldad, excesio y torpemente grave" (2:483).

3. *Aut.*: "Inorme. Lo mismo que enorme, que es más comun" (2:276).

4. Cov.: "Irse a la mano, reportarse" (786). "Reportarse. Vale bolver uno sobre sí y refrenar su cólera" (905).

5. In the manuscript, "incriminada."

6. Cov.: "Ponderación, exageración y encarecimiento" (876).

7. Torcer: "Metaphoricamente vale desviarse o apartarse del camino recto de la virtud y de la razon . . . Se dice tambien de los Jueces, que se inclinan a las partes, que tienen menos justicia . . . Mudar el dictamen, o intencion que alguno tenia de favorecer a otro por obligacion o palabra que tenia contrahida . . . Se dice tambien del vino, que estando hecho o faltandole poco, se vuelve vinagre" (*Aut.*, 3:300).

8. Pozuelo: Possibly Pozuelo de Alarcón or Pozuelo del Rey (two small towns on the outskirts of Madrid).

9. Cov.: "Jumento . . . en nuestro castellano tan sólo se toma por el asno o la borrica; y para dezir a uno que sabe poco, usamos deste término" (722).

10. *Aut.*: "Parla. Expedición en el hablar. Tómase también por la demasía en el hablar" (3:131). Parla is a small town located south of Madrid.

11. Cov.: "Renaquajo. Una mala sabandijuela, que se cría en el agua estancada o limpia del limo de la tierra . . . Un muchacho mal tallado y enfadoso dezimos que es un renaquajo" (904).

12. Cov.: "Mosquito. Mosca pequeña . . . Bien se sabe quantos mosquitos se crían en las bodegas aficionados al vino dellas, y assí para dar a entender que una persona es amiga deste licor, suelen llamarle mosquito" (815).

13. Cov.: "Güero. Vide güevo" (666). "Güevo. Se dixo del nombre latino *ovum* . . . Las aves y los pezes comúnmente sacan su cría en güevos" (668). *Aut.*: "Huero. Lo que está vacío o tiene dentro cosa inútil y sin substancia. Dixose propriamente del huevo corrompido y de que no sale pollo. . . .Se llama por analogía el hombre enfermizo y que no sale de casa por temor de los temporales, que le molestan y fatigan" (2:186). "Estéril" (Chamorro, 471). Los Hueros is a small town on the outskirts of Madrid, near Pozuelo del Rey.

14. Cov.: "Se dixo capón, assí al hombre a quien han sacado los testículos" (257). "Al hombre capado llamámosle capón y castrado; pero el nombre que particularmente le compete es eunuco o espadón" (294).

15. *Aut.*: "Hombre blando, se entiende el afeminado" (1:618). "Cobarde," "pene," "cornudo," "afeminado" (Chamorro, 154).

16. Cov.: "Albarda . . . es la cobertura y el fuste de la bestia de carga . . . al que tienen por necio dezimos que es un albarda" (66–67).

17. Cov.: "Muchos labradores ay que si en algún camino les preguntáys de donde son, responden: De allá arriba, de allá abaxo, sin querer dezir el lugar de donde son" (151).

18. "Caramanchel. Probablemente por camaranchel, de cámara" (*Diccionario etimológico de la lengua castellana*, 480). "Cámara. . . .en número plural significa flujo de vientre . . . encorvado, retorcido, por los movimientos espasmódicos o retortijones de tripas que a veces coinciden con las cámaras" (469). "Mancebía," "prostituta" (Chamorro, 209). Most likely a pun on a small village near Madrid during the seventeenth century, Caramanchel de Abajo, mentioned by Alonso de Castillo Solórzano in his 1631 *Las harpías en Madrid y coche de las Estafas* (cited in Simón Díaz, 229).

19. *Aut.*: "El vino moscatel, hecho por si solo, es malo, por ser mui dulce . . . Llaman al hombre que fastidia por su falta de noticias e ignorancia" (2:614).

20. There is a small town just west of Granada called Ambroz.

21. *Aut.*: "Cortes. adj. Atento, comedido, afable, urbano . . . e por ende fue en España siempre acostumbrado de los homes honrados de enviar sus fijos a criar a las cortes de los Reyes, porque apriesiessen a ser corteses" (1:629). "Cornudo" (Chamorro, 275). *Dicc. etim.*: "Corte es término provincial que significa también establo donde se recoge de noche el ganado" (544).

22. *Aut.*: "Una especie de peon en figura cónica y sin punta de hierro: el qual baila azotado de una corréa . . . Llaman tambien al que es chiquito y bullicioso" (3:209).

23. Cov.: "Faltas en la muger preñada, los meses que ha tenido faltos de su regla" (583).

24. Cov.: "Llamamos comadre a la que ayuda a parir. . . .La muger enojada, y aun sin enojarse, no sabe guardar secreto" (340).The line may also be a play on "Comadrero. El hombre que anda metido con mugeres y gusta sólo de la conversación de unas y de otras, por entretenerse; es mucho de viejos o de hombres fríos y maricones" (340).

25. *Aut.*: "Zarambeque. Tañido, y danza mui alegre, y bulliciosa, la qual es mui frequente entre los Negros" (3:562).

## APPENDIX 2A

1. *Jubón* refers to a clothing article similar to a vest. In addition, according to *Aut.*, "In a joking style it means the lashings on the back given by the authorities" [En estilo jocoso vale los azotes que se dan por Justicia en las espaldas] (2:324).

2. Since *cruzado* plays on multiple meanings, such as a coin of monetary value as well as variations on cross imagery (such as criss-crossed lash marks), I have left the signifier ambiguous ("payment of two hundred") to reflect the original pun.

# Works Cited

Adams, Alice E. *Reproducing the Womb: Images of Childbirth in Science, Feminist Theory, and Literature*. Ithaca: Cornell University Press, 1994.
Adelman, Janet. *Suffocating Mothers: Fantasies of Maternal Origin in Shakespeare's Plays*, Hamlet to The Tempest. New York: Routledge, 1992.
Aeschylus. *The Oresteia*. Translated by David Grene and Wendy Doniger O'Flaherty. Chicago: University of Chicago Press, 1989.
Alemán, Mateo. *Guzmán de Alfarache I*. Edited by José María Micó. Madrid: Cátedra, 1987.
Alfonso X (el Sabio). *Cantigas de Santa María*. Edited by Walter Mettmann. 3 vols. Madrid: Castalia, 1986.
———. *Las Siete Partidas*. Translated by Samuel Parsons Scott. Chicago: Commerce Clearing House, 1931. Reprint, edited by Robert I. Burns, Philadelphia: University of Pennsylvania Press, 2001.
———. *Las Siete Partidas del rey don Alfonso el Sabio*. Edited by la Real Academia de la Historia. Madrid: Atlas, 1972.
———. *Songs of Holy Mary of Alfonso X, The Wise*. Translated by Kathleen Kulp-Hill. Tempe: Arizona Center for Medieval and Renaissance Studies, 2000.
Alonso y de los Ruizes de Fontecha, Juan. *Diez previlegios de preñadas*. Alcalá de Henares: Luis Martinez, 1606.
Andrade, Alonso de. *Libro de la guia de la virtud y de la imitación de nuestra Señora, . . . Tercera parte*. Madrid: Diego Díaz de la Carrera, 1646.
Aristotle. *Generation of Animals*. Translated by A. L. Peck. Cambridge: Harvard University Press, 2000.
Arons, Wendy. Introduction to *When Midwifery Became the Male Physician's Province: The Sixteenth Century Handbook the Rose Garden for Pregnant Women and Midwives*, by Eucharius Rösslin. Jefferson, NC: McFarland, 1994.
Aulnoy, Madame d.' *Travels into Spain*. Edited by R. Foulché-Delbosc. London: Routledge, 1930.
Avellaneda, Alonso Fernández de. *Don Quixote de La Mancha (Part II)*. Translated and edited by Alberta Wilson Server and John Esten Keller. Newark: Juan de la Cuesta, 1980.
———. *El ingenioso hidalgo don Quijote de la Mancha, que contiene su tercera salida*

*y es la quinta parte de sus aventuras*. Edited by Fernando García Salinero. Madrid: Castalia, 1987.

Azpilcueta Navarro, Fr. Martín. *Manual de confesores y penitentes*. Salamanca: Andrea Portonarijs, 1556.

Babuscio, Jack. "Camp and the Gay Sensibility." In *Camp Grounds: Style and Homosexuality*, edited by David Bergman, 19–38. Amherst: University of Massachusetts Press, 1993.

Bakhtin, Mikhail. *Rabelais and His World*. Translated by Hélène Iswolsky. Bloomington: Indiana University Press, 1984.

Barrett, Deirdre. *The Pregnant Man and Other Cases from a Hypnotherapist's Couch*. New York: Times Books, 1999.

Barrionuevo, Jerónimo de. *Avisos*. 2 vols. Madrid: Atlas, 1969.

Bass, Laura. "Framing the Margins on Center Stage." In "The Drama of the Portrait: Theater and Visual Culture in Early Modern Spain" (unpublished manuscript, consulted 2005).

Bennassar, Bartolomé. *Inquisición española: poder politico y control social*. Barcelona: Editorial Crítica, 1981.

Benshoff, Harry M. *Monsters in the Closet: Homosexuality and the Horror Film*. Manchester: Manchester University Press, 1997.

Berceo, Gonzalo de. *Milagros de Nuestra Señora*. Edited by Michael Gerli. Madrid: Cátedra, 1997.

———. *Miracles of Our Lady*. Translated by Richard Terry Mount and Annette Grant Cash. Lexington: University Press of Kentucky, 1997.

Bergman, David. "Strategic Camp: The Art of Gay Rhetoric." In *Camp Grounds: Style and Homosexuality*, 92–109. Amherst: University of Massachusetts Press, 1993.

Bergman, Hannah E. "Juan Rana se retrata." In *Homenaje a Rodríguez-Moñino*, 65–73. Madrid: Castalia, 1966.

———. *Luis Quiñones de Benavente y sus entremeses con un catálogo biográfico de los actores citados en sus obras*. Madrid: Editorial Castalia, 1965.

Bergmann, Emilie L. "Monstrous Maternity in Fray Antonio de Guevara's *Relox de Príncipes*." In *Brave New Worlds: Studies in Spanish Golden Age Literature*, edited by Edward Friedman and Catherine Larson, 39–49. New Orleans: University Press of the South, 1996.

*Bewitched*. Directed by Nora Ephron. Sony Pictures, 2005. DVD release date: October 25, 2005.

Bicks, Caroline. *Midwiving Subjects in Shakespeare's England*. Aldershot: Ashgate, 2003.

Blumenfeld-Kosinski, Renate. *Not of Woman Born: Representations of Caesarean Birth in Medieval and Renaissance Culture*. Ithaca: Cornell University Press, 1990.

Boccaccio, Giovanni. *The Decameron*. Translated by G. H. McWilliam. New York: Penguin, 1983.

Bovistau, Pedro, Claudio Tesserant, and Francisco Belleforest. *Historias prodigiosas y maravillosas*. Translated by A. Pescioni. Madrid: Luis Sánchez, 1603.

Braidotti, Rosi. *Metamorphoses: Towards a Materialist Theory of Becoming.* Cambridge: Polity, 2002.
———. *Nomadic Subjects: Embodiment and Sexual Difference in Contemporary Feminist Theory.* New York: Columbia University Press, 1994.
Bravo-Villasante, Carmen. *La mujer vestida de hombre en el teatro español (Siglos XVI-XVII).* Madrid: Temas, 1976.
Brockliss, L. W. B. "The Embryological Revolution in the France of Louis XIV: the Dominance of Ideology." In *The Human Embryo: Aristotle and the Arabic and European Traditions,* edited by G. R. Dunstan. Evanston: Northwestern University Press, 1990.
Brooks, Lynn Matluck. *The Art of Dancing in Seventeenth-Century Spain: Juan de Esquivel Navarro and His World.* Lewisburg: Bucknell University Press, 2003.
Brown, Peter. *The Body and Society: Men, Women, and Sexual Renunciation in Early Christianity.* New York: Columbia University Press, 1988.
Bruhm, Steven. *Reflecting Narcissus: A Queer Aesthetic.* Minneapolis: University of Minnesota Press, 2001.
Buckley, F. H. *The Morality of Laughter.* Ann Arbor: University of Michigan Press, 2003.
Burshatin, Israel. "Elena alias Eleno: Genders, Sexualities, and Race in the Mirror of Natural History in Sixteenth-Century Spain." In *Gender Reversals and Gender Cultures: Anthropological and Historical Perspectives,* edited by Sabrina Petra Ramet, 105–22. New York: Routledge, 1996.
———. "Written on the Body: Slave or Hermaphrodite in Sixteenth-Century Spain." In *Queer Iberia: Sexualities, Cultures, and Crossings from the Middle Ages to the Renaissance,* edited by Josiah Blackmore and Gregory S. Hutcheson, 420–56. Durham: Duke University Press, 1999.
Bynum, Caroline Walker. *Jesus as Mother: Studies in the Spirituality of the High Middle Ages.* Berkeley: University of California Press, 1982.
Camarena Laucirica, Julio. *Cuentos tradicionales de León.* Madrid: Universidad Complutense de Madrid, 1991.
Cameron, Vivian. "Political Exposures: Sexuality and Caricature in the French Revolution." In *Eroticism and the Body Politic,* edited by Lynn Hunt, 90–107. Baltimore: Johns Hopkins University Press, 1991.
Camille, Michael. "Manuscript Illumination and the Art of Copulation." In Lochrie, McCracken, and Schultz, *Constructing Medieval Sexuality,* 58–90.
Canavaggio, Jean. "Los disfrazados de mujer en la comedia." In *La mujer en el teatro y la novela del siglo XVII.* Toulouse: Université de Toulouse-Le Mirail, 1979.
Carbón, Damián. *Libro del arte de las comadres o madrinas.* Majorca: n.p., 1541.
Caro Baroja, Julio. *Ensayo sobre la literatura de cordel.* Madrid: Revista de Occidente, 1969.
Carranza, Alonso de. *Rogación al Rey D. Felipe IV, y a sus supremos Consejos de Justicia y Estado, en detestación de los grandes abusos en los trajes y adornos nuevamente introducidos en España.* Madrid: María de Quiñones, 1636.

Carrasco, Rafael. *Inquisición y represión sexual en Valencia. Historia de los sodomitas (1565–1785).* Barcelona: Laertes, 1985.

Cartagena Calderón, José. " 'El es tan rara persona.' Sobre cortesanos, lindos, sodomitas y otras masculinidades nefandas en la España de la temprana Edad Moderna." In Delgado and Saint-Saëns, *Lesbianism and Homosexuality*, 139–75.

———. "*El Retablo de las Maravillas* y la construcción cultural de la masculinidad en la España de Miguel de Cervantes." *Gestos* 27 (1999): 25–41.

Casa, Frank P., Luciano García Lorenzo, and Germán Vega García-Luengos, eds. *Diccionario de la comedia del Siglo de Oro.* Madrid: Castalia, 2002.

Casey, James. *Early Modern Spain: A Social History.* London: Routledge, 1999.

Castiglione, Baldassare. *El cortesano.* Edited by Mario Pozzi. Madrid: Cátedra, 1994.

Castiglione, Baldesar. *The Book of the Courtier.* Translated by Charles S. Singleton. Garden City: Anchor Books, 1959.

Castro, Miguel de. "Vida de Miguel de Castro." In *Autobiografías de soldados (siglo XVII)*, edited by José María de Cossío. Biblioteca de Autores Españoles 90:487–627. Madrid: Atlas, 1956.

Cervantes, Miguel de. *Don Quixote.* Translated by J. M. Cohen. New York: Penguin, 1980.

———. *El ingenioso hidalgo don Quijote de la Mancha.* Edited by Luis Andrés Murillo. Madrid: Castalia, 1982.

Céspedes, Elena de, manuscript documents regarding. Sección Inquisición, Tribunal de Toledo: Legajo 234, Expediente 24. Archivo Histórico Nacional, Madrid.

Chamorro, María Inés. *Tesoro de villanos: Diccionario de germanía.* Barcelona: Herder, 2002.

Churchwell, Gordon. *Pregnant Man: How Nature Makes Fathers out of Men.* New York: Quill, 2000.

Cody, Lisa Forman. *Birthing the Nation: Sex, Science, and the Conception of Eighteenth-Century Britons.* Oxford: Oxford University Press, 2005.

Colker, Ruth. *Pregnant Men: Practice, Theory, and the Law.* Bloomington: Indiana University Press, 1994.

*The Cosby Show.* "The Day the Spores Landed." NBC. November 9, 1989 [Season 6].

Cordoba, Pierre. "L'homme enceint de Grenade: Contribution a un dossier d'histoire culturelle." *Mélanges de la Casa de Velázquez* 23 (1987): 307–30.

Cotarelo y Mori, Emilio. *Bibliografía de las controversias sobre la licitud del teatro en España.* Granada: Archivum, 1997.

———. *Colección de entremeses, loas, bailes, jácaras y mojigangas desde finales del siglo XVI a mediados del XVIII.* Nueva Biblioteca de Autores Españoles Tomo 17. Madrid: Bailly/Bailliere, 1911.

Covarrubias, Sebastián de. *Emblemas morales.* Madrid: Luis Sánchez, 1610.

———. *Tesoro de la Lengua Castellana o Española.* Barcelona: Editorial Alta Fulla, 1989.

Cowans, Jon, ed. *Early Modern Spain: A Documentary History*. Philadelphia: University of Pennsylvania Press, 2003.
Crane, Mary Thomas. "Male Pregnancy and Cognitive Permeability in *Measure for Measure*." *Shakespeare Quarterly* 49, no.1 (1998): 269–92.
Cruz, Anne J. *Discourses of Poverty: Social Reform and the Picaresque Novel in Early Modern Spain*. Toronto: University of Toronto Press, 1999.
D'Ancona, Mirella Levi. *The Iconography of the Immaculate Conception in the Middle Ages and Early Renaissance*. New York: College Art Association of America, 1957.
Dangler, Jean. *Mediating Fictions: Literature, Women Healers, and the Go-Between in Medieval and Early Modern Iberia*. Lewisburg: Bucknell University Press, 2001.
Daston, Lorraine, and Katharine Park. "The Hermaphrodite and the Orders of Nature: Sexual Ambiguity in Early Modern France." *Journal of Lesbian and Gay Studies* 1, no. 4 (1995): 419–38.
De Armas, Frederick A. "Deflecting Desire: The Portrayal of Ganymede in Arguijo's Art and Poetry." In Delgado and Saint-Saëns, *Lesbianism and Homosexuality*, 234–56.
Delgado, María José, and Alain Saint-Saëns. *Lesbianism and Homosexuality in Early Modern Spain*. New Orleans: University Press of the South, 2000.
Deleito y Piñuela, José. *La mala vida en la España de Felipe IV*. Madrid: Alianza, 1994.
———. *La mujer, la casa y la moda (en la España del rey poeta)*. Madrid: Espasa-Calpe, 1966.
Delpech, François. "La patraña del hombre preñado: algunas versiones hispánicas." *Nueva Revista de Filología Hispánica* 34, no. 2 (1985–86): 548–98.
Díaz Escovar, Narciso. *Historia del teatro español: Comediantes, escritores, curiosidades escénicas*. Barcelona: Montaner y Simón, 1924.
*Diccionario de Autoridades* (Real Academia Española). Madrid: Gredos, 1963.
*Diccionario etimológico de la lengua castellana*. Buenos Aires: El Aleneo, 1944.
Díez Fernández, J. Ignacio. *La poesía erótica de los Siglos de Oro*. Madrid: Laberinto, 2003.
Diz, M. Ana. "Berceo y Alfonso: la historia de la abadesa encinta." *Cantigueiros* 5 (1993): 85–96.
Donaldson, Peter S. "Shakespeare in the Age of Post-Mechanical Reproduction: Sexual and Electronic Magic in *Prospero's Books*." In *Shakespeare, The Movie: Popularizing the Plays on Film, TV, and Video*, edited by Lynda E. Boose and Richard Burt, 169–85. London: Routledge, 1997.
Donnell, Sidney. *Feminizing the Enemy: Imperial Spain, Transvestite Drama, and the Crisis of Masculinity*. Lewisburg: Bucknell University Press, 2003.
Duque de Estrada, Diego. "Memorias de D. Diego Duque de Estrada." In *Autobiografías de soldados (siglo XVII)*. Biblioteca de Autores Españoles 90:251–484. Edited by José María de Cossio. Madrid: Atlas, 1956.
Dworkin, Andrea. *Right-wing Women*. New York: Perigee, 1983.
Dyer, Richard. *Stars*. London: British Film Institute, 1998.

El Saffar, Ruth Anthony. *Rapture Encaged: The Suppression of the Feminine in Western Culture*. London: Routledge, 1994.
Emery, David. "Art Imitates Tabloids." *Urban Legends and Folklore*. www.urbanlegends.about.com/library/weekly/aa100400a.htm (accessed October 5, 2000).
Ettinghausen, Henry. "The Illustrated Spanish News: Text and Image in the Seventeenth-Century Press." In *Arts and Literature in Spain: 1600–1800; Studies in Honour of Nigel Glendinning*, edited by Charles Davis and Paul Julian Smith, 117–33. London: Támesis, 1993.
———. *Noticias del siglo XVII: Relaciones españolas de sucesos naturales y sobrenaturales*. Barcelona: Puvill Libros, 1995.
Ezcaray, Antonio de. *Vozes del dolor nacidas de la multitud de pecados que se cometen por los trages profanos, afeytes, escotados, y culpables ornatos . . .* Sevilla: Thomas López de Haro, 1691.
Faliu-Lacourt, Christiane. "La madre en la comedia." In *La mujer en el teatro y la novela del siglo XVII*. Toulouse: Université de Toulouse-Le Mirail, 1979.
Fidalgo Francisco, Elvira. " 'La abadesa preñada' (Berceo 21); Seis versiones románicas y tres en latín." *Medioevo y literatura; actas del V Congreso de la Asociación Hispánica de Literatura Medieval* 2 (1995): 329–44.
Finucci, Valeria. *The Manly Masquerade: Masculinity, Paternity, and Castration in the Italian Renaissance*. Durham: Duke University Press, 2003.
———."Maternal Imagination and Monstrous Birth: Tasso's Gerusalemme liberata." In Finucci and Brownlee, *Generation and Degeneration*, 41–77.
Finucci, Valeria, and Kevin Brownlee, eds. *Generation and Degeneration: Tropes of Reproduction in Literature and History from Antiquity through Early Modern Europe*. Durham: Duke University Press, 2001.
Flocker, Michael. *The Metrosexual Guide to Style: A Handbook for the Modern Man*. Cambridge: Da Capo Press, 2003.
Flynn, Maureen. *Sacred Charity: Confraternities and Social Welfare in Spain, 1400–1700*. Ithaca: Cornell University Press, 1989.
Forelle, Helen. *If Men Got Pregnant, Abortion Would be a Sacrament*. Canton: Tesseract, 1991.
Fraenger, Wilhelm. *Hieronymus Bosch*. New York: Dorset Press, 1983.
Frazer, R. M. "Nero the Singing Animal." *Arethusa* 4 (1971): 215–18.
Freud, Sigmund. *Three Case Histories*. New Cork: Collier Books, 1993.
Fudge, Erica, Ruth Gilbert, and Susan Wiseman, eds. *At the Borders of the Human: Beasts, Bodies and Natural Philosophy in the Early Modern Period*. New York: Palgrave, 2002.
Fuentelapeña, Fray Antonio de, *El ente dilucidado: Discurso único, novísimo que muestra hay en la naturaleza animales irracionales invisible, y cuáles sean*. Biblioteca de visionaries, heterodoxos y marginados 4. Edited by J. Ruiz. Madrid: Editora Nacional, 1978. First published 1676 by Imprenta Real.
Galindo, Pedro. *Primera parte del directorio de penitentes, y práctica de una buena y prudente confesión*. Madrid: Juana de Chaves, 1682.
Garcés, María Antonia. *Cervantes in Algiers: A Captive's Tale*. Nashville: Vanderbilt University Press, 2002.

Garza Carvajal, Federico. *Butterflies Will Burn: Prosecuting Sodomites in Early Modern Spain and Mexico*. Austin: University of Texas Press, 2003.

———. "Silk Laced Ruffs and Cuffs: An Inherent Link between 'Sodomie' and Notions of Effeminacy in Andalucía and México 1561–1699." *Thamyris* 7, no.1–2 (2000): 7–39.

———. *VIR: Perceptions of Manliness in Andalucía and México 1561–1699*. Amsterdam: Amsterdamse Historische Reeks, 2000.

Gassier, Pierre, and Juliet Wilson. *The Life and Complete Work of Francisco Goya*. New York: Reynal, 1971.

Gélis, Jacques. *History of Childbirth: Fertility, Pregnancy and Birth in Early Modern Europe*. Boston: Northeastern University Press, 1991.

Gibson, Gail McMurray. "Scene and Obscene: Seeing and Performing Late Medieval Childbirth." *Journal of Medieval and Early Modern Studies* 29, no. 1 (1999): 7–24.

Gilbert, Ruth. *Early Modern Hermaphrodites: Sex and Other Stories*. London: Palgrave, 2002.

———. "Masculine Matrix: Male Births and the Scientific Imagination in Early-Modern England." In *The Arts of 17th-Century Science: Representations of the Natural World in European and North American Culture*, edited by Clair Jowitt and Diane Watt, 160–76. Aldershot: Ashgate, 2002.

González Alcantud, José A. "Monstruos, imaginación e historia. A propósito de un romance." Centro de Estudios Moriscos de Andalucía, September 12, 2002. www.alyamiah.com/cema/modules.php

González Palencia, Ángel, ed. *Noticias de Madrid 1621–1627*. Madrid: Ayuntamiento de Madrid, 1942.

Gossy, Mary S. "Aldonza as Butch: Narrative and the Play of Gender in *Don Quijote*." *Cervantes* 16, no. 2 (1996): 4–28.

Goya, Francisco. *Drawings: The Complete Albums*. Edited by Pierre Gassier. Translated by James Emmóns and Robert Allen. New York: Praeger, 1973.

Granjel, Luis S. *La medicina española del siglo XVII*. Salamanca: Universidad de Salamanca, 1978.

Greer, Fergus. *Leigh Bowery Looks*. London: Violette Editions, 2002.

Greilsammer, Myriam. "The Midwife, the Priest, and the Physician: The Subjugation of Midwives in the Low Countries at the End of the Middle Ages." *Journal of Medieval and Renaissance Studies* 21, no. 2 (1991): 285–327.

*Grey's Anatomy*. "Something to Talk About." ABC. November 6, 2005 [Season 1].

Guevara, Fray Antonio de. *Obras completas, II: Relox de príncipes*. Madrid: Biblioteca Castro, 1994.

Hale, Rosemary Drage. "Joseph as Mother: Adaptation and Appropriation in the Construction of Male Virtue." In *Medieval Mothering*, edited by John Carmi Parsons and Bonnie Wheeler, 101–16. New York: Garland, 1996.

Haraway, Donna. *Simians, Cyborgs, and Women: The Reinvention of Nature*. London: Routledge, 1991.

Heiple, Daniel. "Góngora and the Myth of Ganymede" In Delgado and Saint-Saëns, *Lesbianism and Homosexuality*, 219–32.

Heise, Ursula K. "Transvestism and the Stage Controversy in Spain and England, 1580–1680." *Theatre Journal* 44 (1992): 357–74.
Hernández Alcántara, Antonio. *Estudio histórico de la obra toco-ginecológica y pediátrica de Damián Carbón*. Salamanca: Anaya, 1957.
Herrera Puga, Pedro. *Sociedad y delincuencia en el Siglo de Oro: Aspectos de la vida sevillana en los Siglos XVI y XVII*. Granada: Universidad de Granada, 1971.
Huarte de San Juan, Juan. *Examen de ingenios para las ciencias*. Edited by Guillermo Serés. Madrid: Cátedra, 1989.
Huerta Calvo, Javier. *El nuevo mundo de la risa: Estudios sobre el teatro breve y la comicidad en los Siglos de Oro*. Barcelona: Oro Viejo, 1995.
Huet, Marie-Hélène. *Monstrous Imagination*. Cambridge: Harvard University Press, 1993.
Ibero, Alba. "Imágenes de maternidad en la pintura barroca." In *Las mujeres en el Antiguo Régimen: Imagen y realidad (S. XVI-XVIII)*, edited by Isabel Pérez Molina, Marta Vicente Valentín, Alba Ibero, Eva Carrasco de la Fuente, and Antonio Gil, 91–119. Barcelona: Icaria, 1994.
Jammes, Robert. "La risa y su función social en el Siglo de Oro." In *Risa y sociedad en el teatro español del Siglo de Oro*, edited by Y.-R. Fonquerne, 3–11. Paris: Centre National de la Recherche Scientifique, 1981.
Jiménez Patón, Bartolomé. *Discurso de los tufos, copetes y calvas*. Baeza: Juan de la Cuesta, 1639.
———. *Reforma de trages: Doctrina de frai Hernando de Talavera*. Baeza: Juan de la Cuesta, 1638.
*Junior*. Directed by Ivan Reitman. Universal, 1994. MCA Home Video, release date January 23, 1996.
Kagan, Richard L. and Abigail Dyer, eds. *Inquisitorial Inquiries: Brief Lives of Secret Jews & Other Heretics*. Baltimore: John Hopkins University Press, 2004.
Kamen, Henry. *Inquisition and Society in Spain in the Sixteenth and Seventeenth Centuries*. Bloomington: Indiana University Press, 1985.
Katz, Melissa R. "Regarding Mary: Women's Lives Reflected in the Virgin's Image." In *Divine Mirrors: The Virgin Mary in the Visual Arts*, edited by Melissa R. Katz and Robert A. Orsi. Oxford: Oxford University Press, 2001.
Keller, James R. *Queer (Un)Friendly Film and Television*. Jefferson, NC: McFarland & Company, 2002.
Keller, John Esten, and Annette Grant Cash. *Daily Life Depicted in the "Cantigas de Santa Maria."* Lexington: University Press of Kentucky, 1998.
Kitch, Aaron W. "Printing Bastards: Monstrous Birth Broadsides in Early Modern England." In *Printing and Parenting in Early Modern England*, edited by Douglas A. Brooks, 221–36. Aldershot: Ashgate, 2005.
Knight, Rhonda. "Procreative Sodomy: Textuality and the Construction of Ethnicities in Gerald of Wales's *Descriptio Kambriae*." *Exemplaria: A Journal of Theory in Medieval and Renaissance Studies* 14, no.1 (2002): 47–77.
Kruger, Barbara. *Barbara Kruger*. Cambridge: MIT Press, 1999.
Lanini Sagredo, Francisco Pedro. *El parto de Juan Rana*. MS 14.089–43: 425–35, Biblioteca Nacional, Madrid.

———. *El parto de Juan Rana*. Edited by Peter Thompson. *Comedia Performance: Journal of the Association for Hispanic Classical Theater* 1, no. 1 (Spring 2004): 219-37.
Lanning, John Tate. *The Royal Protomedicato: The Regulation of the Medical Professions in the Spanish Empire*. Durham: Duke University Press, 1985.
Laquer, Thomas. *Making Sex: Body and Gender from the Greeks to Freud*. Cambridge: Harvard University Press, 1990.
Larsen, Ernest. "The Fetal Monster." In Morgan and Michaels, *Fetal Subjects*, 236–50.
*Legend of Leigh Bowery*. Directed by Charles Atlas. Atlas Films, 2001. Lions Gate, DVD release date: July 13, 2004.
Lichtenstein, Therese. "Images of the Maternal: An Interview with Barbara Kruger." In *Representations of Motherhood*, edited by Donna Bassin, Margaret Honey, and Meryle Mahrer Kaplan, 198–201.
Lobato, María Luisa. "Un actor en Palacio: Felipe IV escribe sobre Juan Rana." *Cuadernos de Historia Moderna* 23 (1999): 79–111.
———. "Juan Rana." *Diccionario de la comedia del Siglo de Oro*. Edited by Frank Casa, Luciano García Lorenzo, and Germán Vega García-Luengos, 187–88. Madrid: Castalia, 2002.
Lochrie, Karma, Peggy McCracken, and James A. Schultz, eds. *Constructing Medieval Sexuality*. Minneapolis: University of Minnesota Press, 1997.
Lochrie, Karma. "Mystical Acts, Queer Tendencies." In Lochrie, McCracken, and Schultz, *Constructing Medieval Sexuality*, 180–200.
Lopez, Gregorio. *Las siete partidas del sabio rey Don Alonso el Nono, nuevamente glosadas por el licenciado Gregorio Lopez, del Consejo Real de Indias de Su Magestad*. Madrid: Boletín Oficial del Estado, 1974.
López Terrada, María Luz. "Los tribunales del protomedicato y el protoalbeiterato." In *Historia de la ciencia y de la técnica en la corona de Castilla. Siglos XVI y XVII*, edited by José María López Piñero. Salamanca: Junta de Castilla y León, 2002.
Lovkrona, Inger. "The Pregnant Frog and the Farmer's Wife." In *ARV Scandinavian Yearbook of Folklore* 45 (1989): 73–124.
Luna, Lola, ed. *Valor, agravio y mujer*, by Ana Caro. Madrid: Castalia, 1993.
Manchego, Pedro. *Retrato de un monstruo, que se engendró en un cuerpo de un hombre, que se dize Hernando de la Haba, vezino del lugar de Fereyra, Marquesado de Cenete, de unos hechizos que le dieron. Parteole Francisca de León, comadre de parir, en veynte y uno de Junio, de 1606, por la parte tras ordinaria. Compuestas por Pedro Manchego, vezino de Granada*. Barcelona: Sabastian de Cormellas al Call, 1606.
Maravall, José Antonio. *Culture of the Baroque: Analysis of a Historical Structure*. Minneapolis: University of Minnesota Press, 1986.
Mariscal, George. *Contradictory Subjects: Quevedo, Cervantes, and Seventeenth-Century Spanish Culture*. Ithaca: Cornell University Press, 1991.
Marshall, P. David. *Celebrity and Power. Fame in Contemporary Culture*. Minneapolis: University of Minnesota Press, 1997.

Martín, Adrienne L. "Images of Deviance in Cervantes's Algiers." *Cervantes* 15 (1995): 5–15.

Martínez Ripoll, Antonio. " 'El Conde Duque con una vara en la mano' de Velázquez, o la 'praxis' olivarista de la Razón de Estado, en torno a 1625." In *La España del Conde Duque de Olivares*, edited by John Elliot and Angel García Sanz, 45–79. Valladolid: Universidad de Valladolid, 1990.

Matthews, Sandra, and Laura Wexler. *Pregnant Pictures*. New York: Routledge, 2000.

Maus, Katharine Eisaman. "A Womb of His Own: Male Renaissance Poets in the Female Body." In *Printing and Parenting in Early Modern England*, edited by Douglas A. Brooks, 89–108. Aldershot: Ashgate, 2005.

Mazzoni, Cristina. *Maternal Impressions: Pregnancy and Childbirth in Literature and Theory*. Ithaca: Cornell University Press, 2002.

McLaren, Angus. *A History of Contraception: From Antiquity to the Present Day*. Oxford: Basil Blackwell, 1992.

Medina, Antonio. *Cartilla nueva, útil y necesaria para instruirse las matronas que vulgarmente se llaman comadres, en el oficio de partear*. Madrid: Antonio Sanz, 1750.

Mejía, Vicente. *Saludable instrucción del estado del matrimonio*. Córdoba: Juan Baptista Escudero, 1566.

Mellor, Anne. *Mary Shelley: Her Life, Her Fiction, Her Monsters*. New York: Routledge, 1989.

Millner, Sherry. " 'Womb with a View': Script and Stills." In Morgan and Michaels, *Fetal Subjects*, 201–35.

Moncada, Sancho de. *Restauración política de España*. Madrid: Luis Sánchez, 1619.

Montauban, Jannine. *El ajuar de la vida picaresca*. Madrid: Visor Libros, 2003.

Monter, William. *Frontiers of Heresy: The Spanish Inquisition from the Basque Lands to Sicily*. Cambridge: Cambridge University Press, 1990.

Morgan, Lynn M., and Meredith W. Michaels. *Fetal Subjects, Feminist Positions*. Philadelphia: University of Pennsylvania Press, 1999.

Moreto, Agustín. "Loa de Juan Rana." In *Ramillete de entremeses y bailes nuevamente recogido de los antiguos poetas de España: Siglo XVII*, edited by Hannah E. Bergman, 431–40. Madrid: Castalia, 1970.

Morley, S. Griswold, and Courtney Bruerton. *The Chronology of Lope de Vega's Comedias*. New York: Modern Language Association, 1940.

Morreall, John, ed. *The Philosophy of Laughter and Humor*. Albany: State University of New York Press, 1987.

Morwood, James. *A Dictionary of Latin Words and Phrases*. Oxford: Oxford University Press, 1998.

Musacchio, Jacqueline Marie. *The Art and Ritual of Childbirth in Renaissance Italy*. New Haven: Yale University Press, 1999.

Navas, Juan de. *Elementos del Arte de Partear*. Madrid: Sancha, 1815. First published 1750 by Imprenta Real.

Navascués, Javier de, ed. *Discurso de mi vida*, by Alonso de Contreras. Madrid: Ediciones Internacionales Universitarias, 2004.

Newman, Barbara. *From Virile Woman to WomanChrist: Studies in Medieval Religion and Literature*. Philadelphia: University of Pennsylvania Press, 1995.
Newman, William R. *Promethean Ambitions: Alchemy and the Quest to Perfect Nature*. Chicago: University of Chicago Press, 2004.
Newman, Karen. *Fetal Positions: Individualism, Science, Visuality*. Stanford: Stanford University Press, 1996.
*New Yorker* Cartoon Caption Contest (February 13 & 20, 2006) 178.
Niebylski, Dianna. *Humoring Resistance: Laughter, Bodies and Excess in Contemporary Latin American Fiction*. Albany: State University of New York, 2004.
Nieremberg, Eusebio. *Curiosa filosofía y tesoro de maravillas de la naturaleza examinada en varias cuestiones naturales*. Madrid: Imprenta del Reyno, 1630.
Núñez, Francisco. *Libro del parto humano, en el qual se contienen remedios muy utiles y usuales para el parto dificultoso de las mugeres, con otros muchos secretos a ello pertenecientes, y a las enfermedades de los niños*. Madrid: Tomas Iunti, 1621.
Oliver, Kelly. *Family Values: Subjects Between Nature and Culture*. New York and London: Routledge, 1997.
O'Neill, John. *Incorporating Cultural Theory: Maternity at the Millennium*. Albany: State University of New York Press, 2002.
Ortiz, Teresa. "La educación de las matronas en la Europa Moderna: ¿Liberación o subordinación?" In *De leer a escribir: La educación de las mujeres: ¿libertad o subordinación?* edited by Cristina Segura Graiño, 155–70. Granada: Asociación Cultural AL-Mudayna, 1996.

———. "From Hegemony to Subordination: Midwives in Early Modern Spain." In *The Art of Midwifery: Early Modern Midwives in Europe*, edited by Hilary Marland, 95–114. London: Routledge, 1994.

———. "Protomedicato y matronas: Una relación al servicio de la cirugía." *Dynamis* 16 (1996): 109–20.
Pacheco, Francisco. *Arte de la pintura*. Edited by Bonaventura Bassegoda i Hugas. Madrid: Cátedra, 1990.
Pardo Tomás, José. *Ciencia y Censura: La Inquisición española y los libros científicos en los siglos XVI y XVII*. Madrid: Consejo Superior de Investigaciones Científicas, 1991.
Paré, Ambroise. *On Monsters and Marvels*. Translated by Janis L. Pallister. Chicago: University of Chicago Press, 1982.
Pasamonte, Jerónimo de. "Vida y trabajos de Jerónimo de Pasamonte." In *Autobiografías de soldados (siglo XVII)*. Biblioteca de Autores Españoles 90. Edited by José María de Cossío. Madrid: Atlas, 1956.
Paun de García, Susan. "Zayas's Ideal of the Masculine: Clothes Make the Man." In *Women in the Discourse of Early Modern Spain*, edited by Joan F. Cammarata, 253–71. Gainesville: University Press of Florida, 2003.
Penttila, Chris. "Hot Market: Metrosexuals." *Entrepreneur* (December 2003): 91.
Pérez Escohotado, Javier. *Sexo e Inquisición en España*. Madrid: Temas de Hoy, 1993.
Perreault, Jeanne. "Male Maternity in *Ulysses*." *English Studies in Canada* 13, no.3 (1987): 304–14.

Perry, Mary Elizabeth. *Crime and Society in Early Modern Seville.* Hanover: University Press of New England, 1980.

———. *Gender and Disorder in Early Modern Seville.* Princeton: Princeton University Press, 1990.

———. "The 'Nefarious Sin' in Early Modern Seville." In *The Pursuit of Sodomy: Male Homosexuality in Renaissance and Enlightenment Europe*, edited by Kent Gerard and Gert Hekma, 67–89. New York: Harrington Park Press, 1988.

———. "The Politics of Race, Ethnicity, and Gender in the Making of the Spanish State." In *Culture and the State in Spain 1550–1850*, edited by Tom Lewis and Francisco J. Sánchez, 34–54. New York: Garland, 1999.

Phillips, Robert. *The Pregnant Man.* Garden City: Doubleday, 1978.

Pineda, Juan de. *Diálogos familiares de la agricultura cristiana.* Biblioteca de Autores Españoles 161. Edited by J. Meseguer Fernández. Madrid: Atlas, 1963.

Pinto-Correia, Clara. *The Ovary of Eve: Egg and Sperm Preformation.* Chicago: University of Chicago Press, 1997.

Pliny the Elder. *Natural History: A Selection.* Translated by John F. Healy. New York: Penguin, 1991.

Pomata, Gianna. "Menstruating Men: Similarity and Difference of the Sexes in Early Modern Medicine." In Finucci and Brownlee, *Generation and Degeneration*, 109–52.

*Por tu propio bien.* Directed by Icíar Bollaín. In *Hay Motivo* [a collective film project produced by José Luis Cuerda]. First aired March 5, 2004. www.elmundo.es/fotografia/2004/02/hay_motivo3/foto20.html.

*Queer As Folk.* "Episode 13, Season 5." Showtime. August 7, 2005.

Quevedo, Francisco de. "Entremés primero de Bárbara." In *Obra poética: Teatro y traducciones poéticas*, edited by José Manuel Blecua, 4:19–28. Madrid: Castalia, 1981.

———. "España defendida, y los tiempos de ahora." In *Obras completas en prosa*, edited by Luis Astrana Marín, 341–72. Madrid: Aguilar, 1945.

———. "The Swindler." In *Two Spanish Picaresque Novels.* Translated by Michael Alpert. New York: Penguin, 1981.

———. *La vida del Buscón llamado Don Pablos.* Edited by Domingo Ynduráin. Madrid: Cátedra, 1987.

*Rabbit Test.* Directed by Joan Rivers. Nelson Entertainment, 1977. Video release date: February 23, 1989.

Rael, Juan Bautista. *Cuentos españoles de Colorado y Nuevo Méjico: Spanish Tales from Colorado and New Mexico.* Stanford: Stanford University Press, 1957.

Rallo Gruss, Asunción. *Coloquios matrimoniales del licenciado Pedro de Luján.* Madrid: Anejos del Boletín de la Real Academia Española, 1990.

Read, Kirk. "Mother's Milk from Father's Breast: Maternity without Women in Male French Renaissance Lyric." In *High Anxiety: Masculinity in Crisis in Early Modern France*, edited by Kathleen P. Long, 71–92. Kirksville: Truman State University Press, 2002.

Redondo, Augustin. "Del personaje de Aldonza Lorenzo al de Dulcinea del Toboso:

Algunos aspectos de la invención cervantina." *Anales Cervantinos* 21 (1983): 1–22.
Reed, Richard K. *Birthing Fathers: The Transformation of Men in American Rites of Birth.* New Brunswick: Rutgers University Press, 2005.
Restrepo-Gautier, Pablo. "Afeminados, hechizados y hombres vestidos de mujer: la inversión sexual en algunos entremeses de los Siglos de Oro." In Delgado and Saint-Saëns, *Lesbianism and Homosexuality*, 199–215.
Riddle, John M. *Contraception and Abortion from the Ancient World to the Renaissance.* Cambridge: Harvard University Press, 1992.
Río Parra, Elena del. *Una era de monstruos: Representaciones de lo deforme en el Siglo de Oro español.* Madrid: Iberoamericana, 2003.
Ríos Izquierdo, Pilar. *Mujer y sociedad en el siglo XVII a través de los avisos de Barrionuevo.* Madrid: Dirección General de la Mujer, 1995.
Rivilla Bonet y Pueyo, Joseph. *Desvíos de la naturaleza o tratado de el origen de los monstruos.* Lima: Joseph de Contreras, 1695.
Rodríguez Cuadros, Evangelina. *La técnica del actor español en el Barroco: Hipótesis y documentos.* Madrid: Castalia, 1998.
Rosenberg, Debra. "The War Over Fetal Rights." *Newsweek* (June 9, 2003): 40–47.
Rösslin, Eucharius. *When Midwifery Became the Male Physician's Province: The Sixteenth Century Handbook: The Rose Garden for Pregnant Women and Midwives, Newly Englished.* Translated by Wendy Arons. Jefferson, NC: McFarland, 1994.
Rostoker-Gruber, Karen, and Gail Panzer-Salmanowitz. *If Men Had Babies . . .* Chatsworth: CCC Publications, 2001.
Rufo, Juan. *Las seiscientas apotegmas y otras obras en verso.* Edited by Alberto Blecua. Madrid: Espasa-Calpe, 1972. First published 1596.
Ruyses de Fontecha, Juan Alonso de los. *Diez previlegios para mugeres preñadas.* Alcalá de Henares: Luis Martínez Grande, 1606.
Sáez Raposo, Francisco. *Juan Rana y el teatro cómico breve del siglo XVII.* Madrid: Fundación Universitaria Española, 2005.
Saintyves, Pierre. *Las madres vírgenes y los embarazos milagrosos: Ensayo de mitología comparada.* Madrid: Akal, 1985.
Salomon, Noël. *Lo villano en el teatro del Siglo de Oro.* Madrid: Castalia, 1985.
Sánchez Imizcoz, Ruth. *El teatro menor en la España del siglo XVII: La contribución de Agustín Moreto y Cabaña.* New Orleans: University Press of the South, 1998.
Sanders, Barry. *Sudden Glory: Laughter as Subversive History.* Boston: Beacon Press, 1995.
Sanders, Julie. "Midwifery and the New Science in the Seventeenth Century: Language, Print, and the Theatre." In Fudge, Gilbert, and Wiseman, *At the Borders*, 74–90.
Sandoval-Sánchez, Alberto. "Undoing Abjection after Migration: AIDS and Mariconería Latina in the Cultural Imaginary." Paper presented at "Race, Ethnicity, and Civic Identity in the Americas: A Symposium," University of Kentucky, Lexington, March 26, 2004.

Saslow, James M. *Ganymede in the Renaissance: Homosexuality in Art and Society.* New Haven: Yale University Press, 1986.
Saunders, Michael William. *Imps of the Perverse: Gay Monsters in Film.* Westport: Praeger, 1998.
Sawday, Jonathan. *The Body Emblazoned: Dissection and the Human Body in Renaissance Culture.* London: Routledge, 1995.
———. " 'Forms Such as Never Were in Nature': the Renaissance Cyborg." In Fudge, Gilbert, and Wiseman, *At the Borders*,171–95.
Scarborough, Connie L. "Verbalization and Visualization in MS. R.I.1 of the *Cantigas de Santa Maria*: The Theme of the Runaway Nun." In *Studies on the Cantigas de Santa Maria: Art, Music, and Poetry*, 135–54. Madison: The Hispanic Seminary of Medieval Studies, 1987.
———. "The Virgin as Midwife: Verbalization and Visualization in Alfonso X's *Cantigas de Santa María*." *Michigan Academician* 15. no. 1 (1982): 137–44.
———. *Women in Thirteenth-century Spain as Portrayed in Alfonso X's Cantigas de Santa Maria.* Lewiston: Edwin Mellen Press, 1993.
Schindehette, Susan, and Eileen Finan. "Ultrasound, Ultrasafe?" *People* (June 14, 2004): 111–13.
*Scrubs.* "My Big Bird." NBC. January 24, 2006 [Season 5, Episode 8].
Serralta, Frédéric. "Juan Rana homosexual." *Criticón* 50 (1990): 81–92.
Shapiro, Jerrold Lee. *When Men are Pregnant: Needs and Concerns of Expectant Fathers.* New York: Delta, 1993.
Shaviro, Steven. *The Cinematic Body.* Minneapolis: University of Minnesota Press, 1993.
Shergold, N. D., and J. E. Varey, eds. *Genealogía, origen y noticias de los comediantes de España.* London: Tamesis, 1985.
Shrage, Laurie. *Abortion and Social Responsibility: Depolarizing the Debate.* Oxford: Oxford University Press, 2003.
Sieber, Harry. *Language and Society in 'La vida de Lazarillo de Tormes.'* Baltimore: Johns Hopkins University Press, 1978.
Simón Díaz, José. *Fuentes para la historia de Madrid y sus provincias: Textos impresos de los siglos XVI y XVII.* Madrid: Instituto de Estudios Madrileños, 1964.
*A Slightly Pregnant Man.* Directed by Jacques Demy. Simitar Entertainment, 1973. Video release date: March 7, 1998.
Smith, Paul Julian. *The Body Hispanic: Gender and Sexuality in Spanish and Spanish American Literature.* Oxford: Clarendon Press, 1989.
Sones, Bill and Rich Sones. *Can a Guy Get Pregnant? Scientific Answers to Everyday (& Not-So-Everyday) Questions.* New York: Pi Press, 2006.
Stallybrass, Peter. "Transvestism and the 'body beneath': Speculating on the boy actor." In *Erotic Politics: Desire on the Renaissance Stage*, edited by Susan Zimmerman, 64–83. London: Routledge, 1992.
Stein, Louise K. *Songs of Mortals, Dialogues of the Gods: Music and Theatre in Seventeenth-Century Spain.* Oxford: Clarendon Press, 1993.
Stephanson, Raymond. *The Yard of Wit: Male Creativity and Sexuality, 1650–1750.* Philadelphia: University of Pennsylvania Press, 2004.

Stoichita, Victor I. *El ojo místico: Pintura y visión religiosa en el Siglo de Oro español.* Madrid: Alianza, 1996.
Stott, Andrew. *Comedy.* New York: Routledge, 2005.
Stratton, Suzanne L. *The Immaculate Conception in Spanish Art.* Cambridge: Cambridge University Press, 1994.
Stroud, Matthew D. "Comedy, Foppery, Camp: Moreto's 'El lindo Don Diego.' " In Delgado and Saint-Saëns, *Lesbianism and Homosexuality,* 177–95.
Suárez de Figueroa, Cristóbal. *Varias noticias importantes a la humana comunicación.* Madrid: Tomás Junti, 1621.
Surtz, Ronald E. *The Guitar of God: Gender, Power, and Authority in the Visionary World of Mother Juana de la Cruz (1481-1534).* Philadelphia: University of Pennsylvania Press, 1990.
———. "The Privileging of the Feminine in the Trinity Sermon of Mother Juana de la Cruz." In *Women's Voices and the Politics of Spanish Empire,* edited by Jeanne L. Gillespie, Jennifer Eich, and Lucia Guzzi Harrison. New Orleans: University Press of the South (forthcoming).
Terrón González, Jesús. *Lexico de cosméticos y afeites en el Siglo de Oro.* Salamanca: Unversidad de Extremadura, 1990.
Thompson, Peter. "Crossing the Gendered Clothes-line: Lanini y Sagredo's *El parto de Juan Rana.*" *Bulletin of the Comediantes* 53, no.2 (2001): 317–33.
———. "Juan Rana, A Gay Golden Age *Gracioso.*" In *A Society on Stage: Essays on Spanish Golden Drama,* edited by Edward H. Friedman, H. J. Manzari, and Donald D. Miller, 239–51. New Orleans: University Press of the South, 1998.
———. *The Triumphant Juan Rana: A Gay Actor of the Spanish Golden Age.* Toronto: University of Toronto Press, forthcoming.
Tilley, Sue. *Leigh Bowery: The Life and Times of an Icon.* London: Hodder & Stoughton, 1997.
Tomás y Valiente, Francisco. "El crimen y pecado contra natura." In *Sexo barroco y otras transgresiones premodernas,* edited by F. Tomás y Valiente, B. Clavero, J. L. Bermejo, E. Gacto, A. M. Hespanha, and C. Alvarez Alonso, 33–55. Madrid: Alianza, 1990.
Torquemada, Antonio de. *Jardín de flores curiosas.* Edited by Giovanni Allegra. Madrid: Castalia, 1982.
Trujillo, Tomás de. *Libro llamado reprobación de trajes, y de abuso de juramentos: Con un tratado de limosnas.* Zaragoza: Francisco Curteti, 1563.
Tuttle, Leslie. "Fecund Fathers and Invisible Mothers: The Gender Politics of Seventeenth-Century Natalism" (unpublished manuscript, consulted 2000).
Valencia, Pedro de. *Discurso contra la ociosidad.* BNM (Biblioteca Nacional de Madrid) Ms. 13348. Madrid: 1618.
Vega, Lope de. "Las batuecas del Duque de Alba." In *Obras de Lope de Vega,* edited by Marcelino Menéndez Pelayo, 351–403. Madrid: Atlas, 1968.
———. "La octava maravilla." In *Obras dramáticas,* 247–85. Madrid: Sucesores de Rivadeneyra, 1930.
Velasco, Sherry. "Interracial Lesbian Erotics in Early Modern Spain: Catalina de Erauso and Elena/o de Céspedes." In *Tortilleras: Hispanic and U. S. Latina*

Lesbian Expression, edited by Lourdes Torres and Inmaculada Pertusa-Seva, 213–27. Philadelphia: Temple University Press, 2003.

———. *The Lieutenant Nun: Transgenderism, Lesbian Desire, and Catalina de Erauso*. Austin: University of Texas Press, 2000.

———. "Performing Male Pregnancy in Early Modern Spain: *El parto de Juan Rana*." *Comedia Performance* 1, no. 1 (2004): 192–218.

———. "Reading Male Pregnancy in *Don Quijote* within its Early Modern Context." In *Don Quijote Across Four Centuries: 1605-2005*, edited by Carroll B. Johnson. Newark: Juan de la Cuesta, 2006. 185–93.

Vélez-Quiñones, Harry. "Deficient masculinity: 'Mi puta es el Maestre de Montesa.'" *Journal of Spanish Cultural Studies* 2, no. 1 (2001): 27–40.

———. *Monstrous Displays: Representation and Perversion in Spanish Literature*. New Orleans: University Press of the South, 1999.

Vigil, Mariló. *La vida de las mujeres en los siglos XVI y XVII*. Madrid: Siglo Veintiuno de España, 1986.

Villa, Antonio Rodríguez. *La corte y monarquía de España en los años de 1636 y 1637*. Madrid: Luis Navarro, 1886.

Warner, Marina. *Alone of All Her Sex: The Myth and the Cult of the Virgin Mary*. New York: Vintage Books, 1983.

Warren, Nancy Bradley. "Pregnancy and Productivity: The Imagery of Female Monasticism within and beyond the Cloister Walls." *Journal of Medieval and Early Modern Studies* 28, no. 3 (1998): 531–52.

Wiesner, Merry E. "Early Modern Midwifery: A Case Study." In *Women and Work in Preindustrial Europe*, edited by Barbara A. Hanawalt, 94–113. Bloomington: Indiana University Press, 1986.

———. *Women and Gender in Early Modern Europe*. Cambridge: Cambridge University Press, 1993.

*Wigstock: The Movie*. Directed by Barry Shils. Metro Goldwyn Mayer, 1995. DVD release date: June 3, 2003.

*Will & Grace*. NBC.
"William, Tell" (November 9, 1998) [Season 1].
"The Unsinkable Mommy Adler" (February 9, 1999) [Season 1].
"Seeds of Discontent" (January 25, 2000) [Season 2].
"Hey La, Hey La, My Ex-boyfriend's Back" (March 14, 2000) [Season 2].
"Moveable Feast" (November 22, 2001) [Season 4].
"Marry Me a Little" (November 21, 2002) [Season 5].
"Dames at Sea" (September 25, 2003) [Season 6].
"Cop to It" (January 26, 2006) [Season 8].

Winston, Robert. *The IVF Revolution: The Definitive Guide to Assisted Reproductive Techniques*. London: Vermilion, 2000.

Woliver, Laura R. *The Political Geographies of Pregnancy*. Urbana: University of Illinois Press, 2002.

Yerushalmi, Yosef Hayim. *From Spanish Court to Italian Ghetto: Isaac Cardoso; A Study in Seventeenth-Century Marranism and Jewish Apologetics*. New York: Columbia University Press, 1971.

Zapperi, Roberto. *The Pregnant Man*. Translated by Brian Williams. London: Harwood, 1991.
Zoja, Luigi. *The Father: Historical, Psychological and Cultural Perspectives*. Translated by Henry Martin. New York: Brunner-Routledge, 2002.
Zayas, María de. *Desengaños amorosos*. Edited by Alicia Yllera. Madrid: Cátedra, 1983.

———. *The Disenchantments of Love: A Translation of the Desengaños amorosos*. Translated by H. Patsy Boyer. Albany: State University of New York Press, 1997.

———. *The Enchantments of Love: Amorous and Exemplary Novels*. Translated by H. Patsy Boyer. Berkeley: University of California Press, 1990.

Zayas y Sotomayor, María de. *Novelas amorosas y ejemplares*. Edited by Julián Olivares. Madrid: Cátedra, 2000.
Ziomek, Henryk. *Lo grotesco en la literatura española del Siglo de Oro*. Madrid: Ediciones Alcalá, 1983.

# Index

abortifacients, xv, 60, 68–69, 71–72
abortion, xv, xvii–iii, 13–14, 20–23, 65, 67–72, 163n8, 166n46, 167n47; Alfonso X's *Siete partidas*, 163n5, 166n37, 166n42–47; Pope Sixtus V, 67; Pope Innocence XI, 67; moralists, 68–69; Queen Christina of Sweden, 69; *aborto*, 72, 165n36, 166n46, 166n49, 167n57. *See also* birth control.
Adelman, Janet, 6–7, 157n15
adultery, 88–92, 115, 163n5
alchemy, 17–18
Alfonso X, *Cantigas*, 51, 53–55, 162n1–3, 163n4, 163n8, 164n9; *Las Siete Partidas*, 43, 52, 54, 68, 90–91, 163n5–7, 170n92, 171n94–96
Alonso de los Ruyzes, Juan, 57, 60, 80
Andrade, Alonso de, 90, 170n93
androgyny (androgynes), 34, 95, 99–100
Aristotle, xvii–xviii, 4, 45, 63–65, 68, 79–80, 98, 101, 121, 161n38, 165n36, 168n67, 178n5, 180n24
Arons, Wendy, 58, 166n41
Athena, 2, 78
Atlas, Charles, 24
Aulnoy, Madame d,' 73–74
Azpilcueta Navarro, Martín, 47–48

Babuscio, Jack, 178n6
Bakhtin, Mikhail, xvii, 7; carnivalesque humor 124
Barrett, Deirdre, 9
Barrionuevo, Jerónimo de, 61–62, 69, 81–82, 164n21–22, 168n59, 169n69
*Bearded Lady* (Magdalena Ventura), 100–102
Benshoff, Harry M., 18
Bergman, David, 124, 126
Bergman, Hannah, 35, 38, 121
Bergmann, Emilie, 74
Bicks, Caroline, 60, 164n19
birth control (antifertility), xiii, xv, xviii, 15, 20, 60, 67–69, 71, 163n8
birthing room (delivery room), xv, xvii, 57, 58–60, 62, 123; Isabel de la Cavallería, 61–62, 165n27
Blumenfeld-Kosinski, Renate, 57
Boccaccio, Giovanni: *Decameron*, 3, 31–33
Bollaín, Icíar: *Por tu propio bien*, 22–23
Bovistau, Pedro, xiv, 96–97, 172n6–9
Bowery, Leigh, 24–25
Braidotti, Rosi: alchemy, 17–18; monsters, 18
Brockliss, L.W. B., 166n38
Brooks, Lynn Matluck, 161n41
Brown, Peter, 99

Buckley, F. H., 125
Burshatin, Israel, 103–4
Bush, George W., 21–22
Bynum, Carolina Walker, 3, 156n3

Caesarean operation, 57
Camarena Laucirica, Julio, 4
Camargo, Ignacio de, 111
Cameron, Vivian, 161n39
camp, 21, 23–24, 26, 124, 126
Canavaggio, Jean, 160n18
*Cantigas de Santa María*, See Alfonso X.
Carbón, Damián, 57–59, 79, 164n18, 164n20, 169n67
Carducho, Vicente: *Diálogos de la pintura*, 38
carnivalesque, (*See also* Bakhtin), xiii, 17, 28, 49, 124, 178n5
Caro Baroja, Julio, 170n82
Carranza, Alonso de, 74, 76, 167n55
Carrasco, Rafael, 115, 118, 159n4, 177n63
Cartagena-Calderón, José, 35, 106, 113, 158n32, 160n16, 161n29, 175n43
Casey, James, 77
Castiglione, Baldesar, 43, 90, 106–7, 174n31
Cervantes, Miguel de, 5, 28, 118, 156n8, 157n9, 157n11
Céspedes, Eleno/a de, 101, 103–4, 173n21, 173n23–28
Chamorro, María Inés, 176n50, 179n12, 179n14, 179n17, 179n20, 181n13, 181n15, 181n18, 181n21
child mortality (infant mortality), 51, 72, 163n8
childbirth, xiii, xv, xvii, 8–9, 13, 15, 23, 35, 45–46, 50–51, 54–60, 64, 66, 72, 78–80, 103, 126, 155n6, 157n16, 163n8, 164n11; pain in, 12, 33, 44, 58; as metaphor for literary act, 4–5, 8, 28, 156n6, 158n16, 159n1; Bakhtin, 7; couvade, 8

Churchwell, Gordon, 8
class (economic issues), 61–62, 74, 76, 87, 90–91, 93, 106–11, 119–20, 157n8, 168n59, 168n62
clothing, 1, 13–14, 24, 26–27, 30, 37–38, 41, 43, 45, 47, 62, 74–76, 88, 91, 98–99, 107–8, 112, 118–19, 132–33, 156n8, 160n20–21, 161n39, 174n32, 174n36, 182n1. *See also* cross-dressing.
Cody, Lisa Forman, 6, 65, 157n14
Colker, Ruth: equality theory, 20
comedy, xvi, 1, 14–16, 19, 21, 23, 28, 33–34, 39, 41, 43–44, 48, 51, 56, 85, 98, 116, 121, 123–26, 178n3–5; Aristotelian theory of, xvii, 38–39, 121, 125, 178n5. *See also* humor.
conception, xiii, xv, 4, 7, 46, 48, 51–52, 60, 64–65, 71, 79–80, 88, 98, 109, 124–25, 155n1, 157n15; immaculate, 43–44, 54–55, 161n39, 162n1
conjoined twins, 84
Cordoba, Pierre, 169n75, 169n77, 170n80, 170n82
*Cosby Show*, 14
Cotarelo y Mori, Emilio, 37, 39, 41, 45, 111–12, 121, 160n19, 175n42, 176n44
couvade, 8, 56, 158n18
Covarrubias, Sebastián: *Emblemas morales*, 31, 100, 159n7; *Tesoro*, 33–34, 42–43, 99, 101, 113, 129, 157n10, 161n32–33, 173n19, 176n48–49, 176n51, 179n10–13, 179n15–16, 180n26, 180n4, 180n6, 180n9
Cowans, Jon, 114
Crane, Mary Thomas, 6
Critchley, Simon, 125–26
cross-dressing, 24; punishment for sodomy, 1, 109, 119–20; on stage, 36, 123; men dressed as women, 26–27, 37, 39, 41, 108–10,

112–13, 117, 125; women dressed as men, 98, 114, 157n8, 159n4. *See also* clothing.
Cruz, Anne J., 168n62

D'Ancona, Mirella Levi, 164n12
De Armas, Frederick A., 161n28
Deleito y Piñuela, José, 120, 177n65–66
Delpech, François, 3, 159n13, 169n77, 170n84, 179n12
Demy, Jacques: *A Slightly Pregnant Man*, 13–14
Díaz Escovar, Narciso, 168n60
Diz, M. Ana, 164n8
Donaldson, Peter S., 7
Donnell, Sidney, 108, 111–12
drag queen: pregnant, 24, 31, 123; in Kentucky ("Aisha"), 2, 26–27; in Granada, 2; Leigh Bowery, 25. *See also* cross-dressing.
Dryden, John: *The Wild Gallant*, 6, 157n14
Dworkin, Andrea, 19
Dyer, Richard, 121, 173n21

effeminacy: male, xiii–xviii, 1, 34, 40, 93, 96–97, 108–9, 111, 113, 119–21, 123, 125; female, 109–11. *See also* feminization, metrosexuality.
El Saffar, Ruth, 78
emblem, of gluttony, 39; Covarrubias: *Emblemas morales* ("Only by force"), 31, 159n7; androgyny, 100
embryo, xviii, 2, 17, 19, 24, 65, 71, 88, 165n36, 166n42, 166n46
embryology (embryological debates), xv, 4, 33, 64–65, 67
Emery, David, 17, 158n20, 178n2
*entremés* (interlude, one-act play), xiii, 1–2, 11, 27–29, 31, 33, 41, 45, 47–49, 61, 76–77, 90, 93, 111–12, 123, 125–26, 155n1, 176n46, 178n4–5; and danger to morals, 112

Escamilla, Manuela de, 41
Ettinghausen, Henry, 82, 89, 169n70, 169n73, 174n29
eunuch, 33, 97–100, 179n13
*Examen de ingenios para las ciencias*, 28, 89. *See also* Huarte de San Juan.
Ezcaray, Fray Antonio de, 75, 107, 167n56

Faliu-Lacourt, Christiane, 78
feminization (*see also* effeminacy, metrosexuality) of men, xiii, xvi, xviii, 92, 99, 106–7, 109, 111, 114; fertility control, 5–6, 15, 29, 34, 42, 71, 98
fetal homicide, 52–53
fetal rights, 21, 51–52, 68
fetus, xviii, 11, 14, 32–35, 52, 64–66, 68–71, 73, 78, 83, 90, 94, 109, 166n37, 166n40–41, 167n59; iconography of, 52, 66–67
Finucci, Valeria, xiv, 64, 90, 156n2, 156n4, 161n38, 166n35, 170n43, 178n1
Flocker, Michael, 108, 171n1
Flynn, Maureen, 77
Forelle, Helen, 20
Fraenger, Wilhelm, 34
Frazer, R.M., 35
Freud, Sigmund, 9, 11, 158n18, 178n5; and Daniel Paul Schreber, 9
frogs, 18, 33–36, 46, 81, 162n42; sexuality, 33–36; and Juan Rana, 18, 33–35; tadpoles, 33–34
Fuentelapeña, Fray Antonio de, 65, 95, 104, 166n30, 171n47

Galen, 64, 71, 79, 101, 165n36
Galindo, Pedro, 47–48, 68–69, 91, 162n45–46
Ganymede, 40
Garcés, María Antonia, 118, 177n62, 177n64
Garza Carvajal, Federico, 106, 109, 113, 174n30, 176n47

Gassier, Pierre, 9, 158n17
Gélis, Jacques, 8, 167n48
gender transgression: *See* clothing, cross-dressing, effeminacy in men, masculinity, and feminization.
generation, 2, 12, 18, 65, 79–80; when human life begins, 64–65; preformationism, 4, 66; Aristotle, 63–64; Avicenna, 64, 79
Gilbert, Ruth, xv, 2, 4, 32, 65, 87, 101, 158n21
gluttony, emblem of, 39, 74; *The New Yorker*, 44
Gonzáles Alcantud, José, 85, 169n75
Gossy, Mary S., 159n5
Goya, Francisco de,: *Loco pícaro*, 9–10
Gracián, Baltasar, 117
Granjel, Luis S., 64, 165n35
Greer, Fergus, 24–25, 158n31, 159n32
Greilsammer, Myriam, 63
*Grey's Anatomy*, 17
*Guardainfante*, 74, 76–77. *See also* clothing.
Guevara, Antonio de, 73–75, 167n52
gynecology, xv, 50, 56, 66, 71

hairstyles, 37, 40, 97–98, 106–11, 119–20, 174n36. *See also* feminization of men.
Hale, Rosemary Drage, xvi, 56,
Haraway, Donna, 19
Heiple, Daniel, 113, 161n28–29
Heise, Ursula K., 113–14
hermaphrodites (*see also* androgynes, intersexed), xvi, xviii, 29, 93, 95, 99, 101, 159n4, 172n19; Ovid, 32; emblems of, 32, 101–2; male pregnancy, 29, 95, 100; Céspedes, 101–4
Herrera Puga, Pedro, 115
Hippocretes, 64, 72, 89, 99
homosexuality (gay, queer), xvi, 1, 9, 11–12, 18, 22–24, 26, 33, 35–37, 39–41, 49, 93, 97, 108, 116–19, 124, 126, 155n1–2, 160n16, 174n36, 178n6. *See also* sodomy.
homunculus, 17–18
Huarte de San Juan, Juan, 5, 28, 40, 42, 46, 89–90, 94, 97–99, 105–6, 156n7, 159n2, 161n34, 162n43–44, 171n2, 172n14–15
Huerta Calvo, Javier, 48–49, 162n47
Huet, Marie Hélène, 44, 46, 170n89
humor, xvii, 14, 16, 19, 23, 28, 33–34, 39, 41, 43–44, 48, 51, 56, 85, 116, 121, 123–26, 178n4–5. *See also* comedy.

Ibero, Alba, 54–56, 155n5
iconography, xvi, 3, 5, 15, 34, 50, 65–67, 92; Marian, 50, 54–56. *See also* visual representations.
Immaculate Conception, 43–44, 54–56, 161n39, 162n1
infant mortality: *See* child mortality.
infanticide, xvii, 51, 54, 70, 76–77, 90, 163n8
infertility, 51, 54, 68, 74–75, 98, 109
inheritance, 43, 48, 61–62, 69, 90–91
intersexed bodies, xiii, xvi, xviii, 82, 99. *See also* hermaphrodite and androgynes.

Jiménez Patón, Bartolomé, 40, 76–77, 107, 160n26, 168n61, 174n33
Joseph as mother, xvii, 54, 56, 164n15. *See also* visual representation of.
Juan Rana: *See* Rana, Juan.
*Junior*, 15–16, 23, 33, 39. *See also* Schwarzenegger.

Kagan, Richard L. (and Abigail Dyer), 173n21
Katz, Melissa R., 164n14
Keller, James R., 126
Keller, John (and Annette Cash), 164n9
Kitch, Aaron W., 87
Knight, Rhonda, 157n12
Kruger, Barbara, 20–22

Index   205

Laguna, Andrés, 43, 72
Lanini Sagredo, Francisco Pedro, xiii, 6, 28, 49, 90
Lanning, John Tate, 165n31
Laquer, Thomas, 4, 95, 161n38
Larsen, Ernest, 15, 33, 39
León, Francisco de, 108, 120
León, Pedro de, 115, 119
Lichtenstein, Therese, 21
Lipkin, Joan (and Tom Clear: *He's Having Her Baby*), 21, 158n23
Lobato, María Luisa, 160n22
Lochrie, Karma, 3
López Terrada, María Luz, 165n29
López, Gregorio, 68
Lovkrona, Inger, 34
Luján, Pedro de, 75, 167n57
Luna, Lola, 34

male femininity: *See* effeminacy.
male pregnancy: (male matrix, male reproduction, male maternity, male delivery, male autogenesis), xiii–xvii, as metaphor for literary or intellectual creativity, 1, 4–8, 12, 28–29, 156n6, 157n16, 159n1; Greek mythology, 2, 28; Bible, 2–3; Juana de la Cruz, 3; political vehicle, 1, 12–13, 15, 19–23, 29–31, 79, 161n39; psychological disorder, 9–11; theater, 2, 7, 41, 61, 79, 86–88, 168n65; film, 2, 7, 12–16, 18, 22–24, 33, 39, 161n36, 169n78; television, 2, 13–14, 17, 23, 126; camp versions, 21, 23–24, 26, 124, 126; cyberspace 2, 17; comic entertainment, 1–2, 12–17; female fantasy, 12–13; male fantasy, xiii–xlv, xvii, 2, 11, 13, 15, 17, 47, 50, 92; scientific plausibility of, 17–20; gullibility, 6, 31, 86; false or deceptive (pseudocyesis), 9, 20; metaphor for AIDS, 11–12; as phallic image, 28–29; hermaphroditic condition, 29, 95, 100; man as sole progenitor, 2, 56, 95; visual image of 2, 7, 20–25, 37, 50, 87, 100–101, 157n8 (*see also* visual representation); witchcraft, xiv, 84–87; news pamphlets, 84–87, 100
Manchego, Pedro, 84, 86, 145, 149, 169n75–76, 169n78, 170n81, 170n83
Maravall, José Antonio, 108
Mariana, Queen: reproduction, 60–61, 168n59
Marshall, P. David, 120
Martín, Adrienne, 112, 118, 120, 161n28, 177n62
Martínez Ripoll, Antonio, 30, 159n7
masculinity, male, xiii, 2, 30, 32, 65, 106, 108, 110–11, 160n16, 160n26–27, 174n36; female, 105, 175n41;
maternity, 23, 54, 56, 79, 84, 88, 168n65. *See also* reproduction, procreation, monstrous births, conception.
Matthews, Sandra (and Laura Wexler), 15–16
Maus, Katharine Eisaman, 5
Mazzoni, Cristina, 11
McLaren, Angus, 167n48
Medina, Antonio: *Cartilla nueva*, 70–71, 166n46
Mejía, Vicente, 69
Mellor, Anne, 18
menstruation: male, 42–43, 46, 97, 180n23; female, 61, 98–99
metrosexuality, xviii, 93, 108, 171n1, 174n36
midwives, (midwifery, *comadre*), xvii, 41–42, 50, 54, 57–63, 66–67, 70–71, 79, 82, 84–85, 103, 133, 141, 145–47, 149–50, 152, 162n2, 180n26, 165n31, 166n47, 168n66, 165n24, 169n75, 180n26, 182n24
Millner, Sherry: *Womb with a View*, 12–13

Mingwei, Lee: "The First Male Pregnancy," 17
miscarriage, xvii, 32, 52, 61, 68, 72–76, 168n59–60
*mola*, 4, 79
Moncada, Sancho de, 108, 174n37
monsters, (monstrous births), xiii, xvii, 2, 4, 11–12, 15, 18, 34, 39, 44–47, 49, 67, 74, 79–88, 92, 94–95, 145–50, 152, 168n67, 169n68–69, 169n74–75, 173n20
Montauban, Jannine, 29, 159n1, 165n32
Monter, William, 115
moralists, xiv, xviii, 47–48, 57, 69, 73, 76, 106, 112, 118, 120, 123, 177n63
Moreto, Agustín, *El lindo don Diego*, 35; *Loa de Juan Rana*, 41
*moriscos* (Moors), 85, 117–19
Morley, S. Griswold (and Courtney Bruerton), 170n84
Morreall, John, 170n5, 178n5
mother's imagination, 45–46, 80, 88, 94, 98
Muñoz, Ana, 168n60
Muñoz, María, 105. *See also* transmutation.
Musacchio, Jacqueline Marie, 164n11

Narcissus, 40
Navas, Juan de, 63
Nero, 34–35, 96–97
New Science, xv, 65
Newman, Barbara, 3
Newman, Karen, 66, 166n40
Newman, William, 18
news pamphlets (*relaciones*, broadsides), xiv, 82, 84–87, 89–90, 105, 169n70, 169n75
Niebylski, Dianna, 124
Nieremberg, Eusebio, 88, 170n88
Núñez, Francisco, 57, 60, 66–67, 72–73, 79, 84, 164n16, 168n66, 169n68, 169n74

O'Neill, John, 9
Oliver, Kelly, 15
Ortiz, Teresa, 57, 60, 63, 165n31, 168n66
Ovid, 32, 35

Pacheco, Francisco, xv, 54–56, 164n10, 164n13
Pardo Tomás, José, 72, 167n49
Paré, Ambroise, 34, 45–46, 80–81, 83, 87–89, 94, 97, 99, 171n3
*Parto de Juan Rana, El* (John Frog Gives Birth), xiii, xvi–ii, 1, 4, 12, 15, 21, 23–24, 27–28, 43, 50, 79, 82, 85, 93, 120, 124–25; control of female sexuality and reproduction, 49–50; sodomy (same-sex desire, homosexuality), 13, 30–31, 37–38, 41–42, 93, 121, 123–26, 155n2, 160n16; gender transgression (gender-blurring), 1, 13, 21, 27–28, 30–32, 35, 41–44, 49, 93, 121, 178n5; intellectual fecundity, 1, 4, 28; gluttony, 44; midwives (*comadres*), 41–42, 82, 180n26, 182n24; paternity anxiety, 1, 43, 45–47, 50, 89; and resemblance, 1, 38, 45, 47, 89; Huarte de San Juan, 28, 40, 42; Aristotle, 4, 45, 121, 125, 161n38, 178n5, 180n24
paternity, xiii–xiv; and anxiety (false paternity) 1–2, 5, 28, 43, 45–48, 50, 62, 85–86, 88–91, 123–24, 155n1, 156n1, 164n9, 168n65. *See also* resemblance.
Paun de García, Susan, 110
Penttila, Chris, 108
Pérez Escohotado, Javier, 32, 68, 77, 115, 166n44, 167n47
Pérez, Cosme, *See* Rana, Juan.
Perreault, Jeanne, 2, 157n16
Perry, Mary Elizabeth, 62, 76, 92, 115, 118–19, 155n5, 164n10, 167n47
Phillips, Robert, 157n16
picaresque, 9–10, 49, 116–17, 168n62

pictorial images, *See* visual representations.
Pineda, Juan de, 64, 72, 91, 165n36, 167n50
Pinto-Correia, Clara, 33, 166n38
Pliny, 64, 71, 80, 99, 161n38, 180n24
politics, (political power), male pregnancy, 1–2, 14, 27, 29–31, 44, 65, 79, 93; moriscos, 118; identity and gender politics, 31, 44, 93, 106, 110–11, 124; 159n3, 161n39; women's reproductive options, 13–15, 19–22, 27, 44, 166n42; homoeroticism, 12, 93, 106, 174n36
Pomata, Gianna, 161n37
*Por tu propio bien*, 22–23
pregnancy: female, xvii, 3, 50–54, 58, 61, 64, 66, 68–73, 75–79, 81–82; male: *see* male pregnancy. *See also* witchcraft.
pregnant man: *See* male pregnancy.
Primerose, James: *Popular Errours, or the Errours of the People in Physick*, 6
procreation, xiii–xiv, xvii, 2, 17, 28, 45, 49–51, 61–62, 64. *See also* childbirth.
*Protomédicos* (*protomedicato*), 62–63

*Queer As Folk*, 24
Quevedo, Francisco de, 48, 112–14, 116–17, 162n47, 176n52, 176n57, 177n60

*Rabbit Test*, 14, 23, 161n36
Rael, Juan Bautista, 156n5
Rana, Juan, (Cosme Pérez), xiii, 1, 6, 11, 28–31, 33, 35, 41–47, 49, 112, 124–27; and sodomy, xvi, 35, 37–38, 104, 120–21; professional life, 38–41, 120–21; physical appearance, 35–36, 39; effeminate mannerisms, 2, 41, 93, 111
Read, Kirk, 4–5
Redondo, Augustin, 159n5

Reed, Richard K., 8–9
reproduction: male, 2, 17–19, 49; (*see also* male pregnancy); human, xvii–iii, 4–5, 8, 11, 15, 33, 50, 56, 63, 68, 74, 79–80, 87, 89, 92, 161n39, 164n9, 165n32, 168n59
reproductive medicine and health, xiii–xv, 1–2, 5, 12–15, 19, 22–23, 27, 44, 50, 57, 85, 88, 123–27, 161n39, 168n59, 169n78; rights and options, xiv–xv, xvii, 14, 20–22, 27, 77–78, 81, 91, 155n6; technology, 18–19, 33, 49–50; professionalization of, xv, 56–71, 74–76;
resemblance, 1, 38, 45–47, 80, 88–89, 103
Restrepo-Gautier, Pablo, 37, 160n19, 160n24, 176n46, 178n4
Ribera, José de: *The Bearded Lady*, 101–2
Riddle, John M., 71, 155n4
Río Parra, Elena del, 100, 157n9, 158n17, 161n40, 169n75
Ríos Izquierdo, Pilar, 166n45, 168n59
Rivers, Joan: *See Rabbit Test*.
Rivilla Bonet y Pueyo, Joseph, 44–45, 161n40
Robledo, Diego Antonio de, 64
Rodríguez Cuadros, Evangelina, 38, 40, 159n10, 160n23, 160n25, 161n30, 168n60
*Roe v. Wade*, 13, 20–21
Rosenberg, Debra, 53
Rösslin, Eucharius, 57–58, 66

Rostoker-Gruber, Karen, (and Gail Panzer-Salmanowitz): *If Men Had Babies . . .* , 13
Rufo, Juan: *Las seiscientas apotegmas y otras obras en verso*, 5–6

Sáez-Raposo, Francisco, 37, 155n112
Saintyves, Pierre, 161n38
Salomon, Noel, 159n8

same-sex desire, 31, 34, 37–38, 41, 97, 100, 112, 115–17, 121, 155n2, 176n46. *See also* homosexuality and sodomy.
Sanders, Barry, 125
Sanders, Julie, xv, 57, 60
Sandoval-Sánchez, Alberto, 11–12
Saslow, James, 40–41
Saunders, Michael William, 39
Sawday, Jonathan, 158n22, 166n39
Scarborough, Connie L., 162n2, 164n8
Schneegans, G., 7
Schreber, Daniel Paul, 9, 11
Schwarzenegger, Arnold, 15–16, 33, 39
*Scrubs*, 13
Serralta, Frédéric, 35, 123, 178n3
sex assignment, xiv, xvi, 2, 27, 92–94, 97–106, 111, 121, 123
sex changes (transmutations), xiv, xvi, 31, 49, 93–97, 103–5
sexuality, female: xvii, 15, 34, 43, 50, 90; male: *See* homosexuality and same-sex desire.
Shakespeare, *Measure for Measure*, 6–7; *The Tempest*, 6; *All's Well That Ends Well*, 7
Shapiro, Jerrold Lee, 155n1, 156n1
Shaviro, Steven, 126
Shelley, Mary: *Frankenstein*, 15, 18
Shergold, N.D. (and J.E. Varey), 41
Shrage, Laurie, 21
*A Slightly Pregnant Man*, 13–14
sodomy (sodomite, *pecado nefando, lindo, maricón, marimarica, afeminado, bujarrón, sodomita, putillo, bugre, garzón, horadado*), xiii, xvi, xviii, 1, 5, 13, 31, 34–38, 41–42, 93–96, 103–6, 109, 112–26, 155n2, 157n12, 160n16, 160n22, 173n24, 174n36, 176n45, 176n50, 177n61, 177n63. *See also* homosexuality and same-sex desire.
soldiers's autobiographies, 117, 176n50
Sones, Bill (and Rich Sones), 19–20
spectators (theatergoers, viewers, audience), xiii, 6–7, 18, 20–22, 26–27, 31, 34–35, 37–43, 46, 50, 61, 67, 74, 78, 80, 84, 93, 100, 111–12, 119, 121, 123, 168n60
Stallybrass, Peter, 100
Stein, Louise K., 161n41
Steinbock, Bonnie, 52–53
Stephanson, Raymond, 4, 156n6, 166n39
Stoichita, Victor I., 54
Stott, Andrew, 178n5
Stratton, Suzanne, 55
Stroud, Matthew D., 161n29
Suárez de Figueroa, Cristóbal, 112, 176n45
Surtz, Ronald, 3, 156n3

theater, and male pregnancy, 2, 7, 41, 61, 79, 86–88, 111, 168n65; English stage, 6–7; Spain, 28, 35, 37–41, 48, 61, 78–79, 93, 111–12, 118, 120–24, 127, 168n60, 160n59; AIDS, 11–12; Nero 35; medieval, 50–51, 56; effeminacy, 93, 111–12. *See also* spectators.
Thompson, Peter, 29, 31, 35, 37, 135, 155n1, 159n15, 161n31
Tilley, Sue, 24
Torquemada, Antonio de, 97–98, 172n11
transgender, xvi, 178n4
transvestism: *See* cross-dressing.
transmutation: *See* sex change.
Trujillo, Tomás de, male cross-dressing, 37–38; sodomy 37, 107–8, 160n20

Valencia, Pedro de, 109, 115, 175n38
Vega, Lope de, 86, 170n82, n85
Velasco, Sherry, 157n10, 173n22, 175n41
Vélez-Quiñones, Harry, 35, 159n15, 160n16, 173n20, 174n36, 177n61
Vigil, Mariló, 69, 72, 90–91, 174n35
Virgin Mary, xv, 43–44, 50–56, 89, 162n1–2, 163n5

visual representations (pictorial representations, illustrations), pregnancy and childbirth, xv–xvi, 1, 51–56, 164n11; Mary, xv, 50, 54; Joseph, xv, 54, 56; monsters (monstrous births), xvii, 45–46, 80–88, 98, 101; emblems, 31–32, 100–101; Caesarean operation, 57; *Cantigas*, 51–55, 162n1–2, 163n8; Carbón, 59–60; William Harvey, 65; Paré, 45–46, 81, 83, 87, 89; disembodied fetus, 20–21, 66–67, 166n40, 166n42; frogs, 33–34; *relación* and new pamphlets 82, 84; Rosslin, 67, 166n41; Núñez 66–67; visual culture, 2, 24; visual impact, 7, 88, 98, 157n8; bearded lady, 100–102

Warner, Marina, 51, 56, 164n15
*Weekly World News*, 17
Wiesner, Merry E., 70, 76

*Wigstock*, 24
*Will & Grace*, 23–24, 126, 158n29
Winston, Robert, 19
witchcraft (witches), xiv, 34, 60, 69, 77, 84–87, 169n78
Woliver, Laura R., 20
womb, 2, 4–5, 32, 34, 52, 64–66, 68, 72–73, 79–81, 88, 92, 94, 98, 109, 125,166n41, 166n42; womb envy, 8, 11–12, 33; men's womb, 5, 24, 47, 156n6; expectant fathers, 8, 13, 75, 156n1, 166n42
women's reproductive health: *See* reproductive medicine and health.

Zapperi, Roberto, 3, 35, 156n3, 159n9
Zayas, María de, feminization of men, 110–11, 175n39; reproduction, 77–78, 168n63; paternity, 90; homosexuality, 115, 176n55

www.ingramcontent.com/pod-product-compliance
Lightning Source LLC
Chambersburg PA
CBHW030111010526
44116CB00005B/190